"*Redeeming Violent Verses* is grounded in excellent scholarship, but the author's practical good sense and deep pastoral commitment make the book eminently suited for use in real-world settings. In this lucidly written and well-thought-out study, Eric Seibert has done a notable service to churches. I hope it reaches the widest possible audience."

—**PHILIP JENKINS**, Distinguished Professor of History, Institute for Studies of Religion, Baylor University, and author of *Laying Down the Sword: Why We Can't Ignore the Bible's Violent Verses*

"I've read my fair share of books and articles addressing the violence of the Old Testament, and, as a pastor and educator, I have to say that I have never encountered anything nearly as practically helpful as *Redeeming Violent Verses*. I am confident that anyone who is disturbed by the violent texts of the Old Testament will benefit from this very readable work. But if you are a person whom God has called to use the Bible to influence others, in any capacity, whether adults or children, I *implore* you to deeply digest this bold and insightful work!"

—**GREGORY A. BOYD**, pastor and author of *The Crucifixion of the Warrior God: Interpreting the Old Testament's Violent Portraits of God in Light of the Cross*

"Eric Seibert's *Redeeming Violent Verses* challenges the church to engage seriously and honestly with the problem of violence in the Bible, and he offers thoughtful, simple (though never simplistic), and, above all, practical guidance for this difficult work. Seibert's hospitable style and inimitable clarity model good practices of naming, questioning, and learning from violent texts. Pastors, Sunday school teachers, and Bible readers who struggle to understand and explain violence in the Bible will find this book a valuable resource."

—**CARYN A. REEDER**, Professor of New Testament, Westmont College

"Eric Seibert takes on one of the most challenging issues in Scripture—the violence attributed to God and to God's people. He offers eminently practical guidance on how to engage these texts with people of all ages in the church. Every pastor and those responsible for teaching children and youth in the church should read this book."

—**ADAM HAMILTON**, pastor and author of *Wrestling with Doubt, Finding Faith* and *Making Sense of the Bible*

"Denial and avoidance: that's how we usually deal with descriptions of human and divine violence in Scripture. Seibert not only allows church leaders to help their members take an honest look at biblical violence but also offers honest, healthy, and practical ways to interpret and use these texts in various tasks of ministry. This is a must-read for anyone who wants to take the whole Bible seriously in the life of the church."

—**O. WESLEY ALLEN JR.**, Lois Craddock Perkins Professor of Homiletics, Perkins School of Theology, Southern Methodist University

"Eric Seibert's expertise in the interpretation of violence and the Bible is well established. In this book, he offers what few have been able to: a practical, insightful, and useful guide to *using* texts that are often avoided or dismissed. His love for communities of commitment and for those who have suffered violence is as evident here as his exegetical acumen."

—**AMY C. COTTRILL**, Professor of Religion, Reinhardt University

Redeeming Violent Verses

Redeeming Violent Verses

*A Guide for Using Troublesome Texts
in Church and Ministry*

Eric A. Seibert

WESTMINSTER
JOHN KNOX PRESS
LOUISVILLE · KENTUCKY

First Edition
Published by Westminster John Knox Press
Louisville, Kentucky

23 24 25 26 27 28 29 30 31—10 9 8 7 6 5 4 3 2 1

Unless otherwise indicated, Scripture quotations are from the New Revised Standard Version of the Bible, copyright © 1989 by the Division of Christian Education of the National Council of the Churches of Christ in the U.S.A., and are used by permission. Scripture quotations marked NRSVue are from the New Revised Standard Version, Updated Edition, copyright © 2021 National Council of Churches of Christ in the United States of America. Used by permission. All rights reserved worldwide.

Some material in this book was adapted from Eric A. Seibert, *Disturbing Divine Behavior: Troubling Old Testament Images of God* (Minneapolis: Fortress, 2009), and *The Violence of Scripture: Overcoming the Old Testament's Troubling Legacy* (Minneapolis: Fortress, 2012). Used by permission.

Parts of chapter 6 are adapted from Eric A. Seibert, "Preaching from Violent Biblical Texts: Helpful Strategies for Addressing Violence in the Old Testament," *Perspectives in Studies* 42 (2015): 247–57. Used by permission.

Excerpts in chapter 6 from "The Jericho Woman" by Ulrike Bechmann from Ulrike Bechmann, "The Woman of Jericho: Dramatization and Feminist Hermeneutics," in *Faith and Feminism: Ecumenical Essays*, ed. B. Diane Lipsett and Phyllis Trible (Louisville, KY: Westminster John Knox, 2014) are used by permission.

Book design by Sharon Adams
Cover design by Mark Abrams
Cover photo by Pawel Czerwinski on Unsplash

Library of Congress Cataloging-in-Publication Data is on file
at the Library of Congress, Washington, DC.

ISBN-13: 978-0-664-26468-0

To all who minister,

with hope that you will take this book to heart,

put its teachings into practice,

and use violent verses responsibly,

so that you, and those in your care, can benefit from all they have to offer.

And . . .

To all who have been harmed by the Bible,

with anger and sadness that this happened to you,

and with hope that you may still experience the overwhelming goodness and love of God,

despite the pain caused by those who used Scripture against you.

Contents

Acknowledgments

Writing a book is always a communal project, even when only one name appears on the front cover. This book is certainly no exception. Many people have influenced, assisted, and supported me along the way. I owe each and every one of you a debt of gratitude—both those named below and countless others.

In the fall of 2016, Henry Carrigan asked if a paper I was giving at the annual Society of Biblical Literature meeting in San Antonio might be part of a larger project. That conversation was a catalyst for this book. Thank you, Henry, for your interest in my work at that early stage and for setting the wheels in motion.

I was fortunate to have a number of people read and comment on a draft of this book (or some part of it) prior to publication. To these individuals—Michelle Curtis, David Flowers, Denise Fogelsanger, Stephen Gallaher, Melanie Howard, Jay McDermond, Don Murk, Dave Perry, Elisa Seibert, Hannah Sledge, Zach Spidel, and J. Blair Wilgus—I offer my sincere and heartfelt thanks. Thank you for so generously giving of your time to help me in this way. Your feedback was invaluable and contributed to a much better final product than would otherwise have been possible. I incorporated many of your suggestions into the book—and probably should have included many more! I hope you can take some satisfaction in knowing how much your time and efforts helped. Thanks also to Kimberly Steiner in Interlibrary Loan at Murray Library for help securing resources and to Shelly Skinner for suggesting some resources.

I also want to say a word of thanks to my mom and my dad (who passed away while this book was being written) for creating time for me to write by watching grandchildren, doing chores around the house, bringing food, and just generally making life more pleasant in so many ways. I am incredibly blessed to have you in my life, Mom. I just wish Dad was still with us as well.

My immediate family deserves special thanks for the many ways they make my work both possible and enjoyable. To my three wonderful children,

Nathan, Rebecca, and Hannah: Thank you for being such great kids and for bringing so much joy and laughter into our home. I enjoy spending time with each one of you and treasure our relationship. And finally, to Elisa, my best friend and partner for life, thank you for cheering me on and believing I have something worth saying. Your support and encouragement mean so much to me. I am forever grateful we get to journey through life together. I love you!

It has been wonderful working with Westminster John Knox Press on this project, and I am so glad it found a home here. I was delighted to get to know Bridgett Green early in the process. Thank you, Bridgett, for successfully shepherding my proposal through to acceptance. I also had the good pleasure of working with Julie Mullins at many stages throughout this process. Thank you for fielding my many questions along the way with grace and wisdom, and thank you for lending your keen editorial skills and abilities to my writing. The book is considerably better because of you! I also want to express my appreciation to José Santana for help with marketing. I am convinced your sole mission in life now is to make this book a national bestseller. Thanks also to Julie Tonini for moving this book through production and to Tina E. Noll for her exceptionally fine copyediting work. Finally, I want to thank S. David Garber and Jen Weers for completing the tedious task of preparing the indexes.

I am sure there are many other people I should thank—teachers, scholars, authors, friends—people who have helped form me as a writer and people who have contributed ideas that in one form or another appear in this book. I am grateful for you all!

I sincerely hope this book will be of service to the church and to all who minister in various capacities. May you be inspired to find new and creative ways to use violent biblical texts constructively so that you, and those to whom you minister, may by spiritually enriched by them.

PART I

Understanding Why the Church
Should Not Ignore Violent Verses

1

A Violent Bible and Vanishing Verses

Introducing the Problem

> One of the greatest challenges the church faces today is to interpret
> and explain passages in the Bible that seem to promote or encourage
> violence.
>
> —Jerome F. D. Creach, *Violence in Scripture*[1]

Hardly a book in the Old Testament, and very few in the New Testament, does not contain explicit references to violence in one form or another. There are accounts of cannibalism, child sacrifice, kidnapping, enslavement, incest, murder, rape, and dispossession. Politically motivated killings are not uncommon, and stories of warfare and slaughter occur with alarming frequency. Violence is so prominent in the Old Testament that one scholar has suggested it "is a central, if not *the* central, issue for the entire text."[2] And passages recounting the beheading of John the Baptist, the crucifixion of Jesus, the stoning of Stephen, and the gruesome death of King Herod remind us that violence is often present in the New Testament as well.[3] There is no denying it. Violent verses run throughout the Bible. So why don't they appear more often in church?

WHERE HAVE ALL THE VIOLENT VERSES GONE?

In the course of a regular Sunday morning, most churchgoers are unlikely to encounter very many violent biblical texts. They will probably never hear about the mutilation of Adoni-bezek (Judg. 1:1–7), the kidnapping of Shilonite women who were then forced to marry their abductors (Judg. 21:15–24), the

3

gruesome slaying of King Agag (1 Sam. 15:33), the beating and incarceration of Jeremiah (Jer. 37:11–16), or the bone-crushing destruction of men, women, and children in the lions' den (Dan. 6:24). Nor will most churchgoers be introduced to imprecatory psalms that wish harm upon their enemies, hoping their children will become orphans who "wander about and beg" with none "to pity" them (Ps. 109:9–10, 12). Likewise, many of the most terrifying judgment oracles, like this one from Jeremiah, seldom get any airtime:

> Thus says the LORD: I am about to fill all the inhabitants of this land—the kings who sit on David's throne, the priests, the prophets, and all the inhabitants of Jerusalem—with drunkenness. And I will dash them one against another, parents and children together, says the LORD. I will not pity or spare or have compassion when I destroy them. . . .
>   I will scatter you like chaff driven by the wind from the desert. . . .
>   I myself will lift up your skirts over your face, and your shame will be seen. (Jer. 13:13–14, 24, 26)

Texts like these are not welcome in church.

When was the last time you heard a sermon about the woman from Thebez who mortally wounded Abimelech by throwing a millstone on his head, which crushed his skull (Judg. 9:53)? Or have you ever heard someone preach about the slaughter in Samaria when Jehu treacherously massacred scores of Baal worshipers (2 Kgs. 10:18–27)? Likewise, sermons about Judas committing suicide (Matt. 27:1–10), or about an angel of the Lord mortally striking Herod, who is "eaten by worms" (Acts 12:20–23), are not standard fare in most churches. Preachers tend to avoid these texts like the plague.

Similarly, most Sunday school classes, even *adult* Sunday school classes, won't touch certain parts of the Bible. Who wants to talk about the book of Nahum, a short prophetic book that gleefully anticipates the total destruction of the Ninevites? How many Sunday school teachers are interested in embarking on a prolonged study of the conquest narrative, with its merciless stories of devastation and the systematic annihilation of the entire Canaanite population (Josh. 6–11)? Very few.

As a result, large portions of the Bible never see the light of day in most congregations. Of course there are exceptions—the pastor who decides to preach through the Minor Prophets, or the Sunday school class that undertakes a study of the book of Exodus, plagues and all. But by and large, the majority of churchgoers rarely encounter violent verses on Sunday morning.

This creates real difficulties for people who attempt to read and study the Bible on their own. They find themselves ill-equipped to interpret these troubling texts in responsible ways and are left with little or no guidance for using them constructively. This is precisely what happened to Canadian professor of historical theology Randal Rauser. He writes:

> When I grew up I was given absolutely no direction to read these vio-
> lent narratives. And so I learned to overlook or avoid them, and I got
> really good at it. As a result I remained blissfully ignorant of much of
> the violence that fills the pages of Scripture. . . . My pastors and teach-
> ers growing up simply didn't equip me to grapple with the diversity,
> intensity, and frequency of violence within the Good Book. I had no
> tools even to *recognize* it let alone to figure it out.[4]

Like Rauser, many people have very little significant contact with violent biblical texts in church. This leaves them unsure how to handle violent verses and
deprives them of an opportunity to learn from them. It also creates a potentially dangerous situation. Without instruction, people are liable to misappropriate these verses, and some may even use them to justify violent behavior
toward others. Unfortunately, church history bears this out.[5]

SANITIZING AND JUSTIFYING VIOLENT VERSES

To be sure, not every violent passage is absent on Sunday morning. Some
well-known stories of death and destruction are frequent guests in Sunday
school classes and pulpits: Noah's ark, Joshua and the Battle of Jericho, David
and Goliath—to name just a few. Yet more often than not, when these violent stories do appear in church, they are not handled particularly well. Very
little attention is paid to the brutality they contain, much less to problems this
violence raises for many readers. Instead, when these stories (and others like
them) are used, ministers routinely sanitize them or justify the violence they
contain.[6] This does not serve the church well.

Sanitizing Violence in the Bible

When violent biblical passages are sanitized, the troubling parts of the story
are omitted or mentioned only briefly in passing. There is no real discussion
of the violence they contain or of the kind of problems that violent verses raise
for modern readers. The horrors of bloodshed and killing are conveniently
kept at a safe distance, and our attention is directed to the "happy" parts of
the passage. What results is a sparkling clean version of the story that feels sort
of like a family-friendly G-rated Disney film.[7]

Take the story of Noah's ark, for example. Usually, when this story is used
in church, we are meant to be encouraged by God's deliverance of Noah, his

family, and a boatload of animals. We are not normally invited to consider the fate of those stranded *outside* the ark. Typically, they are not even mentioned. Similarly, when the story of Joshua and the Battle of Jericho shows up on Sunday morning, we are expected to celebrate Israel's victory, not to inquire about the fate of the terrified inhabitants slaughtered inside the city walls. Instead, pastors and Sunday school teachers direct our attention to Israel's obedience to God—marching around the walls of the city, blowing trumpets, and shouting—and to God's miraculous intervention that results in city walls collapsing. But what about Joshua 6:21?

> Then they [the Israelites] devoted to destruction by the edge of the sword all in the city, both men and women, young and old, oxen, sheep, and donkeys.

This verse is seldom mentioned. Most ministers do not invite us to imagine the terror these city dwellers felt. They do not encourage us to linger over the carnage, let alone feel any compassion for the countless lives lost in this bloody massacre. Instead, they say, in effect, "Move along, move along. Nothing to see here." But there *is* something to see. And we *should* look. Indeed, we *must* look. While some degree of sanitizing is understandable when teaching violent stories like these to preschoolers or young children, it is inadequate when talking about these texts with teens and adults.[8] Sanitizing violent texts conceals their problematic nature and fails to help us come to terms with the moral and ethical difficulties they raise.

Justifying Violence in the Bible

The other thing that often happens when violent verses appear on Sunday morning is that pastors and lay leaders try to justify the bloodshed. This is especially true when the violence is condoned in the text or at least appears to have the writer's approval. For example, when God is portrayed behaving violently, many ministers take it upon themselves to defend God from charges of wrongdoing by explaining why it was *right* for God to engage in this kind of behavior. They "explain" *why* it was necessary for God to kill virtually every living thing in a worldwide flood, and they offer justifications for why God commanded the people of Israel to slaughter Canaanites without mercy. They do so in order to make violent biblical texts more palatable, to convince churchgoers that despite appearances to the contrary, these acts of violence are morally acceptable.

But apologetic efforts like these come at a high price. On the one hand, they reinforce the notion that God is violent and that God uses violence to achieve divine purposes. While some Christians have no problem with this view of God, others find it difficult, if not impossible, to reconcile it with other portrayals of God in Scripture.[9] In addition, efforts to justify violence in the Bible have the unfortunate effect of reinforcing the idea that violence is appropriate and even commendable in certain situations. Again, while some Christians may not be troubled by this, others believe violence is *not* a virtue and should be rejected by all who follow the nonviolent way of Jesus. While sanitizing and justifying biblical violence often make people feel better about violent verses, these practices sidestep the real issues and fail to grapple seriously enough with the text.

Rather than ignoring violent passages, or trying to whitewash or defend the violence they contain, it is important to address them honestly and openly, acknowledging their problematic dimensions while exploring their positive possibilities.[10] To that end, the primary purpose of this book is to help religious practitioners—pastors, priests, church leaders, Christian educators, lay leaders, and ministers of all stripes—find constructive ways to use violent biblical texts responsibly when preaching, teaching, and leading worship.[11]

WHO SHOULD READ THIS BOOK?

In the past fifteen years or so, a number of books from different perspectives have been published to help people make sense of "God's" violent behavior in the pages of Scripture. I myself have contributed to this growing body of literature.[12] Yet not much has been written about how to use these—and a host of other—violent biblical texts in church. This leaves those who minister at a real disadvantage. What should they do with stories that sanction genocide or praise individuals for killing others? How can they use these texts in sermons, liturgies, Christian education classes, and elsewhere *without* promoting the violent ideologies they contain? Very little attention has been given to questions like these.

Redeeming Violent Verses seeks to remedy this undesirable state of affairs and is designed for *all* who serve in church and ministry. It is for both clergy *and* laity, for those in paid positions and those in volunteer roles. If you use Scripture to preach, teach, lead Bible studies, give devotionals, or facilitate worship, this book has been written with you in mind. In the pages that follow, you will find helpful insights and practical suggestions that will enable you to use violent biblical texts in creative and responsible ways.

While clergy and lay leaders are the primary audience for this book, others engaged in various forms of ministry will benefit as well. Many of the examples and suggestions offered here are easily adaptable to other contexts, such as parachurch organizations, Christian secondary schools, and Christian institutions of higher learning such as colleges, universities, and seminaries.

In addition, since violent biblical texts trouble a broad range of individuals, anyone who is bothered by all the killing and bloodshed in the Bible, or has struggled to find anything beneficial in these violent verses, will be rewarded by reading this book.

THE VALUE OF USING VIOLENT VERSES
IN CHURCH AND MINISTRY

As I have suggested, ministers and lay leaders who ignore violent biblical texts leave them open to misinterpretation and misappropriation. Without guidance or instruction, people are more likely to use these passages in harmful ways, to justify violent behavior or to conceive of God as an angry judge, ready to punish sinners at a moment's notice. Ignoring these verses also deprives churchgoers of the many benefits that result from using these passages constructively. This is unfortunate, to say the least, since so much good comes from reading these verses responsibly.

The pages that follow are filled with helpful hints and creative strategies for using violent biblical texts in positive, faith-affirming ways. This provides a helpful new perspective on violent verses in the Bible, one that regards them as valuable texts to be explored, not just problems to be solved. It also reminds us that *all* parts of the Bible can be spiritually edifying, even those parts that might initially seem most troubling and intimidating.

I am convinced that significant benefits come from using violent verses responsibly in worship services, Christian education programs, and other ministry settings. Pastors and lay leaders can demonstrate their value and usefulness by incorporating them into sermons and by talking about them in Sunday school classes. For example, many violent biblical texts vividly demonstrate the destructive and harmful nature of violence. Texts like these can be used in efforts to persuade people to avoid violent "solutions" and to seek nonviolent alternatives instead. These verses also serve as an excellent starting point for in-depth conversations about various forms of violence in the modern world—capital punishment, suicide, intimate partner violence, sexual assault, and so forth. Violent biblical texts provide a natural entrée into discussions about sensitive topics like these that ministers are often hesitant to broach. Exploring these verses also provides opportunities to encourage people to develop compassion for victims of violence in the pages of the Bible. This can have a profound impact on the way we see people, even our enemies, and how we treat them.

These ideas (and others) are developed more fully in chapter 2, where I make a more extensive case for the importance and value of using violent verses in church and ministry. Suffice it to say for now, there is much to be gained by bringing violent biblical texts out of the shadows and using them creatively.

THE BIBLICAL TEXTS UNDER CONSIDERATION

This book focuses almost exclusively on texts from the Old Testament.[13] My decision to concentrate on this part of the Bible is not meant to imply that there are not many violent texts in the New Testament, or that those which do appear are surprisingly easy to interpret. Violent biblical texts pose a formidable challenge regardless of where they reside in the canon. I have chosen to focus on the Old Testament because that is where the problem is often most intensely felt and because that is my area of specialty. Happily, many of the suggestions offered throughout this book apply equally well to difficult verses in both Testaments, and those who wish to use violent passages from the New Testament in ministry will find it easy to adapt much of what follows.

Throughout the book, I will use phrases like "violent biblical texts," "violent passages," and "violent verses" interchangeably. For our purposes, it is unnecessary to establish a precise definition of violence that allows us to determine exactly which verses qualify as *violent* verses and which do not. This would be important if we were undertaking a comprehensive study of violence in the Bible, but that is not the purpose of this book. Instead, I am interested in exploring Old Testament texts that contain actions which few people, if any, would question as being violent.

Specifically, I am interested in considering Old Testament texts that describe *physical* violence. Though violence takes many forms—psychological, emotional, relational, verbal—most of the texts discussed here depict, or envision, some form of physical violence that causes injury or harm, and that may result in death.

I am keenly aware that many biblical texts contain violent ideologies (e.g., patriarchy, sexism, racism, ethnocentrism) which are not always manifested in the text as *physical* violence. I am also painfully aware that many Old Testament texts have a long and violent history of interpretation, regardless of whether the text itself describes an act of violence or contains the threat of violence. While I am gravely concerned about the way these kinds of texts are used (and misused), they are not the primary focus of this particular study.[14]

My decision to concentrate primarily on biblical texts that contain physical acts of violence is largely a practical consideration. It provides focus and coherence and helps keep the book within manageable proportions. It also addresses biblical texts that initially tend to create the greatest problems for the majority of readers.

The Old Testament texts considered here primarily describe violence that is done to, or directed toward, *people*. Obviously, the effects of violent behavior are not limited to people alone. Many Old Testament texts describe violence against animals and the environment. Given the way human behavior has often had very negative consequences for the animal kingdom and the natural world, we would be wise to consider carefully how we might use these texts to inform our attitudes and actions going forward.[15] The way we treat the world around us matters immensely—a point that has become unmistakably clear as we routinely witness the deleterious effects of climate change in our world.[16] Still, since the most significant problems many people have with the Old Testament come from texts describing violence toward human beings, these passages will be our focus.

VIOLENCE IN THE OLD TESTAMENT

Before proceeding, it may be helpful to make a few general comments about the scope and nature of violence in the Old Testament. No matter how you measure it, the sheer amount of violence in the Old Testament is staggering.[17] Professor Mark McEntire believes that "human violence is the *primary* factor which shapes the biblical story."[18] Similarly, Raymund Schwager contends that "no other human activity or experience is mentioned as often" as violence in the Old Testament. By his count, there are "over *six hundred* passages that explicitly talk about nations, kings, or individuals attacking, destroying, and killing others."[19] The number is even higher when considering passages containing acts of *divine* violence. "Approximately *one thousand passages* speak of Yahweh's blazing anger, of his punishments by death and destruction, and how like a consuming fire he passes judgment, takes revenge, and threatens annihilation."[20] In addition, Schwager claims that "in over one hundred other passages Yahweh expressly gives the command to kill people."[21] That means there are more than seventeen hundred violent passages in the Old Testament!

Divine Violence and Human Violence

One way to categorize violence in the Old Testament is to differentiate between (1) divine violence, (2) divinely sanctioned violence, and (3) human-initiated violence. Strictly speaking, divine violence is something that God performs *without* direct human assistance. When God annihilates virtually all the inhabitants of Sodom and Gomorrah (Gen. 19:24–25), puts Er and Onan to death (Gen. 38:7, 10), obliterates the Egyptian army in the Red Sea (Exod. 14:26–31), and kills many Israelites by sending venomous snakes (Num. 21:6), God works alone. Humans are not involved in these acts of smiting and slaying.[22]

Divinely *sanctioned* violence, on the other hand, refers to human acts of violence that God explicitly commands or condones. For example, after God reportedly commands Moses to "avenge the Israelites on the Midianites" (Num. 31:2), we are told "they did battle against Midian, as the LORD had commanded Moses, and killed every male" (v. 7). In another instance, the text portrays God issuing this command to King Saul: "Go and attack Amalek, and utterly destroy all that they have; do not spare them, but kill both man and woman, child and infant, ox and sheep, camel and donkey" (1 Sam. 15:3). In both cases, God ostensibly commands one group of people to kill another, thus sanctioning the violence that ensues.

Divinely sanctioned violence also includes acts that appear to have God's blessing and approval even when it is not explicitly given. Examples of this are Jael's murder of Sisera (Judg. 4:17–24; 5:24–27) and David's triumph over Goliath (1 Sam. 17). Jael receives no word from God instructing her to drive a tent peg through Sisera's skull, but the text regards her death-dealing blow as an act of faithfulness. Likewise, David is not given a divine directive to slay Goliath, but all indications from the text seem to suggest that killing this man pleased God.

In addition to divine violence and divinely sanctioned violence, the Old Testament also contains numerous examples of human-initiated acts of violence. People engage in a wide range of devastating acts without divine authorization or approval. Cain kills his brother Abel (Gen. 4:8–11). David orders Joab to ensure Uriah is killed in battle (2 Sam. 11:14–17). Amnon rapes his half sister Tamar (2 Sam. 13:1–22). The Jezreelites unjustly convict Naboth and stone him to death (1 Kgs. 21:11–13). There is no indication of God's blessing or support in any of these instances.

These distinctions between divine violence, divinely sanctioned violence, and human-initiated violence are important to keep in mind as we move through the book. As we will see, Old Testament passages that fall into one of the first two categories present unique challenges and require special attention.[23]

Wrongful Violence and "Virtuous" Violence

When reading violent Old Testament texts, it is often possible to distinguish between what I refer to as wrongful violence and "virtuous" violence.[24] Wrongful violence is violence that is portrayed negatively and disapproved of

in the text. It includes violent acts regarded as being inappropriate, unjusti-
fied, and condemnable. Wrongful violence is unsanctioned and unacceptable,
and those who engage in such behavior do so without divine approval.

"Virtuous" violence, on the other hand, is portrayed as being appropriate,
justified, and perhaps even praiseworthy. It is sanctioned and sometimes even
celebrated in the text. Those who engage acts of "virtuous" violence enjoy
God's blessing and are understood to be acting in ways that are congruent
with God's intentions.

Most modern readers easily recognize that the murder of Abel (Gen. 4),
the rape of Tamar (2 Sam. 13), and the stoning of Naboth (1 Kgs. 21) are
examples of wrongful violence. These violent acts, motivated by jealousy, lust,
and greed, are presented in ways that are critical of them. But other violent
accounts, like the slaughter of the Canaanites (Josh. 6–11) and the annihilation of the Amalekites (1 Sam. 15), find approval in the Bible, making them
examples of "virtuous" violence.[25]

When referring to "virtuous" violence, I have placed quotation marks
around the word "virtuous" to indicate that this refers to the *biblical writer's*
perspective about the act in question. It does not reflect my views. Personally,
I do not think violence is ever virtuous. I believe it is always harmful, even
when it is used in an attempt to help others. I have written about this in my
book *Disarming the Church: Why Christians Must Forsake Violence to Follow Jesus and
Change the World*.[26] I believe Jesus lived nonviolently and called his followers to
do the same.

For our purposes here, it is *not* necessary to agree with me on this particular
point to benefit from what is to come. Even if you believe followers of Jesus
can (or even should) use violence for certain reasons—to protect innocent
lives, for self-defense, to prevent a terrorist attack—that does not change the
fact that many biblical texts describe people engaging in acts of violence we
routinely condemn. We still need to figure out how to use these texts carefully
and constructively, in ways that do not perpetuate harm against others.

Recognizing the distinction between wrongful violence and "virtuous" violence is helpful when considering how to use violent verses in church. As we
will see, biblical texts that *condemn* violence are often much easier to use than
texts that *condone* it.

A SHORT SUMMARY OF WHAT LIES AHEAD

Finally, allow me to offer a brief word about the structure and content of this
book. It has three parts. The first of these, "Understanding Why the Church
Should Not Ignore Violent Verses," sets forth the problem (chap. 1) and makes

a case for why it is so vitally important to use—rather than ignore—violent biblical texts in church (chap. 2).

Part 2, "Finding Ways to Use Violent Biblical Texts Responsibly in Church," begins by offering seven ways to use a violent biblical text constructively (chap. 3). This is followed by three chapters dealing with the use of violent verses in different facets of ministry: Christian education (chap. 4), worship (chap. 5), and preaching (chap. 6).

The final part of the book, "Exploring Sample Texts and Talking about Violent Portrayals of God," contains three chapters. Chapter 7 applies some of the suggestions made earlier in the book to a few selected Old Testament passages. This demonstrates how certain strategies work with specific biblical texts. In chapter 8, the focus is exclusively on Old Testament texts containing divine violence. It is helpful to have a separate chapter devoted to this issue because many people find it especially challenging to know how to handle texts that portray God behaving violently. The last chapter of the book (chap. 9) offers some final words of practical advice to those who accept the challenge and heed the call to use violent verses in church and ministry.

CONCLUSION

Though I am not sure what led you to read this book, I am very glad you are here. Maybe you are a pastor who has struggled to preach from violent Old Testament texts. Perhaps you are a Sunday school teacher concerned about how you should retell violent Bible stories to children in age-appropriate ways. Or maybe you are a churchgoer who has been seeking a better understanding of violence in the Bible, given all the problems it raises for many people. It is also possible that you are reading this book because your college or seminary professor required it for class. Or maybe you just found this book while browsing online or wandering through a bookstore and it piqued your curiosity. Whatever the case may be, I sincerely appreciate your willingness to journey with me in the pages that follow. I hope you enjoy this book and trust you find it helpful as you seek to use violent biblical texts creatively and constructively in church and other contexts.

2

Why Bother with Violent Verses?

Making the Case for Using Violent Biblical Texts in Church

> If we are serious about all Scripture being God-breathed, we *can't afford* to ignore difficult texts. We need to preach and ponder the *whole* counsel of God, even the bits that trouble us, *especially* the bits that trouble us.
>
> —Randal Rauser, *What's So Confusing about Grace?*[1]

The primary purpose of this chapter is to make a case for why violent biblical texts *should* be used in church and other ministry settings. The fact that these verses rarely appear in such contexts suggests that some ministers might need a bit of persuasion before they are ready and willing to tackle some of these tough passages in public. What follows should help in this regard.

But before we consider why it is so important and beneficial for those who minister to use violent biblical texts in this way, it is helpful to explore further why these verses rarely show up on Sunday morning. Beyond the fact that hearing stories about people being harmed is disturbing and uncomfortable for many churchgoers, I believe there are other reasons that account for the lack of attention given to violent verses in Christian education programs, sermons, and worship services.

WHY ARE VIOLENT TEXTS MISSING FROM CHURCH?

One reason the vast majority of violent biblical texts do not appear in church has to do with the nature of the Revised Common Lectionary (RCL).[2] The

RCL is a three-year cycle of Scripture readings designed to be used in Sunday morning worship services. These readings are drawn from both the Old and New Testaments. Ministers who follow the lectionary use some, or all, of these passages as their sermon text. One of the advantages of using the lectionary is that it introduces the church to a broad range of biblical texts over a three-year cycle. This helps ensure that some of the main themes of Scripture are presented in church on a regular basis, and it prevents ministers from cherry-picking passages they like while ignoring those they do not.

While this is good in theory, the problem is that the RCL does not include many of the Bible's most violent verses. The glaring absence of these verses from the RCL significantly limits its usefulness, since it means many of these verses will probably never be read or discussed in some churches. As John Thompson observes, "The Revised Common Lectionary . . . bypasses with surgical precision not only even fragmentary imprecations in the Psalter, but also virtually every text that pertains to violence against women."[3] Likewise, Barbara Brown Taylor acknowledges that people who rely on the lectionary when preaching "have never been confronted with Moses' killing of the 3,000 in the wilderness (Ex. 32:25ff.) or Jepthah's [*sic*] murder of his daughter (Judg. 11:29ff.)" because these passages, and others like them, are not found there.[4] Since the lectionary largely excludes violent verses, people who attend main-line churches (which are among those most likely to follow the RCL) are never introduced to many violent biblical texts during Sunday morning worship. This deprives congregations of the opportunity to wrestle with these texts, a practice that is necessary if we are to benefit from these verses and learn how to use them responsibly.

A similar issue exists with regard to Christian education materials for children and youth. Apart from some of the most popular stories—Noah's ark, Joshua and the Battle of Jericho, David and Goliath—a lot of Sunday school curriculum sidesteps, or altogether avoids, violent verses. This leaves Sunday school teachers with little opportunity to address these texts honestly, something I believe is extremely important. While a resourceful youth pastor *might* be able to find some curriculum that discusses violent biblical texts, these materials are few and far between. Although I can't say for sure, I suspect this has something to do with the fact that many people who are commissioned to write these materials are both uncomfortable with violence in Scripture and uncertain how to incorporate it into church-based curricula. This leads to my next point.

A second reason violent biblical texts appear infrequently in church is simply because some ministers just do not know what to do with them. Though they might be familiar with many of these texts, they may find themselves at a loss for how to use them in church. This is poignantly illustrated by an experience Professor Julia O'Brien had a number of years ago at a workshop she was leading on "Reading the Bible as an Adult." O'Brien writes:

> During a break, a retired pastor kindly but firmly grasped my arm and implored, "What can I do with the image of God as a warrior in the Old Testament?" Even though the violence of the Old Testament was not the topic for the day, he desperately hoped that an Old Testament scholar could answer the question that continued to trouble him. *This man was a seminary graduate and a gifted minister who had preached and taught the Bible for more than thirty-five years, but he still had no idea about how to think or talk about the image of God as a violent warrior.*[5]

Ministers who do not feel confident dealing with violent verses or the imagery they contain are unlikely to select them for sermon topics or Sunday school electives.

Third, some ministers and lay leaders believe these texts are of limited theological value. For example, consider the brief story of Nadab and Abihu, Aaron's two sons, who offered "unholy fire" before God and were instantly annihilated when "fire came out from the presence of the LORD and consumed them" (Lev. 10:1–2). Why invest time and energy trying to extract some lesson, moral, or spiritual meaning from such an obscure story buried in an Old Testament book nobody pays much attention to anymore? Or why try to preach from prophetic passages that contain images of God as an abusive husband (Hos. 2:1–13) or that speak of God destroying Israel "like a bear robbed of her cubs," mangling them "as a wild animal would" (Hos. 13:8)? Not only are passages like these relatively unknown to most churchgoers, the violent images they contain are fundamentally at odds with the way most Christians conceive of God. It requires care and skill to discuss these passages well. Many ministers are simply unconvinced it is worth the time and effort. Why bother with bloody Bible stories and terrifying prophetic pronouncements when there are so many unproblematic passages from which to choose?

Another reason many violent verses are routinely overlooked on Sunday mornings is because they deal with topics the church assiduously avoids talking about: sexual misconduct, suicide, domestic violence—the list goes on. Since these are not easy topics to discuss, many ministers are understandably reluctant to teach and preach from passages that deal directly with them. If you are uncomfortable having a conversation about sexual assault, for example, you probably won't be inclined to preach a sermon that deals with the rape of Dinah in Genesis 34. Likewise, if you are hesitant to talk about suicide, 1 Samuel 31:1–4, which describes King Saul's last moments before he kills himself on the battlefield, is probably not going to top your list of potential sermon texts.

Of course, some ministers may choose not to use violent passages in church for pastoral reasons. They are concerned that some of the issues raised in these texts might be distressing for those under their care. Passages dealing with sexual violence or suicide, for example, could be triggering for those who have been sexually assaulted or have lost a family member or friend to suicide. Therefore, they steer clear of such passages to avoid potentially retraumatizing these individuals.

A final reason many violent verses never receive any attention on Sunday mornings is simply because so many of them are concentrated in the Old Testament, a part of the Bible that receives scant attention in most churches.[6] This point is so painfully obvious it hardly needs elaboration.[7] Far more sermons are preached from the New Testament than the Old, for example, and most worship leaders make little liturgical use of the Old Testament beyond the book of Psalms. Obviously, there are exceptions, but by and large, the Old Testament does not play a prominent role in most Sunday morning worship services. Even when the Old Testament does make an appearance, we rarely encounter its most violent verses.

WHY USE VIOLENT TEXTS AT ALL?

As enticing as it might be just to ignore these passages, I do not believe avoiding violent biblical texts is the way forward. Instead, it is crucial for all who minister to find ways to use these texts creatively and constructively. There is real wisdom and great value in using these oft-neglected parts of Scripture in the life of the church.

In what follows, I lay out my case for the importance of using violent verses in church. While each of the reasons given below can stand on its own, when they are taken together I believe they make a compelling argument for why the church should be intentional about using violent verses on a regular basis.

To Teach People How to Read and Interpret the Whole Bible

One of the most basic duties of Christian ministers is to teach people how to read and interpret the Bible responsibly. To do this well, it is important to introduce churchgoers to all parts of Scripture, even—and perhaps especially—its most difficult parts. While it is unrealistic to address every verse in the Bible, ministers should introduce churchgoers to a representative sampling of all the Bible contains: the good, the bad, and the ugly. They should teach and preach from a wide range of passages and should avoid the temptation to pick and choose passages they like while disregarding those they do not. To ignore violent passages would be to ignore huge swaths of the biblical text. It seems to me that ministers who routinely sidestep the difficult parts of Scripture abdicate part of their responsibility.

For better or for worse, people in the pews look to pastors, priests, and other leaders in the church for guidance when it comes to reading and understanding Scripture. They assume these individuals have undergone seminary training or comparable forms of theological education. And they expect them to have acquired tools that enable them to make sense of the Bible. While some of these expectations may be unrealistic (e.g., assuming a pastor is a biblical scholar just because he or she went to seminary), those with formal theological training are uniquely positioned to deal with violent biblical texts in ways others are not. Teaching people how to handle violent verses responsibly is an important part of what it means to be faithful to the task of helping people read the Bible well.

To Have Integrity in What We Assert about Scripture

Second, it is necessary for ministers to address violent biblical texts in church to have integrity in what they claim to be true about the Bible. Most pastors affirm the Bible is inspired by God and authoritative for Christian faith and practice. What they mean by this differs considerably from one tradition to the next, but these core convictions about the nature of Scripture are widely held.[8]

Christians who affirm the inspiration of Scripture often appeal to 2 Timothy 3:16, "All scripture is inspired by God and is useful for teaching, for reproof, for correction, and for training in righteousness." What is unclear, however, is what the writer meant by "all scripture" since the Bible was still in the process of formation. At the time 2 Timothy was written, there was no consensus about which books should be included in the Old Testament, and not all of the New Testament books had been written yet. It is reasonable to assume the majority of books that were eventually included in the Old Testament, plus some others, are in view here. In any case, Christians today often apply this verse broadly to affirm that every part of the Bible is "inspired" and "useful."

But this raises a number of interesting questions. What does it mean to say *violent* biblical texts are inspired and useful? In what sense is the story about the rape of Dinah and its bloody aftermath (Gen. 34) "inspired"? How is the story of Samson's violent revenge on the Philistines (Judg. 16), resulting in three thousand deaths (including his own), "useful" for teaching, reproof, correction, and training in righteousness? And what does it mean to say Old Testament laws requiring the death penalty, or imprecatory psalms filled with expressions of ill will toward enemies, are authoritative?

If we believe every part of the Bible is inspired and useful, it is important to be able to demonstrate how even the most violent biblical texts can be used positively and constructively, in spiritually edifying and faith-affirming ways. Otherwise, our lofty claims about the nature of Scripture seem rather disingenuous.

To Bolster the Church's Credibility

Over the years, I have taught countless students who come from churches that speak about the Bible *only* in glowing terms. All their lives they have been taught that the Bible is perfect, unproblematic, and completely trustworthy. They have never heard a pastor, youth minister, or worship leader acknowledge there are parts of the Bible that are troubling, let alone potentially harmful. Therefore, when they encounter some of these problematic passages for themselves, it can precipitate something of a crisis.

At first, they are shocked by what they discover. They never knew such things were in the Bible, and they have no idea what to do with them. But these initial feelings of shock and confusion soon give way to a more disorienting realization: a sense of betrayal. "If the church wasn't honest with me about this," they wonder, "what else aren't they telling me? How else have I been misled and misinformed?"

Some regard the church's failure to deal forthrightly with violent verses as a fundamental breach of trust. It causes them to question the integrity and motives of their pastors and religious mentors.[9] After all, if the church says nothing about the problematic nature of violence in Scripture—something hidden in plain sight—maybe it hasn't been up front about other things as well. This situation creates lots of questions and doubts and sometimes causes people to distance themselves from the church. Too many young people have left the church because their good questions were rebuffed by religious authorities who told them to stop asking or made them feel like second-class Christians for doing so.[10]

This undesirable state of affairs can be avoided by periodically introducing people to violent biblical texts and by being honest about the very real problems they create for many Christians. Pastors do not need to have all the answers, and they do not always need to get it "right" when it comes to dealing with violent verses. But they do need to be transparent about the challenging nature of violent biblical texts and the problems they generate for many readers. Otherwise, they may unwittingly create a situation that drives people away from the church rather than leading them to it. We give people a huge gift—and dramatically increase their chances of staying connected to the church—when we honor their questions.

To Encourage People to Wrestle with Violent Texts

When pastors, Sunday school teachers, and others wrestle with violent biblical texts in Christian education classes or from the pulpit, they model a "way of being" with these texts. This is possibly one of the greatest gifts the church can give. By being honest with these texts, addressing the violence they contain, and searching for responsible ways to read them, the church gives people permission to do the same. This says to the congregation, "It's OK to struggle with Scripture. It's OK to have disagreements with the Bible. It's OK to critique some of what you read." By modeling a healthy engagement with the hard parts of the Bible, the church encourages its members to do the same.

The presence of "virtuous" violence in the Bible, violence that is approved and sometimes even celebrated by a biblical writer, should bother us a lot. Why? Because God is not violent and does not want us to behave violently. Despite what some texts suggest, the God of the universe never initiates, sanctions, or participates in acts of violence. It is impossible to affirm God is love while simultaneously claiming God is violent since violence and love are mutually exclusive. When Israelites attribute violence to God, they are conveying their beliefs about God rather than revealing what God is really like (more on this to come).

In chapter 8, we will discuss how Jesus himself was selective about which images of God he used and how he used them. He had little use for violent views of God and envisioned God quite differently from many of his contemporaries. Jesus helps us see the love of God with special clarity through his life and ministry, pointing us to a God who does no harm.

Christians should be bothered by the presence of "virtuous" violence in Scripture because violence is *not* a Christian virtue. Though I realize many Christians believe violence is justified in certain situations—to defend the innocent or to participate in a "just" war—behaving violently toward someone is at odds with the call to love our neighbor as ourselves, which Jesus referred to as the second greatest commandment (Matt. 22:39). Violence is also inconsistent with the kind of enemy love Jesus demands of his disciples (Matt. 5:43–45). And violent behavior is ruled out by the Golden Rule. Jesus commands his followers to treat other people the way they want to be treated (Matt. 7:12). Since most people don't want to be treated violently, violence should not be part of Christian ethical behavior.[11]

All this should impact the way we read and evaluate what the Bible says about violence. It makes sense for us to be troubled when the Bible condones violent acts and behaviors that we condemn and that are at odds with the character of God and the nature of Christian discipleship. Affirming the authority of Scripture does not mean blindly accepting its evaluation of things. Rather, we must be ready to engage in critique when we encounter things in Scripture that are ethically or morally askew. This is necessary for one simple and obvious reason: *people* were involved in the formation of the Bible, and people are not perfect (I know, shocking!).

The individuals who produced these texts wrote in ways that reflect their own cultural values and theological assumptions. Sometimes, their writing helps us see God, and God's vision for the world, more clearly (e.g., when they portray God as being loving and relational, and when they stress the importance of community and the value of hospitality). Other times it does not, especially when their writing attributes violence to God or reflects practices and attitudes that are less than God's ideal (e.g., when they condone slavery or perpetuate patriarchy).

This means that those who minister need to help people learn to read discerningly. To use language I have developed elsewhere, we need to be *conversant* readers rather than *compliant* readers.[12]

> Compliant readers are individuals whose basic instinct is to read the Bible trustingly. Those who read this way accept the Bible's claims, adopt its values, and embrace its assumptions without necessarily giving serious consideration to the implications of their consent.[13]

Conversant readers have a different orientation:

> Conversant readers are ready to engage the Bible in a genuine dialogue whose outcome is not predetermined by the ideology of the biblical text. While they might agree with the views and values espoused in this or that Old Testament text, they are just as likely to disagree. Conversant readers are discerning readers who accept what they can and resist what they must.[14]

For many people, realizing they can interact with the Bible like this is liberating and life-giving. It frees them to read the Bible more honestly. It normalizes and validates their struggles with violent verses and gives them permission to critically engage them. Reading conversantly, rather than compliantly, means you do not need to agree with the text's positive assessments of violence, nor do you need to believe that violent portrayals of God reflect God's true nature and character.

To Address Obstacles to Faith

In his book *What's So Confusing about Grace?*, Professor Randal Rauser reflects on the difficulties violent verses pose for the life of faith. He writes:

> Over the last decade I have spent a lot of time interacting with skeptics and atheists. And I've found time and again that one major catalyst for people leaving the church in the first place traces back to dissatisfaction with the various reading strategies they learned in church for dealing with biblical violence.[15]

If ministers are serious about keeping people in church, they need to find intellectually satisfying ways to read and interpret troubling texts. Otherwise, violent texts may become an insurmountable obstacle that leads people away from the church and from God.

Violent portrayals of God in the Old Testament are particularly problematic in this regard. Many people want nothing to do with God *if* God really is the kind of being who wipes out entire cities, commands genocide, and instantaneously kills people for seemingly minor infractions.[16] David Plotz, an agnostic Jew, puts it this way:

> After reading about the genocides, the plagues, the murders, the mass enslavements, the ruthless vengeance for minor sins (or no sin at all), and all that smiting—every bit of it directly performed, authorized, or approved by God—I can only conclude that the God of the Hebrew Bible, if He existed, was awful, cruel, and capricious. He gives us moments of beauty—sublime beauty and grace!—but taken as a whole, He is no God I want to obey, and no God I can love.[17]

Many Christians also struggle with violent portrayals of God. Professor Ted Grimsrud tells a story about one of his brightest students, who lost his faith because of this. The student wanted to disprove pacifism by proving that God was violent. He "began with Genesis," writes Grimsrud, "and by the time he reached Joshua he was undergoing a major crisis of faith. The God of the Bible was so violent that he lost his faith in that God."[18] If violent verses keep some people from coming to faith, and cause others to lose the faith they have, it behooves the church to find a way to deal with these biblical texts that results in a different outcome.

If you are a pastor or lay leader, you can be of significant help in this regard. You can remove some of these obstacles to faith by helping people understand that not every portrayal of God in the Bible reveals what God is actually like. Violent, vindictive, and vengeful images of God in the Old Testament say more about the cultural context from which they emerged than they do about God's true nature and character.

You can help churchgoers see God more clearly by putting violent Old Testament portrayals of God in their broader cultural context and by offering interpretive strategies to deal responsibly with these troubling images. Since God is most fully and clearly revealed in the person of Jesus, you can encourage people to allow the revelation of God in Jesus to guide their thinking about what God is truly like. This has the potential of correcting mistaken notions about God that often arise from violent Old Testament texts and that all too frequently arrest people's faith or keep them from coming to faith in the first place. Since giving careful attention to Old Testament passages containing divine violence and divinely sanctioned violence is so very important, we will devote a chapter to this topic later in the book.[19]

To Help Churchgoers Respond to Criticism of Christianity and the Bible

Some people try to undermine Christian faith by emphasizing the enormous amount of violence and killing in the Bible. This is understandable in many ways, especially when you consider how much violence Christians have committed in the name of God throughout history, often justifying their behavior by appealing to biblical texts. In his book *Drunk with Blood: God's Killings in the Bible*, Steve Wells says, "It is my hope that as God's killings become better known, people will know better than to believe in the Bible. Such belief should be admired by no one and ridiculed by all."[20] Based on texts like these, Richard Dawkins has this to say about God's character:

> The God of the Old Testament is arguably the most unpleasant character in all fiction: jealous and proud of it; a petty, unjust, unforgiving control freak; a vindictive, bloodthirsty ethnic cleanser; a misogynistic, homophobic, racist, infanticidal, genocidal, filicidal, pestilential, megalomaniacal, sadomasochistic, capriciously malevolent bully.[21]

Dan Barker, an evangelical preacher turned atheist, wrote an entire book supporting this oft-quoted sentence by citing some fifteen hundred Old Testament passages that he claims illustrate these nineteen undesirable divine characteristics (and others he adds to the list).[22] All this presents a formidable challenge to Christians who regard the Bible as the word of God.

Churchgoers should be aware of the way violent verses have been used to critique the Bible, God, and Christianity, and they should have some means of responding to critiques like these. Pastors and lay leaders can help people do this by exploring some of the most violent passages in the Bible and offering more informed ways of talking about them. While some may find it disturbing to grapple with passages like these, it is much better to engage them in the context of the church than to be blindsided by someone using them to attack Christianity. Having these conversations in Christian spaces with trusted pastors, mentors, and lay leaders has the advantage of exploring these issues in faith-affirming ways with more depth and intellectual rigor than what typically characterizes the way these verses are used by those who are antagonistic toward Christianity.[23]

To Discourage Using the Bible to Justify Violence

One of the most important reasons for discussing violent verses in the church is to mitigate the harm they have done. Violent biblical texts have been used to justify all sorts of atrocities, such as massacres, executions, dispossession, forced relocation, and warfare. They have been used to legitimate violence against Native Americans, African Americans, women, children, Jews, Muslims, the LGBTQIA+ community, and other minoritized groups. As Greg Boyd observes:

> The tragic persecution and killing of heretics, witches, Muslims, and fellow Christians, along with the endless nationalistic military campaigns that Christians supported and participated in throughout history, were largely rationalized by appealing to violent passages in the OT.[24]

Sadly, this is not just a thing of the past. Christians continue to appeal to the Old Testament to justify all sorts of evil and oppression. Violent verses are used to support capital punishment, sanction warfare, condemn same-sex relationships, abuse children, degrade the environment, and perpetuate patriarchy.[25]

Given these texts' potential to do real harm, it is imperative for the church to talk about them. As William Emilsen and John Squires vividly put it in the book they edited dealing with violence, religion, and sacred texts:

> Ignoring violent texts is like camping on the bank of a crocodile-infested river. It is dangerous. It is naive in the extreme. These Leviathan-like texts should be treated with the utmost respect and caution. They can erupt with violent force when it is least expected.[26]

Neglected verses can all too easily become dangerous verses.

Although the church cannot permanently disarm violent biblical texts, it can do a lot to defuse them. Ministers can lead the way by talking about how these passages should—and should not—be used. They can teach people how to handle violent verses by denouncing any attempt to use them to justify violence and by offering constructive alternatives that encourage faithful Christian living.

To Benefit from All They Can Teach Us

Finally, it is important to find ways to use violent verses in church and ministry because there is so much we can learn from them. Troublesome though they be, these texts yield many valuable insights *when read responsibly*. In fact, the texts we might initially find especially distressing may be the very ones that help us most. As already noted, they can open up space for important conversations that enable us to talk about sensitive topics. They may also raise critical questions about evil, tragedy, and human suffering that are well worth

pondering. They might even help us curb some of our own violent inclinations, especially when we look closely and see more of ourselves in these troubling stories than we might like.

But if we ignore these texts, we remove all these possibilities. What's more,
we deprive ourselves—and those to whom we minister—of all the insight and
wisdom that can come from them.

One of the most rewarding aspects of working with violent biblical texts is
their relative unfamiliarity. While certain biblical stories containing violence
are well known, like the flood narrative and the destruction of Sodom and
Gomorrah, many are not. There is a lot of uncharted territory here, with
many texts waiting to be explored in fresh new ways. Although this takes some
effort and creativity, options for using these passages constructively abound.
The church has much to gain from using violent biblical texts in worship
services and Christian education programs, and those who minister have a
golden opportunity to demonstrate how these texts can be a rich resource for
spiritual growth and reflection.

CONCLUSION

If you started this chapter with questions about the wisdom of using violent
verses in church and ministry, I hope the previous pages have demonstrated
both the value *and* the necessity of bringing these passages to light. If you still
need some additional persuasion, I highly recommend Philip Jenkins's insightful book *Laying Down the Sword: Why We Can't Ignore the Bible's Violent Verses.*
Jenkins stresses the importance of dealing openly and honestly with violent
biblical texts and of finding ways to handle them with care.

Rather than ignoring violent texts, which leaves them open to abuse, ministers can demonstrate the value of engaging these verses responsibly as they
preach, teach, and lead worship. The next chapter lays the groundwork for
this crucial work by offering suggestions for how violent biblical texts can be
used in positive, faith-affirming ways.

PART II

Finding Ways to Use Violent Biblical Texts Responsibly in Church

3

Seven Constructive Ways
to Use a Violent Biblical Text

*Creative Possibilities That Avoid Sanitizing,
Spiritualizing, or Justifying Violence*

> In my experience the one thing that most troubles people about the
> Old Testament is its violence. People regularly plead with me to say
> something positive about the violence of the conquest of the land in
> the book of Joshua, the violence of God's smiting of the people with a
> plague in the book of Numbers, and of course, the violence of God's
> angry tirades in the Prophetic Books.
> —Julia M. O'Brien, *Challenging Prophetic Metaphor*[1]

It's Thursday afternoon. You have just learned that your beloved senior pastor has tested positive for COVID-19 and needs to quarantine for the next several days. As part of the pastoral team, you naturally wonder who they will ask to fill in for her on Sunday morning. Just then, the phone rings. You pick it up and quickly recognize the cheery voice of the new office manager at your church, who has an important message for you from the senior pastor. She has asked if you would be willing to preach the sermon this week. Eager to be helpful, and not wanting to disappoint, you graciously agree and hang up the phone. You have done some preaching before, and you look forward to putting something together, even if it is rather short notice.

A moment later the phone rings again and you find yourself talking to the office manager once more. He says he failed to mention one important detail. The senior pastor would like you to finish the sermon series she has been preaching on the ten plagues in the book of Exodus. This is your Scripture text:

29

> At midnight the LORD struck down all the firstborn in the land of
> Egypt, from the firstborn of Pharaoh who sat on his throne to the
> firstborn of the prisoner who was in the dungeon, and all the firstborn
> of the livestock. Pharaoh arose in the night, he and all his officials and
> all the Egyptians; and there was a loud cry in Egypt, for there was not
> a house without someone dead. (Exod. 12:29–30)

With that, the office manager says good-bye and you are left alone, slightly
panicked as you wonder what in the world you have gotten yourself into.
What can be done with such a violent biblical text? How can you craft an
inspiring sermon from a passage like this? Won't people think God is merciless
and cruel? And what kind of positive applications can you make from verses
like these that are filled with so much death and destruction?

SEVEN CONSTRUCTIVE WAYS TO USE
A VIOLENT BIBLICAL TEXT

If you have ever asked questions like these, take heart. There is hope. In the
pages that follow, we will look at seven options for using violent biblical texts
creatively and constructively in the church and beyond. These options are
given a general introduction here, with subsequent chapters illustrating specific ways they can be applied in Sunday school classes, worship services, and
sermons.

To Demonstrate Why Violence Is So Harmful

Many people today are exposed to so much violence through movies, video
games, novels, music, and the 24/7 news cycle that they become desensitized
to it. When this happens, it is easy to become numb to it and to forget how
horrible and horrifying violence actually is.

This is where violent biblical texts can be quite helpful in the hands of a
skilled minister. These texts can resensitize us to the harmful and destructive
nature of violence. This is especially true of passages that dramatize the *negative*
consequences of violent words and deeds. Ministers can capitalize on this in a
number of ways when preaching and teaching.

For example, numerous Old Testament stories illustrate the sad reality that
violence routinely leads to more violence. This is seen clearly in the story of
David and Bathsheba (2 Sam. 11–12). David abuses his authority as king to
have Bathsheba taken from her home and brought to the palace, where he
sexually assaults her. Later, when he learns that Bathsheba is pregnant, he
recalls her husband Uriah from the battlefield in a desperate attempt to cover

up his sexual transgressions. When that fails, he orders Joab to put Uriah in harm's way and then to withdraw from him during combat. As a result, Uriah is killed in battle precisely as David intended.

After this horrible chain of events unfolds, David is confronted by the prophet Nathan, who minces no words:

> Why have you despised the word of the LORD, to do what is evil in his sight? You have struck down Uriah the Hittite with the sword, and have taken his wife to be your wife, and have killed him with the sword of the Ammonites. Now therefore the sword shall never depart from your house. (2 Sam. 12:9–10a)

Violence plagues David and his family for the rest of his life. It begins with the death of his "illegitimate" child, an event that is portrayed as an act of divine judgment directly linked to David's decision to eliminate Uriah (12:14). Sometime after this, David's oldest son Amnon also engages in an act of sexual violence by raping his half sister Tamar (2 Sam. 13). The placement of the rape of Tamar immediately after the rape of Bathsheba invites us to consider the relationship between these two narratives. Is it meant to imply that David's despicable behavior somehow made Amnon's more possible? Or should this account be understood as partial fulfillment of the judgment that the prophet Nathan pronounced against David? In any case, the rape of Tamar infuriates Absalom, Tamar's full brother. Two years later, Absalom takes his revenge by ordering his servants to murder Amnon (13:28–29). Again, we see how one act of violence leads to another.

These chapters in 2 Samuel could also be used to demonstrate how violence results in enormous pain and grief. Bathsheba suffers sexual trauma *and* the loss of both her husband and child because of David's violent behavior.[2] David spends a week agonizing over his ill son, fasting and praying to no avail while his child's life hangs in the balance (12:16–19). Tamar is raped and cast out of Amnon's house, "crying aloud as she went," with ashes on her head and a torn garment to signify her distress (13:19). And before 2 Samuel 13 comes to a close, Amnon is dead and Absalom has fled, leaving David's house in shambles (v. 37).

Violence creates all sorts of trauma, grief, and brokenness—for both victims *and* perpetrators. Perpetrators of violence sometimes put their own lives at risk. For example, after Cain kills his brother Abel, he fears for his life (Gen. 4:14), and after Moses' not-so-perfect murder becomes known, he must flee from Egypt to keep from being killed (Exod. 2:11–15).

Ministers can use biblical texts like these to demonstrate how harmful violence is and how much pain and suffering it causes. By exposing violence in all its ugliness, pastors and lay leaders can forcefully critique this type of behavior and can encourage their listeners to reject all forms of violence against others.[3]

To Consider Ways to Respond to Violence

The Bible contains an amazingly diverse range of responses to violence and the threat of violence. Paying attention to these responses, and the texts in which they are embedded, can be helpful to church leaders trying to discern the best way to respond to various forms of violence in their own community and around the world.

Numerous passages in the Old Testament illustrate how violence was prevented through bold and creative actions. We read about a woman named Abigail who prevents a massacre (1 Sam. 25) and a prophet named Obadiah who rescues one hundred prophets from certain death (1 Kgs. 18:3–4). There are also stories about heroic Israelites who save individual lives: a group of Israelites save Jonathan's life (1 Sam. 14:43–45), Michal saves David's life (1 Sam. 19:11–17), and Jehosheba saves Joash's life (2 Kgs. 11:1–3).[4] Threats of violence are also overcome through conversation (Josh. 22) and by miraculous nonviolent intervention (2 Kgs. 6).

In addition to inspiring stories like these, we read about courageous individuals who refuse to participate in acts of violence even when ordered to do so. For example, Shiphrah and Puah, two Hebrew midwives, refuse to kill newborn baby boys despite Pharaoh's command (Exod. 1:15–21). Other stories highlight people's resolve to be true to God even when doing so carries the penalty of death. The godly behavior of Daniel and his friends Shadrach, Meshach, and Abednego exemplifies this (Dan. 3 and 6).

In a few cases, as in the story of Joseph, forgiveness is offered in response to violence (Gen. 45:1–15; 50:15–21). Joseph could have chosen to kill the brothers who had planned to kill him, but he does not. Other times, victims of violence lament what has happened, expressing public grief over the pain and suffering they have experienced. King David is inconsolable over the death of his son Absalom (2 Sam. 18:33). The book of Lamentations gives voice to the anguish people felt about the destruction of Jerusalem.

When faced with the imminent threat of violence, some people simply focus on self-preservation. When the Babylonians finally breach the walls of Jerusalem, we are told that "the king with all the soldiers fled by night" (2 Kgs. 25:4).[5] Unfortunately, King Zedekiah's attempt to get away is unsuccessful, and the last thing he sees before his eyes are gouged out is his sons slain (v. 7). Others, like King Hezekiah, look to God for deliverance through prayer and prophetic counsel when facing the threat of destruction (19:1–7, 14–19). And some, like the Ninevites, choose to repent when threatened with annihilation (Jonah 3:5–9).[6]

Ministers may find it helpful to become familiar with different responses to violence in the Old Testament, especially as they consider how to respond to yet another school shooting or racially motivated killing. These violent biblical texts create space to consider the place of lament and protest, forgiveness and resistance, nonviolent action and self-preservation. They can be valuable resources to help people process violence in the world today.

To Develop Compassion for Victims of Violence

Christians generally regard compassion as a virtue, as something that should govern the way we behave toward others. We see this in the book of Colossians when the writer instructs believers to "clothe yourselves with compassion, kindness, humility, meekness, and patience" (3:12). We would be wise to follow this directive. After all, compassion is one of the fundamental attributes of God. The Old Testament repeatedly describes God as compassionate, and the New Testament mentions Jesus' compassion on more than one occasion.[7]

Violent biblical texts provide endless opportunities to cultivate compassion, especially for those who have been most directly harmed by acts of violence.[8] In some cases, our compassion is kindled fairly easily when reading these verses, particularly when we encounter victims who have done nothing wrong. Jephthah's daughter is one obvious example (Judg. 11:29–40).

Unbeknownst to her, her father Jephthah makes a stupid vow. In exchange for victory over the Ammonites, Jephthah promises to make a burnt offering of whatever comes out of his house upon his return (11:31 NRSVue), perhaps thinking it will be one of his animals. Jephthah then goes off to battle and delivers a crushing blow to the Ammonites. When he returns home victorious, he is surprised to discover that his *daughter*, his only child, comes out of his house first to greet him. Bound by the oath he has made—or so he assumes— he fulfills the terms of his reckless vow (v. 39).[9]

It is not hard to feel compassion for Jephthah's daughter, this otherwise unknown young woman who is the victim of being in the wrong place at the wrong time. Her singular request before she dies serves to emphasize the tragedy of it all: "Grant me two months, so that I may go and wander on the mountains, and bewail my virginity, my companions and I" (v. 37). In this case, compassion comes naturally.

But cultivating compassion for other victims of violence in the Bible is often more difficult and can feel counterintuitive, especially when they are traditional enemies of Israel. In typical readings, who cries for the Canaanites ostensibly slaughtered by Joshua and the people of Israel (Josh. 6–11)? Who mourns for the thousands of Moabites who are slain after Ehud assassinates their king (Judg. 3:26–30)? Many readers pass over the deaths of these "evildoers" without feeling any compassion for them. Yet even if readers think their fates were deserved, or regard them as a faceless enemy, it is important to remember that all human life is sacred to God. We should never rejoice over the death of another person, even one who is known to be, or described as being, unusually wicked. This is equally true of people in the Bible *and* people today. While it is natural to feel relief that such a person is no longer able to harm others, every life lost to violence is a cause for grief, not celebration.

Using violent biblical texts to cultivate compassion for others may be one of their most important functions. Why? Because developing compassion for people in the pages of the Bible can help us develop compassion for people in the world around us.[10] This, in turn, can have a significant effect on the way we treat others. Those who feel compassion for people in the biblical text, even those regarded as Israel's "enemies," are likely to exhibit similar levels of compassion toward people in the world today. It is extremely difficult to behave violently toward someone for whom you feel compassion. We will return to this point later and discuss *how* to cultivate compassion for victims of violence in the Old Testament.

To Talk about Difficult Topics

There are many topics the church should address but often actively avoids, including issues like domestic violence, rape, capital punishment, white nationalism, incest and sexual abuse, suicide, and human trafficking. Many people find these issues unpleasant to think about and difficult to discuss, so it's no surprise they are not often featured in Sunday worship services. Still, if the church is to fulfill its commitment to do justice and to love our neighbors, it is important for Christians to have informed conversations about these issues so they know how to respond at home, in church, and throughout society in ways that are congruent with the life and teachings of Jesus.

Many of the Bible's violent texts provide natural opportunities for talking about some of these difficult issues. With care and planning, ministers can use any number of them as convenient entry points into these challenging conversations. Given the sensitive nature of many of these topics, ministers and lay leaders should take steps to prevent unnecessarily triggering individuals who might find them unsettling. When discussing things like suicide, sexual assault, or domestic violence, it is helpful to provide people with some advance warning, ideally many days before the planned conversation, as well as on the day of the conversation itself, for anyone who missed previous notices. That way, if people feel the subject matter is too difficult for them, or believe it is inappropriate for their children, they can choose not to attend the event or worship service where this will be discussed.[11]

To illustrate how violent verses could be used as an entry point into these conversations, let's consider two issues: domestic violence, or intimate partner violence, and suicide. Domestic violence is experienced by women and men all over the world.[12] It crosses all religious, social, economic, ethnic, and national boundaries. It is as widespread among church members as it is among people who have no religious affiliation.[13] Every Sunday morning, both abusers and those who have been abused—or are currently being abused—sit in church pews around the world. It is a problem of epic proportions, yet one that is rarely mentioned in church.

One way to begin a conversation about this issue would be to invite people to look closely at Hosea 2, a biblical text that could be used to profile a domestic abuser.[14] This chapter displays many controlling behaviors that are characteristic of an abuser.[15] These include the threat of sexualized violence (vv. 2–3), forced isolation (vv. 6–7), economic control (vv. 8–9), exclusion from social and religious events (v. 11), and destruction of cherished personal property (v. 12). After all this, the abuser promises to "speak tenderly to her" and give her gifts (vv. 14–15) to encourage her return. Abusers do this all the time. They attempt to calm their partner's fears with words of love and with promises never to hurt them again. But these are empty promises that represent one more way of manipulating and controlling the person they are abusing. Being aware of how abusers operate can help people recognize domestic abuse when they see it or experience it. It can also encourage them to seek help when they, or others they know, are being harmed in this way.

A number of violent verses in the Bible can also be helpful to ministers who want to talk about suicidal ideation and suicide prevention. Seven individuals in the Bible commit suicide (or assisted suicide): Abimelech (Judg. 9:50–54), Samson (Judg. 16:23–31), Saul (1 Sam. 31:1–4), Saul's armor bearer (1 Sam. 31:5), Ahithophel (2 Sam. 16:15–17:23), Zimri (1 Kgs. 16:8–20), and Judas (Matt. 27:3–5; cf. Acts 1:15–18). Any of these passages could be used to discuss why people sometimes take their own life and what can be done to prevent that from happening.[16] For example, the primary factor behind Abimelech's request to be killed (assisted suicide) is fear of shame. While engaged in battle, Abimelech is mortally wounded by a woman who throws a millstone on his head, crushing his skull (Judg. 9:53).

> Immediately he called to the young man who carried his armor and said to him, "Draw your sword and kill me, so people will not say about me, 'A woman killed him.'" So the young man thrust him through, and he died. (v. 54)

After retelling this story, ministers and lay leaders could begin a discussion of suicide by asking questions like these: How prominent a role do you think shame plays in the decision to take one's own life? What other factors contribute to suicidal ideation and the desire to die? What are some of the most common indicators that someone is contemplating suicide, and how should we respond if we suspect someone we know may be thinking of ending their life? Using violent verses to generate conversations about difficult topics like these strikes me as a very promising way to use violent biblical texts responsibly.

Given the complexity and sensitivity of some of these topics, you might want to consider inviting a mental health professional to guide the conversation. Look to people within your own congregation, or reach out to local organizations and see if someone might be available to share their expertise with your church or with your Sunday school or adult education class. Ministers should not be expected to be experts on everything, and it is wise to partner with therapists, social workers, and educators who are knowledgeable in these areas. At the very least, when you explore sensitive topics, be sure to have resources available and referrals ready for those who may need additional support.

To Raise Awareness of Violence and Act to Stop It

Violent biblical texts have the capacity to remind us of how much pain and suffering people have experienced—and continue to experience—at the hands of others. Earlier we talked briefly about two women in the Old Testament who were raped, Bathsheba and Tamar. Tragically, the sexual violence they experienced still happens with alarming frequency. According to the Rape, Abuse and Incest National Network (RAINN), "1 out of every 6 American women has been the victim of an attempted or completed rape in her lifetime (14.8% completed, 2.8% attempted)" and "about 3% of American men—or 1 in 33—have experienced an attempted or completed rape in their lifetime."[17] That means in any church, chances are extremely high that numerous people (both women *and* men, though sexual violence predominately affects women) have experienced some form of sexual assault.

One way to help survivors of rape and sexual assault feel seen and heard is by focusing on stories of women like Bathsheba and Tamar. People who have had similar experiences will appreciate hearing you state clearly and unequivocally that what happened to these women was completely wrong and entirely not their fault. This validates their experience and promotes healing.

Of course, as mentioned above, you need to be very careful how you use biblical texts that contain accounts of sexual violence. As with other sensitive issues, these stories have the potential to be triggering and could traumatize those who have been raped or sexually assaulted. Therefore, if you plan to use texts like these in church and ministry—and I hope you will—it would be wise to prepare for this carefully by being well informed about the topic, by providing people with advance notice, by making additional resources available, and by indicating where survivors can go for counsel and support as needed. You might also consider inviting someone with expertise in sexual assault to address this issue and to be a resource to people in the congregation who have further questions. When done well, expressing compassion for women in the Bible like Bathsheba and Tamar, and acknowledging all the trauma they endured, sends strong signals to people in the pews who themselves might be recovering from some form of sexual assault. It will help them realize that you care for them and are concerned about what they have gone through. It may even prompt some to seek help processing their own experience.

To illustrate one creative way to use violent verses to raise awareness of the kind of gender-based violence many people experience today, consider what Rachel Held Evans and her friend did with some of the most horrifying stories in the Bible. They focused on four women in the Old Testament whose stories Professor Phyllis Trible refers to as "texts of terror" because of the violence against women they contain.[18] As Evans describes it:

> On a chilly December evening, we sat around the coffee table in my living room and lit candles in memory of Hagar [abused by her mistress], Jephthah's daughter [sacrificed by her father], the concubine from Judges 19 [gang-raped and dismembered], and Tamar, the daughter of King David who was raped by her half brother. We read their stories, along with poetry and reflections composed by modern-day women who have survived gender-based violence. My friend built a diorama out of a pinewood box that featured five faceless wooden figures, huddled together beneath a ring of barbed wire, their silhouettes reflected on the backboard by pages cut from a book. Across the top of the box were printed the words of Christ—"As you have done unto the least of these, so you have done to me."[19]

After writing about this in her *New York Times* bestseller *A Year of Biblical Womanhood*, Evans said she "connected with pastors and worship leaders who have incorporated similar liturgies into their services, often during the season of Lent."[20]

The church can use terrible texts like these for remembrance and confession. By focusing on women in the Bible who have suffered unspeakable acts of violence, we are reminded of the enormous amount of violence so many women suffer every day all around the world. Prayers of confession, responsive readings, and words of remembrance could all be included as part of the Sunday morning liturgy. While this could take place any time of the year, it might be especially powerful to include some of these elements during November because November 25 has been designated by the United Nations General Assembly as the International Day for the Elimination of Violence against Women. Participating in these acts of remembrance (and confession) should lead the church to action. It should cause churchgoers to redouble their efforts to stand against all forms of gender-based violence and abuse. As Evans puts it, "If the Bible's texts of terror compel us to face with fresh horror and resolve the ongoing oppression and exploitation of women, then perhaps these stories do not trouble us in vain. Perhaps we can use them for some good."[21]

Violent verses can be a powerful tool to persuade people to take action, not only to prevent violence against women, but to combat all forms of violence and oppression regardless of who is being harmed: BIPOC (Black, indigenous, people of color), members of the LGBTQIA+ community, underrepresented populations generally, the elderly, those who are disabled, women, children— anyone. Though fighting violence with violence is futile, fighting violence with violent texts is not. Some of the Bible's most terrifying texts can be used effectively to raise our awareness of the suffering of others so we might lament, repent, and take action to bring about change.

To Warn against Using Violent Texts to Do Harm

As briefly noted in chapter 1, the church has used violent biblical texts throughout history to justify and, in some cases, instigate terrible acts of violence and killing.[22] It is important for Christians to be aware of this history in order to repent of past transgressions and to pledge never to repeat them. One way the church can educate people in this regard is by discussing some of these past abuses and the biblical passages used to justify them.

For example, a pastor could prepare a sermon dealing with the annihilation of Amalekites in 1 Samuel 15, a deeply troubling text that has been used to justify numerous acts of violence against others.[23] This passage contains one of the most chilling divine directives in the entire Old Testament, one that calls for the utter annihilation of every last Amalekite. The prophet Samuel speaks these words to King Saul:

> "Thus says the LORD of hosts: 'I will punish the Amalekites for what they did in opposing the Israelites when they came up out of Egypt. Now go and attack Amalek, and utterly destroy all that they have; do not spare them, but kill both man and woman, child and infant, ox and sheep, camel and donkey.'" (1 Sam. 15:2–3)

The rationale for this dreadful decree goes back to an incident that took place hundreds of years earlier. Soon after the Hebrew people escaped from Egyptian bondage, they were attacked by the Amalekites (Exod. 17:8–16; Deut. 25:17–19). Now, centuries later, the Amalekites were going to be punished for that act of aggression.

As the story goes, the Israelites kill all the Amalekites except the king (and "the best of the sheep and the cattle" [1 Sam. 15:15]). When Samuel arrives, he is not pleased that Saul has spared the Amalekite king's life and finishes the job himself in an act of butchery that has inspired numerous graphic artistic renderings (1 Sam. 15:33).

This deadly passage was used by colonialists of North America to justify their horrific treatment of Native Americans. On September 1, 1689, Cotton Mather preached a sermon in which he compared the colonists to Israel and the Native Americans to Amalek. As Susan Niditch observes:

> The war against the Indians of New England is justified on grounds both explicit and implicit: they are accused of murdering Christians and therefore are worthy of death . . . but also they are Ammon, Amalek, an indigenous population who will be displaced and disinherited by divine decision to make way for the new Israel. Mather is in a lengthy tradition of Christian preaching on war when he treats the enemy as Amalek and the fighting as justified crusade.[24]

More recently, the same passage was used to inspire Hutu Christians to slaughter their Tutsi friends and neighbors in Rwanda. As Joshua Masusu recalls of one pastor:

> He compared the Tutsis to the Amalekites, and said Saul was rejected by God because he failed to exterminate all of the Amalekites. He said, "If you don't exterminate the Tutsis, you'll be rejected. If you don't want to be rejected by God, then finish the job of killing the people God has rejected. No child, no wife, no old man should be left alive." And the people said "Amen."[25]

This pastor's use of 1 Samuel 15 is particularly shocking when one considers that approximately eight hundred thousand Tutsis were killed, many with machetes, in a period of about three months.

Violent biblical texts have an enormous capacity to harm others. Ministers should be on guard against such abuses, and they should, periodically, remind churchgoers how violent biblical texts have been misused in the past. Hopefully, this will keep the church from repeating its mistakes as people are reminded that such verses should never be used to justify acts of violence or oppression. This is important work even in churches that might consider themselves more "enlightened," or beyond abusing violent texts in such harmful ways. When religious leaders fail to publicly acknowledge the church's past sins in this regard, they—and the people they serve—are more susceptible to being unduly influenced by these violent verses, sometimes even in very subtle ways. Since confession is a core spiritual practice in the Christian tradition, it is helpful for the church to seek forgiveness for the way previous generations of Christians have weaponized the Bible and used it against others, particularly marginalized people. This benefits both those who make and those who receive this kind of confession.

To Make Personal Connections and Applications

One of the most fundamental questions many Christians ask when reading the Bible is, "How does it apply to my life?" For many churchgoers, this is an especially difficult question to answer when it comes to violent biblical texts. What "life lesson" are we to learn from the story of Samson's revenge on the Philistines when he kills roughly three thousand of them (Judg. 16:23–31)? What insight should we apply to our lives after reading the story of David's execution of seven of Saul's sons (2 Sam. 21:1–9)? What should we "take away" from Elijah's slaughter of the prophets of Baal after descending from Mount Carmel (1 Kgs. 18:40)? Questions like these are not easy to answer, and we should proceed with caution. Still, I am convinced there are responsible ways to make relevant applications from even the most violent biblical texts.

To illustrate this, let's consider an especially bloody narrative in 2 Kings 9–10 that describes Jehu's rise to power. Jehu is a military commander who is secretly anointed king by an unnamed prophet from the company of Elijah (9:6). During this clandestine meeting, the prophet speaks to Jehu in the name of the Lord:

> You shall strike down the house of your master Ahab, so that I may avenge on Jezebel the blood of my servants the prophets, and the blood of all the servants of the LORD. (v. 7)

And this is precisely what Jehu does. He orders the officials of Samaria to decapitate Ahab's sons and to bring their heads to him in baskets. After receiving these bloody containers, Jehu eliminates everyone in Jezreel who had any association with Ahab.

> So Jehu killed all who were left of the house of Ahab in Jezreel, and his leaders, close friends, and priests, until he left him no survivor. (10:11)

But Jehu does not stop there. He pays a personal visit to Samaria, where he continues his killing spree.

> When he came to Samaria, he killed all who were left to Ahab in Samaria, until he had wiped them out, according to the word of the LORD that he spoke to Elijah. (v. 17)

While all this violence is ostensibly done with divine sanction and blessing, these are politically motivated killings, plain and simple. History is replete with slaughters like these carried out in the name of God. But they never reflect God's will, since God is not a purveyor of violence, a point we will explore more fully in chapter 8. Regardless of the religious rationale people supply, such killings are motivated by human needs and desires. This one is no different. Jehu wants to be sure none of his potential rivals can threaten his right to rule, and he goes to great lengths to make it so.

On the face of it, a narrative like 2 Kings 9–10 may seem largely irrelevant for modern readers. Who cares how many people some ancient Israelite king killed to secure his hold on power? How are these violent verses "useful for teaching, for reproof, for correction, and for training in righteousness"? Christians will likely struggle to find some deep spiritual insight or practical application in these chapters.

One way to redeem this very violent passage is to encourage people to use it for self-reflection. Consider how far Jehu is willing to go to eliminate *all* his potential rivals. By the end of the narrative, anyone who threatened (or was perceived to threaten) Jehu's hold on power winds up dead. Jehu is ruthless. Why bother to "keep your friends close and your enemies closer" when it is so much easier just to eliminate your opponents?[26] Jehu operates with a political expediency that would make Machiavelli proud!

While most of us would not dream of killing our rivals, the story of Jehu's rise to power raises important questions for us to ponder all the same. It invites us to reflect on the way we treat *our* opponents. Who *are* our rivals? Who are the people who threaten your power and position in some way? Maybe it's the new employee where you work. She is doing a fantastic job and now stands poised to get that promotion you desperately wanted. To what lengths would you go to thwart her? Would you spread damaging rumors? Refuse to cooperate with her? Perhaps even sabotage her work?

Or suppose you are vying for a better church appointment, or competing for a special position within your denomination. Would you inflate your résumé? Would you boast about your great accomplishments even if most of the work was actually done by others? Would you subtly undermine the ministry of other pastors in your area who might be likely to advance ahead of you? Might you even make false accusations against them, insinuating they have been involved in some sort of financial impropriety or sexual indiscretion? In short, how far would you go to promote your own advancement at the expense of others? While most of us would (thankfully) never think of killing our rivals, there is more Jehu in us than we may care to admit.

Using the story of Jehu like this, for self-reflection and introspection, represents one way that stories like these can be used beneficially to make personal connections with the text. It would not be hard to work something like this into a sermon or Sunday school lesson. Using 2 Kings 9–10 in this way can help churchgoers realize the value of violent texts like this one in spite of the numerous challenges they inevitably raise.

IS EVERY VIOLENT BIBLICAL TEXT USABLE?

Throughout this chapter we have explored various ways that violent biblical texts can be used constructively in church and ministry. But does this apply to *every* violent biblical text? Is it reasonable to expect something beneficial can be gleaned from each and every violent verse in the Bible? Or should some of these be avoided? Are some passages so problematic that they are morally and theologically bankrupt?

I do not think so.

Old Testament scholar Ellen Davis was once asked if there was any text she would reject.[27] After considerable reflection she replied:

> No biblical text may be safely repudiated as a potential source of edification for the Church. When we think we have reached the point of zero-edification, then that perception indicates that we are not reading deeply enough; we have not probed the layers of the text with sufficient care.[28]

In fact, rather than rejecting difficult texts, Davis believes we should extend "interpretive charity" to them. She explains:

> Interpretive charity does not mean pity, but rather something more like generosity and patience toward the text. . . . Charitable reading requires considerable effort; it is easier to dispense with the problematic text. Those who regard a text as religiously authoritative are willing to sustain that effort because they perceive that the text comes to them, in some sense, as a gift from God.[29]

Davis invites us to take time to engage even the most difficult texts in the hopes of hearing a word from God.

Thomas Long also encourages us to find something of value in even the most problematic passages. In an article dealing with "difficult preaching texts," Long includes a sermon he preached on 2 Samuel 6:1–7, a passage that describes the fate of an unfortunate Israelite named Uzzah who is instantly annihilated by God when he touches the ark of the covenant to keep it from toppling over while in transit. Long believes that "it would be a serious mistake to dismiss this story with the wave of a hand as a piece of moldy barbarism. . . . Like Jacob wrestling beside the river, *we should not let this story go until it has at least the chance to bless us.*"[30]

Long is alluding to the enigmatic story of Jacob's wrestling match at the Jabbok River recorded in Genesis 32. On the eve of meeting his brother Esau, from whom he fled twenty years prior, Jacob wrestles throughout the night with "a man" many interpreters believe represents God. When daybreak comes, and the "man" asks to be released, Jacob replies, "I will not let you go, unless you bless me" (v. 26). Jacob is tenacious, determined to have something good come from this encounter.

Jacob's wrestling match seems an apt analogy for the way we should interact with violent biblical texts. We wrestle with them—strenuously at times— but we stay in the ring because we are convinced something good will come from the struggle. We believe a blessing awaits, and we will not let go until it is received. This takes work and considerable effort, but it is worth it. I am convinced that even the most unsavory parts of Scripture can yield important insights about life with God, human relationships, and ethical living when they are read responsibly.

To be clear, I am not suggesting that every violent biblical text works equally well in every context; there are settings in which they should be avoided entirely. For example, some texts are not suitable for young children and have no place in elementary Sunday school classes. Other violent verses do not work well as a "call to worship" or as a responsive reading during Sunday morning worship.[31] We need to be prudent about when and how violent biblical texts are used and we should always handle them with care.

That said, I stand by my claim that all violent verses can be used profitably in church and ministry. I have labored this point because I believe staying convinced of the value of these passages is half the battle. If we think violent verses are nothing more than a problem to be solved and believe that they have little, if anything, to offer us, we are unlikely to get much out of them. But if we catch a glimpse of their potential usefulness, and commit ourselves to studying them carefully, we are sure to discover how beneficial they can be.

CONCLUSION

As this chapter has demonstrated, there are many ways violent biblical texts can be used to encourage spiritual growth and to enhance Christian faith. In the chapters to come, we will demonstrate how these ideas can be applied in various contexts by pastors and lay leaders. Specifically, we will consider how violent verses can be used effectively for preaching, teaching, and worship by exploring how to use them as sermon texts or as the basis for Sunday school lessons, and by incorporating them into prayers and readings during worship services.

4

Teaching Violent Bible Stories to Children

How Should We Talk about David and Goliath?

> How we read and interpret the Bible with children may mean the
> difference between whether or not it will continue to be an important
> source for their life of faith as they become young adults.
> —Elizabeth F. Caldwell, *I Wonder*[1]

In her recent book *Violence and Nonviolence in Scripture: Helping Children Understand Challenging Stories,* Catherine Maresca recounts an incident that exemplifies how little thought has been given to the way children should be taught about violence in the Bible. During an interdenominational conference in Washington, DC, someone asked "a panel of respected religious educators and peace activists" this question: "How do we read the violent passages of the Bible with children?"[2] Maresca describes what happened next:

> The entire audience of children and youth ministers leaned forward
> in their pews. Their hunger for good guidance was palpable, but the
> panel had nothing to offer in that regard. Some were prepared to
> address the issue of violence and children; others the issue of violence
> and the Bible; and others children and the Bible. *No one, however, had
> tackled how to present these difficult passages with children* and explore their
> theological meaning.[3]

While the panelists' lack of response is disappointing, it is unsurprising. Not much has been published about teaching violent biblical texts to children. And even less has been written about how to handle the violence in these texts responsibly. There is little to guide the children's pastor, youth minister,

Christian educator, or volunteer who decides to use a violent Bible story in Sunday school class or during children's church.

This undesirable situation is exacerbated by a deeper problem: the scant attention many churches give to how *anything* in the Bible should be taught to children—not to mention its most difficult passages! As Rosemary Cox observes, "Little has been done to examine the principles underlying our use of the Bible with children in the church."[4] This is unfortunate, to say the least, especially given Elizabeth Caldwell's claim in the epigraph that how we use the Bible with children may well determine whether or not they find it spiritually beneficial as they grow older. If this is true, it behooves church leaders to carefully consider the instructional methods and techniques they use to teach the Bible to children and teens.

While the larger issue of teaching the Bible to children is beyond the scope of this book, it is obviously related to the central concern of this chapter, which is to consider how best to teach the *violent* parts of Scripture to children. How can church leaders introduce children and teens to troubling Bible stories in ways that are age appropriate, honest, *and* congruent with the church's core values and beliefs? This is an important question, and one we will explore from various angles in the pages to follow. But before we do, a more basic issue requires our attention.

SHOULD CHILDREN BE TAUGHT VIOLENT BIBLE STORIES?

As we observed, many of the Bible's most popular stories are also some of its most violent ones: Noah's ark, Samson and Delilah, Joshua and the Battle of Jericho, David and Goliath—to name just a few. Stories like these are routinely taught to children. But should they be? Are biblical texts filled with killing, death, and destruction really suitable for children?

At the church I attend, children are given their very own Bible when they "graduate" from first grade. It's helpful when the children's pastor instructs these young recipients to start in the New Testament and focus on Jesus first. That is sound advice.[5] Still, what happens when they leave the Gospels and wander off into some Old Testament story about dismemberment, cannibalism, or incest? Are we sure we even want our children to read this book?[6]

My guess is that most Christians would emphatically declare, "Of course we do! The Bible is indispensable to Christian faith and life. People of *all* ages should read and study it." I agree. I do want people of all ages to read

Scripture and believe even children can learn things from some of its more violent verses. It can help them determine what kinds of behavior are harmful and can provide opportunities to consider how they might respond to whatever acts of violence they encounter or experience. That said, there is no denying that these biblical texts present real challenges for Sunday school teachers and youth workers who decide to use them.

How *much* violence, and what *sort* of violence, should children and adolescents be exposed to? And how should Christian educators talk with them about Bible stories that sanction and justify acts we condemn? Should children be encouraged to praise Joshua for slaughtering everyone in Jericho, "both men and women, young and old," along with their animals (Josh. 6:21)? Should they be taught to see David as a hero for killing an unusually tall man and then slicing off his head (1 Sam. 17:48–51)? Clearly, children are going to need some guidance here.

If the church is going to introduce children to some of these violent stories—and I think it should—then those who teach need to handle them very carefully. Sunday school teachers, children's pastors, and youth ministers need to be intentional about using these stories in ways that are both developmentally appropriate and that promote spiritual growth.

BEST PRACTICES FOR TEACHING VIOLENT BIBLE STORIES TO CHILDREN

The purpose of this chapter is to discuss best practices for teaching violent biblical texts to children and teens, though given how little has been written on this topic, I am unaware of any real consensus on this point. I use the phrase to emphasize things I consider very important, or essential to keep in mind, when talking with children about violence in the Bible.

Since most children have their first encounter with violent verses through Old Testament stories, this will be our focus. Though the Old Testament contains other types of violent texts, such as laws carrying the death penalty and judgment oracles prophesying divine destruction, these are not standard fare in most Sunday school classrooms. Nor are the violent parables, stories, and apocalyptic imagery found in the New Testament.

While the suggestions offered here are primarily designed for those who teach Sunday school or children's church,[7] they are relevant for a broad range of church workers who teach children in a variety of ministry contexts such as vacation Bible school, midweek club programs, and Sunday evening services.[8]

Introduce Violent Stories in Age-Appropriate Ways

As a general rule of thumb, anyone teaching the Bible to children should attempt to do so in age-appropriate ways. Children at different ages are obviously at different stages of cognitive, moral, and spiritual development. This directly impacts—or *should* impact—how one teaches the Bible to children. The way you talk to a first-grader about the story of Noah's ark or David and Goliath, for example, will surely differ from the way you talk about those stories with a high school senior.

While numerous studies have attempted to delineate stages of child development with great care, they have not been without critique.[9] For our purposes, it will suffice to recognize that children at various stages of development have different capacities to process violent biblical texts. In order to offer some guidance in this regard, I will categorize children into three groups based on their age. These groupings, though not hard and fast, provide some means of determining how violent biblical texts should be taught to children of all ages.

> Group 1: Toddlers and early learners (preschool through third grade): ages 2–8
> Group 2: Preteens (fourth through seventh grade): ages 9–12
> Group 3: Teenagers (eighth through twelfth grade): ages 13–18

We can now consider some general guidelines for discussing violent biblical stories with children in each of these groups.

Group 1: Avoid Some Stories, and Selectively Tell Others

If Bible stories were rated according to the guidelines established by the Motion Picture Association, a number of them would be R-rated (or worse!). Young children do not need to hear these stories in Sunday school or children's church. Five- and six-year-olds do not need to learn about the Levite's "concubine" being gang-raped and dismembered (Judg. 19), just as seven- and eight-year-olds do not need to read about the rape of Tamar (2 Sam. 13). Stories about sexual violence in the Bible—or anywhere else for that matter—are not appropriate at these ages. Likewise, biblical stories of genocide, suicide, mutilation, and child sacrifice are best left for when children are older and better able to process such mature themes. After all, what parent would want their child coming home from church with a craft based on the story of Saul's final moments, when he kills himself with his sword after being mortally wounded in battle (1 Sam. 31:1–7)?

Fortunately, those who teach toddlers and early learners almost never need to confront these unseemly stories in Sunday school because they are typically absent from most standard church curricula. Still, some violent stories do appear regularly in church-based curriculum for children. Sooner or later, those who teach children will probably need to find some way to talk with them about stories like the flood narrative and the Battle of Jericho. But how?

A common and effective strategy for teaching violent Bible stories to very young children is to selectively retell them. You can emphasize parts of the story that affirm God's care and protection, rather than those that describe human death and destruction. For example, when telling the story of Noah's ark (Gen. 6–9), focus on Noah and his family who are safely *inside* the ark rather than dwelling on the people dying *outside* it. Talk about how God was present with Noah throughout this ordeal and make connections to the way God is with us today through difficult circumstances.

Or suppose the Sunday school lesson is about Israel's dramatic Red Sea crossing (Exod. 14–15). What would it look like to selectively retell that story? Teachers could emphasize God's guidance and deliverance as they describe how Israelites made their way safely across to the other side on dry ground. They could talk about the way this story illustrates God's great love for the Hebrew people and how God helps them get away from people seeking their harm. In retelling the story, it is not necessary to mention the verse about dead Egyptian soldiers washing up on shore (14:30). Nor must toddlers and early learners be asked to consider all the widows and orphans created as a result of God drowning the entire Egyptian army. For this age-group, it is permissible to leave out these troubling details.

I realize this kind of selective retelling is *precisely* the kind of sanitizing I warned about in chapter 1. As I wrote there, part of the difficulty with sanitizing violent biblical texts is that it "conceals their problematic nature and fails to help us come to terms with the moral and ethical difficulties they raise." While I stand by that claim, I believe it *is* prudent to make an exception in this instance. It is acceptable—even advisable—to selectively retell some of the Old Testament's violent stories *to young children.* Toddlers and early learners do not need to be burdened with the "moral and ethical difficulties" raised by these texts. While it is important to confront these issues as they grow older, they do not need to do so while still in preschool or early elementary school. For young children, it is fine to focus on more positive and redemptive aspects of these texts.

Group 2: Introduce Preteens to a Wider Range of Stories and the Violence They Contain

While texts containing extremely graphic acts of violence should always be handled with great care and are probably still not suitable for children in this age-group, preteens should be introduced to a wider selection of violent stories from the Bible. These stories should *not* be sanitized, and selective retellings should come to an end. Children ages nine through twelve develop the moral capacity to process troubling texts and should not be shielded from them, at least *most* of them. They can handle these stories and are ready to hear about the violence they contain.

At this stage, Christian educators should feel free to talk about violent aspects of these stories without feeling the need to elaborate on them. For example, it would be fine to mention that lots of people died outside the ark and that many lives were lost inside the city of Jericho. But there is no need to focus extensively on the violent dimensions of these stories when teaching children in this age-group. You can acknowledge the death and destruction that is there, and then move on to explore other themes and ideas.

Preteens are likely to have some questions about the violence in these stories. Why did God kill so many in the flood? What happened to all the people living in Jericho after the walls fell down? If they raise questions like these, it is important to engage their questions openly and honestly (more on this momentarily). Learning how to talk about the troubling parts of these stories represents an important step toward dealing with them responsibly.

Group 3: Use Any Story, Problematize the Violence, and Focus on the Victims

Teenagers should be introduced to all parts of the Bible, even its most disturbing verses. In all likelihood, many of them will have already encountered a considerable amount of violence, bloodshed, and death in movies, books, and video games. While they might be surprised at what they find in the Bible, they will not be completely shocked, since these themes will not be new or unfamiliar. More to the point, most teenagers are developmentally ready to have serious discussions about violence in Scripture.

This is a good age to reintroduce some of the Bible stories they learned when they were younger. Only this time, as the stories are retold, more attention should be given to the victims in the text, both seen and unseen. When you discuss the story of Noah's ark with teens, reflect on the fate of those outside the ark. When you revisit the story of Joshua and the Battle of Jericho, talk about the people inside the city who are mercilessly slaughtered by the Israelites. Help them *see* the victims in these texts. Let them *feel* the human tragedy. Consider showing them artwork that depicts the devastation without sensationalizing it. Doing so will create space to talk about the harmful nature of violence as they see its negative impact.

Also, by humanizing the victims of violence in the Bible, teens can learn to develop compassion for them. This is one of the strategies for using a violent text constructively discussed in the previous chapter. Cultivating compassion for victims of violence is an especially valuable skill to develop in a world that frequently views certain kinds of people as expendable.

Since youth ministers often have considerable freedom choosing what topics to discuss with teens, they can intentionally deal with some of the more violent parts of Scripture. Given how triggering some of these topics can be, this would certainly need to be done with significant care and sensitivity (more on that in a moment). They can help teens reflect on the horrors of genocide by discussing the slaughter of Canaanites (Josh. 6–11) or the annihilation of Amalekites (1 Sam. 15). They can spend time talking about sexual violence and sexual assault by exploring disturbing stories like the rape of Dinah (Gen. 34) or Tamar (2 Sam. 13). And they can emphasize the tragedy of suicide by introducing teens to the seldom-heard stories of Ahithophel (2 Sam. 16:15– 17:23) or Zimri (1 Kgs. 16:8–20). Violent Old Testament texts like these provide helpful entry points into extremely important conversations.

Given the sensitive nature of these topics—particularly sexual assault and suicide—it would be wise for youth ministers to communicate with parents and guardians, letting them know what issues you are covering and why. Consider providing a handout beforehand that highlights some of the key points you plan to address and offers guidance for how to respond to questions their teens might raise. Identify resources they can consult if they want to learn more, and let them know you are happy to meet with them to discuss any questions or concerns. Maintaining open lines of communication like this will go a long way toward allaying fears that parents might have, or misunderstandings that might arise, from your decision to deal with these challenging topics and troubling texts.

Before broaching matters like sexual assault and suicide, youth ministers should be sure they know how to talk with teens about sensitive topics that are potentially triggering. Some youth ministers will have received this kind of instruction in college or seminary. But others may have little—if any— training in this area. If this describes you, it is important to educate yourself through books, online resources, and workshops.[10] If you still don't feel capable of addressing these issues, consider inviting an expert to be a guest speaker. Social workers, mental health professionals, clergy, and others who have training and expertise in these areas are an invaluable resource.

Finally, when you have these conversations, be mindful that people might open up to you about their own suicidal thoughts or their own sexual trauma. You should be prepared for this and ready to help as you are able. Also— and very importantly—be sure you know your limits and when to refer teens elsewhere if they need a different level of support and care than you can provide.

Be Honest about Violence in the Bible

When we teach violent biblical stories in church, they should be told honestly.[11] While making certain allowances for toddlers and early learners, as noted above, we should resist the temptation to make these stories kinder and gentler than they actually are, and we should not retell them in ways that minimize or obscure the violence they contain. As Pastor Sarah Hinlicky Wilson puts it:

> We can try to present them [children] an unproblematic Bible. . . . Or we can embrace the problematic Bible and abandon our efforts to control it. . . . We can hand over to our children, out of our own hands and our own control, the messy, shocking, astonishing, inspiring and multifarious holy scripture and let the Spirit use it to awaken their spirits, hearts and minds—including all the problems that come with such inspiration.[12]

Admittedly, this will be hard to do if we *ourselves* are uncomfortable with these violent texts. But we must resist the urge to clean up these stories. Instead, we should tell it like it is and then help children and teens process whatever thoughts and feelings these verses elicit. If we minimize the violence, or ignore it altogether, we rob children of the opportunity to learn from it.

But there is an even more important reason to deal honestly with the troubling aspects of these texts: it builds trust. When children see us being honest with Scripture, even when it makes us uncomfortable or reveals we do not have all the answers, something very significant happens. Children come to see us as people of integrity, people they can trust to take seriously their own questions and doubts, not only about violent verses but about other matters of faith as well.[13] On the other hand, if we play fast and loose with troubling biblical texts, and evade the hard questions children and teens ask us about them, why would they come to us for spiritual guidance and direction in the future?

When adults avoid violent texts or focus only on positive elements within them, children are given the wrong idea about the Bible. This can cause them to feel angry and frustrated later in life when they begin to see Scripture as it really is. Many feel a deep sense of betrayal. Why didn't their beloved pastor, youth minister, or Sunday school teacher talk straight with them? Why weren't they honest about the true nature of the Bible?

While presenting children with an "unproblematic Bible" *might* make things easier for Christian educators in the short term, it creates larger and more intractable problems down the road. Yet this is completely avoidable if those entrusted with the religious education of children are willing to be honest about the Bible. While this must be done in age-appropriate ways, as I have stressed, there comes a time when people need to realize that the flood narrative is not some happy-go-lucky colorful children's story about a floating zoo. It is divine destruction on such a global scale that it makes the COVID-19 pandemic pale by comparison. Children need to encounter the real Bible, not some sugarcoated version that minimizes or removes all the difficulties.

I realize that my insistence on "being honest" with these texts doesn't provide specific guidance for how to respond to questions children might raise about *why* God would wipe out virtually every living thing in a flood or *why* God commanded Israelites to mercilessly slaughter Canaanites. Nor does it offer advice for what to do with these passages in an instructional setting. We will get to that. My point here is to stress how crucial it is to be totally honest with these texts and the violence they contain. At the end of the day, isn't it better to have children who trust you to help them wrestle with the theological, moral, and ethical issues these texts raise than to have children who doubt your integrity and question the church's credibility because you were unwilling or unable to be honest about the Bible's difficulties?[14]

Refuse to Regard Violent Individuals as Heroes

When teaching children, it is important to consider carefully which biblical characters we hold up as role models or heroes and why. In my office, I have a Little Golden Book titled *Bible Heroes of the Old Testament*. In greatly abbreviated form, it tells the story of fourteen "heroes" of the Old Testament: Adam, Noah, Joseph, Miriam, Moses, Joshua, Samson, Deborah, David, Solomon, Elijah, Esther, Daniel, and Jonah. Based on this lineup, one can legitimately wonder what criteria the author used to determine who qualified as a hero. Adam does not strike me as heroic in any sense of the word. Nor does Jonah, a man who ran from God and couldn't stand the idea of God showing mercy to his enemies. But what I find most disturbing is the inclusion of cold-blooded killers like Samson, Joshua, and David who are responsible for so many deaths.

I realize that the individuals we routinely consider heroic in modern Western culture are those who take bold and decisive *violent* action when "necessary." This is reflected in popular culture, particularly in films and television shows that glorify women and men who use violence to stop evil (think *Star Wars* or the Marvel Universe). But as Christians who are called to follow the nonviolent way of Jesus, the Prince of Peace, doesn't it seem more than a little odd to valorize people in the Bible with so much blood on their hands?

The cover art of *Bible Heroes of the Old Testament*, which features Samson just moments before his death, is particularly unfortunate. As you may remember, Samson is captured by the Philistines, the people he once terrorized, after foolishly revealing that the secret of his great strength lies in his uncut hair. Once he is shorn, the Philistines promptly gouge out his eyes and humiliate him. Samson is hungry for revenge and bides his time as his hair slowly begins to grow back. Then, at an opportune moment, Samson prays, asking God to give him strength to punish the Philistines for the loss of his eyesight.

> Lord GOD, remember me and strengthen me only this once . . . so that with this one act of revenge I may pay back the Philistines for my two eyes. (Judg. 16:28)

The picture on the front of the book depicts this tragic moment at the end of Samson's life. Samson is shown pushing down the central pillars holding up the roof of the building where he has been brought to amuse thousands of Philistines. Samson stands alone on the book cover, inaccurately depicted with his eyes intact. (I can only assume the publisher deemed gouged-out eyes too graphic for the front cover of a children's book.) The Philistines who are just moments from death are conspicuously absent from the cover.

After uttering his final words—"Let me die with the Philistines"—Samson literally brings down the house (v. 30). Everyone dies—including the young boy who had led Samson to the supporting pillars. The body count for Samson's vengeance, *a deed not unlike that of a suicide bomber,* is approximately three thousand souls.[15] His actions make a mockery of Israel's legislation designed to restrict disproportionate retaliation.[16] Instead of taking an eye for an eye, Samson takes six thousand eyes for two! Bottom line: the final act of Samson's life is not heroic. It is revenge, plain and simple. That Samson is said to be divinely appointed as a deliverer—or that he prays moments before his death—doesn't change that. Nor does the fact that the writer of Hebrews praises Samson (along with five other individuals) in Hebrews 11:32–34. Samson's positive assessment by this New Testament writer does not suggest that everything he did was good or worthy of emulation. David also appears in this lineup, and his life was far from perfect. Samson is clearly not the kind of person we should be holding up to children as a hero, even *if* one believes some aspects of his life were commendable.

Instead of valorizing violent men and women in the Bible, we should look for other role models. As I have written elsewhere:

> We should help children think of heroes as people who *save* lives rather than destroy them. They are brave individuals who resolve conflict without resorting to violence, and who take significant risks to help people without harming others in the process. We should be on the lookout for people who behave in these ways since their stories can be quite useful for promoting the kinds of values and virtues we wish to encourage in children (and adults!). Thus, rather than celebrating the violence of Jael, who kills a man by driving a tent peg through his skull, we ought to praise the nonviolence of Abigail, who prevents a massacre through her courageous words and deeds. Or rather than

praising David for killing a Philistine, we ought to praise Joseph for forgiving his brothers.[17]

Whatever else we do with troublesome texts, we should not uphold individuals as heroes for their violent behavior. There may be other aspects of their lives that are good and praiseworthy, and we can certainly celebrate these. But it is inconsistent to claim to follow the nonviolent way of Jesus while at the same time venerating those whose lives are characterized by violence, bloodshed, and killing.

Emphasize That Our Views about Violence Differ from Ancient Israel's

When we teach Bible stories to children, we always want to be careful not to endorse the violence within them. This is quite easy when dealing with passages containing examples of "wrongful" violence. No thoughtful Sunday school teacher would discuss the story of Cain and Abel and then say, "Go and do likewise!" Nor would anyone talk about the rape of Dinah and then praise Shechem for his sexual prowess. That would be offensive and completely inappropriate. These stories clearly show us what is wrong with violence.

But things get a lot more difficult when the text implicitly, or explicitly, approves of the violence it contains. Stories like Noah's ark, Joshua and the Battle of Jericho, and David and Goliath work on the assumption that violence is sometimes necessary and commendable.[18] Unfortunately, too many people share this assumption, making it difficult for them to critique violence in the Bible. As a student once quipped, "If killing was good enough for Joshua, then it's good enough for me!"[19] That is precisely the kind of message we do *not* want children taking away from these texts. I would hope that even those Christians who believe killing is warranted in certain situations—such as in the heat of battle or perhaps in self-defense—would be disturbed by this sort of simplistic justification for killing today. So what can be done to keep children from making such dangerous and misguided connections?

In addition to refusing to valorize men and women who behave violently in the Bible, we can also help children realize that some of our views about violence are going to differ from those expressed in Scripture. That is to be expected, given the enormous historical and cultural distance between the ancient world in which these texts were written and our own. Moral values and ethical standards of right and wrong change considerably over time, and they vary from one culture to another. We do not think exactly the same way people did in antiquity. We evaluate things differently and are likely to disagree with some of the views we encounter in Scripture.[20]

To help children grasp this idea, you could demonstrate some concrete ways our thinking has changed over time. For example, people in ancient Israel believed the world was flat (Isa. 11:12; Rev. 7:1; 20:8), and they were certain the sun revolved around the earth (Josh. 10:12–14). We think differently today and no longer accept these ancient cosmological assumptions. Israelites believed it was permissible to own slaves (see Lev. 25:44–46; cf. Exod. 21:20–21); we do not. Polygamy and arranged marriages are sanctioned in Scripture, but most Christians and Jews disapprove of such practices today. People in ancient Israel believed natural disasters and sickness were signs of divine punishment. Today we attribute such things to naturally occurring weather patterns and microscopic organisms. Even Jesus rejected the idea that all human suffering was the result of sinning (Luke 13:1–5; John 9:1–5), even though this belief was deeply embedded in Israel's psyche (see especially Deut. 28).[21]

When children begin to understand that people living today see the world quite differently from ancient Israelites, they are better equipped to evaluate Old Testament passages that sanction violence. It helps them realize they are not obligated to regard violence as virtuous just because it finds approval in the pages of Scripture. Many of our views about warfare and killing, and about violence and nonviolence, have changed over time. Certain types of violence that are condoned in the Bible, such as capital punishment, blood vengeance, and genocide, are now widely condemned.

While ancient Israelites sanctioned and even celebrated violence in certain situations, we should remember that neither the Jewish tradition nor the Christian faith celebrates violence. Rather, both Jews and Christians have a strong ethic of life, one that emphasizes helping people, not harming them. Christians are to conduct themselves "in a manner worthy of the gospel of Christ" (Phil. 1:27) and should not hate, dominate, or retaliate. Rather, they are to love and serve others, to practice forgiveness and reconciliation, and to "overcome evil with good" (Rom. 12:21).

This means that great care must be taken when teaching children Old Testament stories containing "virtuous" violence. We should do everything in our power to help children understand that some of our most central Christian values differ from those we find embedded in these ancient texts—both Old *and* New Testament. Instead of reinforcing positive views of violence, we should use the Old Testament to emphasize such things as forgiveness (e.g., the story of Joseph), compassion (e.g., the story of Jonah), and nonviolent conflict resolution (e.g., the story of Abigail), and we should make it clear that the teachings of Jesus point in a different direction than violence, one that encourages love of enemy and prayer for persecutors (Matt. 5:44).[22] If children leave our Sunday school classroom or children's church program thinking that violence is acceptable because certain Bible stories sanction it, we are surely doing something wrong.

Encourage Questions and Curiosity

In his intriguingly titled book, *How Not to Totally Put Your Children off God*, Howard Worsley reflects on his memories of encountering the Bible as a child.[23] He recounts a profoundly spiritual experience he had as a ten-year-old while reading the neglected book of Habakkuk—an experience that led him to pray on his own for the first time. He also remembers how his dad read long passages from the book of Proverbs at the breakfast table early in the morning. And he recalls hearing the Bible read at Wednesday evening church services, though, he describes those occasions as very unsatisfying.

> Much to my dismay, the questions I wanted to ask were not asked, and if I pitched in with a question, it was not given a satisfactory answer. I wanted to know why anything done by people in the Bible was somehow virtuous. Was it OK for David to use a sling to overcome a thug called Goliath when maybe he could have talked him down? Was it OK for Samson to be so violent, or for Solomon to have so many wives? I got the impression that there was a subtext that the adults knew and I did not know, and as an adult looking back, I think I was correct in my assumption.[24]

It is unfortunate that Worsley did not experience church as a place that addressed his questions or encouraged his curiosity.

Children and young adults should know they are allowed to ask whatever questions they have about the Bible. And they should experience church as a safe space where their questions will be honored and taken seriously, where they will not be scolded or shamed for asking them.

For that to happen, Sunday school teachers, children's church volunteers, vacation Bible school workers, children's pastors, youth workers, and others will need to teach these stories in ways that make space for such questions to emerge. One way to accomplish this is to utilize what Elizabeth Caldwell refers to as "a wondering model" of teaching the Bible, something she adapts from Jerome Berryman's idea of "Godly play."[25] As Caldwell describes it:

> This model invites and expects an approach to biblical texts that is honest and curious, open to inquiry and interpretation. Its focus and intent is on how a child is first introduced to biblical story in a way that encourages their questions, curiosities, and all of their imagination. It

supports a child's spiritual development as they grow with a story, in understanding its meaning and the possible connections it has for their life. It is a model of engaging the biblical text that values open-ended responses rather than right or wrong answers. As such it seeks to empower children and the adults who read with them with the ability to see the connections between these old stories and how we see God revealed in them.[26]

Many children's Bibles and Christian education materials reduce stories to a single, simplified, moral truth, prepackaged and ready to deliver in one easy dose. Yet this way of reading the Bible stifles curiosity and limits what can be gleaned from it. It tames the text by erecting boundaries around what it can and cannot mean.[27]

By contrast, a wondering model of reading opens up the biblical text and encourages exploration and discovery. It helps children actively engage biblical stories in ways that do not predetermine the outcome or keep new insights from emerging. This prevents young learners from getting bored with the text when they return to it in the future.

Here's how Caldwell explains the way the wondering model works. A teacher begins by reading a story from the Bible or an adaptation of it from a children's Bible or storybook. Alternatively, teachers might choose to retell the story in their own words, or perhaps even show a dramatized version of it if one is available. Next, the teacher raises several open-ended questions about the story.

- Who is in the story and what happens to them?
- What do you think this story is about?
- What kind of story is this?
- How is this story different from the time and place in which we live?
- Why do you think this story is important?
- How do you connect with the story or what does this story have to do with your life? Or, when would be a good time to remember this story?[28]

These questions that Caldwell suggests leave open a wide range of responses and do not foreclose what the text means. This is especially valuable for dealing with violent biblical texts because it gives children both space *and permission* to comment on some of the more difficult parts of the story if they wish. This, in turn, provides teachers with wonderful opportunities to talk with children about real-life issues these texts raise such as anger, death, loss, suffering, killing, war, violence, betrayal, jealousy, and revenge. Even if some of these conversations are challenging, they are important. It helps children know they can talk honestly about these stories and the questions they have about them. This not only keeps them engaged with the Bible; it might even save their faith.

Help Children Imagine Nonviolent Versions of Violent Stories

Another way to use violent Old Testament narratives with children and teens involves inviting them to use their imagination to envision a violence-free version of the story. Ask them to imagine how things might have turned out differently if the main characters in the story had *not* resorted to violence. For example, what might have happened between Cain and Abel if Cain had *not* killed his brother? How could Cain have managed his anger better? What other options did he have to deal with his frustrations? Questions like these help children develop their own moral intuition as they explore various possibilities for how the story could have unfolded differently. They also set the stage to ask children some personal questions. What do *you* do when you feel angry? Do *you* sometimes hurt other people when you get mad? What might be some better ways to behave when you get upset?

This creative approach is especially useful with Old Testament stories that approve of the violence they contain. For example, rather than heaping praise on David for killing Goliath, teachers can encourage children to imagine other ways these two individuals might have resolved their differences. You might begin with open-ended questions that allow them to express whatever feelings they have about the story, followed by more directed questions. For instance:

- What do you think about this story? What do you like about it? Dislike about it?
- What are some other ways David and Goliath could have worked out their differences?
- Tell me about a time when someone threatened to hurt you. What happened, and how did you feel?
- Tell me about a time when you hurt someone. Why did you behave this way, and how did you feel afterward?
- If Jesus had been alive during this time, what do you think he might have said to Goliath? To David?
- How do you think God would have liked this story to end?

Rather than simply reinforcing notions of "virtuous" violence, questions like these open up the text for deeper exploration. They help children reflect on the problematic nature of violence and encourage them to consider other options for navigating conflict.[29]

Be Judicious about the Songs, Crafts, and Dramas You Use

There are many creative ways to teach children stories from the Bible. Songs, crafts, puppets, visual aids, and drama can be fabulous teaching tools that enable children, especially preteens, to "experience" Scripture in fun, easy-to-understand ways. Teens can also benefit greatly from a range of music, role plays, and art. Church leaders should encourage Sunday school teachers (and others) to do all they can to make the Bible as interesting and accessible as possible.

Still, caution is in order when using these creative techniques with violent stories. Before you ask your preteens to dramatize a violent Bible story, for example, consider carefully your intended purpose. Why are you having them do this? What messages (both intended and unintended) might the drama communicate? If the purpose of the dramatization is to *problematize* the violence described in the text, that is fine. But if the drama only serves to reinforce the "virtue" of violence—to celebrate Israel's conquest of Canaan or David's victory over Goliath, for instance—then it should be avoided.

We should also be certain that the songs children sing, and the crafts they make, in association with biblical texts do not celebrate death and destruction. Randal Rauser recalls a time when his daughter was young and sang a song titled "100% Chance of Rain" in the children's choir at church. Randal describes the song as "a playful retelling of the flooding of the earth and drowning of all living things."[30] Rauser also mentions a music video by the Cedarmont Kids that uses the African American spiritual "Joshua Fought the Battle of Jericho" to reenact the story.[31]

> The video features children marching around a fortress made of foam colored bricks as they wield their toy spears. Eventually, the walls are knocked down to gales of laughter and joy. Not surprisingly, no Canaanites ever made an appearance. Presumably, the tear-stained cheeks of terrified civilians pleading for their lives wouldn't fit the ethos of the video.[32]

Songs and reenactments like these seriously complicate our efforts to deal responsibly with the violent dimensions of these Old Testament stories.

While using various forms of media can be a helpful way to introduce children to some of these stories, every effort should be made to avoid using songs, crafts, or dramatizations that justify or glorify violence. Otherwise, they may get the impression that violence sometimes *is* virtuous and *can* be used to accomplish God's will.

One resource some teachers might find helpful to creatively and visually introduce children to violent Bible stories is the Brick Bible (thebrickbible. com) by Elbe Spurling.[33] Spurling's Lego-based illustrations of various parts of the Bible take seriously the violence they contain. Spurling helps us notice things we might prefer to ignore, and she refuses to shy away from the violent dimensions of these stories. The scenes she creates can be jarring and disturbing, but using Legos provides a way into these stories and should make it easier to discuss them, especially with children.[34]

ANSWERING HARD QUESTIONS CHILDREN ASK ABOUT GOD'S BEHAVIOR

So far, we have considered a number of best practices that children's ministers, Sunday school teachers, youth workers, and others can use when talking about violent stories in the Old Testament. Yet we have largely avoided the question of what should we say when children and adolescents ask hard questions about *God's* violent behavior in the Bible? Sooner or later, they will begin to wonder why God is involved in so much killing in the Old Testament. Didn't God care about the people drowning outside the ark? Was it really necessary for God to destroy all the inhabitants of Sodom and Gomorrah—save four? Why did God smite every firstborn child in Egypt? Weren't they made in God's image also? And what made God hate Canaanites so much that God commanded Israel to slaughter every last one of them without mercy? Questions like these are difficult for trained theologians and biblical scholars to answer. What is a fifth-grade Sunday school teacher or a volunteer leading children's church supposed to do with them?

Since this is such an important issue, and one with significant complexity, we will devote an entire chapter to it later. In light of that, my response here is provisional but hopefully still useful to those of you on the front lines who must field difficult questions like these from inquisitive youngsters.

The first thing you should do when a child asks a question about God's violent behavior in the Old Testament is to honor the question itself (even if it terrifies you!). Say, "That's a great question. I'm so glad you asked. Let's think about this together." To reiterate a point made earlier, *how* you respond to them might be just as important as *what* you say in response. A *gracious* response, one that indicates that you respect them and welcome their curiosity, signals that questions are OK and that it is safe to raise them. Obviously, what we say in response to their questions also matters a great deal. There are a number of ways to approach this, and some of these are likely to be more effective with certain age-groups than with others.

One way to *begin* a response to a question about why God behaves violently in a particular passage is to invite children to engage in a close reading of the text to see what they can discover. What does the text itself say (if anything) about why God behaved a certain way? In the book of Genesis, for example, the worldwide flood is described as God's response to human evil and violence (6:5, 13). It is not arbitrary or spiteful, and there is no indication that

God takes any pleasure or delight in humanity's destruction. Indeed, when the floodwaters subside, God promises to never flood the world again (9:8–17).

Granted, this still leaves many questions unanswered. How could a morally perfect being drown helpless infants and vulnerable elderly people? Why couldn't God find a less violent way to deal with the evil inclinations of the antediluvian population? Still, encouraging children to read the Bible closely clarifies the nature of the problem and helps them know more precisely where the difficulties reside.

A second way to respond would be to tell them that Christians have different opinions about how to understand God's violent behavior in the Old Testament and then to introduce some of these. Suppose a teenager in the youth Sunday school class is really bothered by God's divine directive to kill all the Canaanites without mercy. You could begin by validating their discomfort with this deadly decree, letting them know Christians have struggled with this for centuries. You could then introduce them to various ways Christians have tried to make sense of these passages. For instance, some believe God was justified in issuing this command to punish Canaanites for their wickedness. Others say God's actions are not fully understandable but are morally right because everything God does is good and right. Still others—who disagree with the notion that God said or did everything the Bible claims—do not believe God ever issued this command in the first place, despite what the text says.

Sharing a wide range of options, even ones you do not agree with, and doing this in age-appropriate ways can be very beneficial for children and young adults.[35] It indicates others have asked the same questions they are asking about God's behavior, and it provides them with a quick overview of some of the explanations that have been proposed. This gives them an opportunity to compare and contrast these approaches as they weigh pros and cons and develop their own beliefs.

Introducing children to multiple possibilities has the added benefit of teaching them to value and respect views that differ from their own. It helps them realize there is not just one single position on issues of theological importance. Christians have diverse views about the nature of God and the practice of biblical interpretation. Being aware of various perspectives can help children and young people have respectful conversations rather than demonizing those who have a different point of view. It also helps them have a more robust faith, one that is not put in crisis when they encounter views that do not align with their own.

Using the "Christians think differently on this topic" approach is especially helpful if you want to answer a difficult question *without* revealing your personal views. This can be particularly useful if your beliefs are at odds with the church or Christian organization you serve. Going public with personal views that are contrary to those of the religious institutions and stakeholders to whom you are accountable can have serious and costly consequences.[36] However we choose to navigate this particular issue, it is important to send children a clear message that violent biblical texts should never be used to justify violent behavior toward others. Sunday school teachers, like all ministers and lay leaders in the church, should encourage ways of reading the Bible that promote love and mercy, not death and destruction.

A third way to respond to concerns about God's violent behavior in the Bible is to question the theological accuracy of these portrayals. While I think it is appropriate to raise this question in some form or other with children of various ages, especially once they become preteens, most teenagers are developmentally ready to have a serious conversation about this, and youth pastors should give focused attention to it. Questioning the theological accuracy of violent portrayals of God involves challenging two assumptions about the Old Testament: that all the stories are historically accurate, and that God said and did whatever the text claims. But what if some of these stories were never meant to be historical, at least not in the same way we think about history today? And what if God did *not* say and do everything the text claims? If these two commonly held assumptions are misguided, then it stands to reason that some of these Old Testament portrayals of God do not accurately reflect God's character. This opens up a whole new way of approaching these troubling depictions of God, though it will raise other questions about traditional ways of understanding the inspiration and authority of Scripture. This is a very important option, and one we will explore at length in chapter 8.

Finally, if you are really unsure how to respond to hard questions children are asking about God's behavior in the Bible—maybe because you find yourself asking the same questions—it is fine to be totally honest with them and admit you do not have it all figured out.[37] You can tell them you too have wondered why God would order Abraham to sacrifice his beloved son and command Israelites to slaughter Canaanites. You can let them know you also are bothered by the story of God killing firstborn children in Egypt and then drowning the Egyptian army in the Red Sea. Like them, you have a hard time believing that an infinitely creative, all-loving God would resort to such brutal and bloody tactics. If you are working with younger children, I think it would be important to reassure them of God's goodness—and especially God's great love and care for them—even if you can't make sense of everything the Bible says about God. This should be the primary focus for toddlers and early learners.

Telling children you wonder about some of the same things they do normalizes their questions. It helps them realize they are not weird, bad, or unchristian for raising questions like these or for being confused about God's violent behavior in the Old Testament. After all, if their trusted Sunday school teacher is asking the same questions they are, then surely those questions are important and worthwhile even if they prove difficult to answer.

Obviously, part of a teacher's job is to help young people find answers to the questions they are asking. If you do not know how to respond to a question, you can always tell them you will look into it and get back to them. This gives you space to do some research and to consult with others. If you do not have the time or energy to invest in this, see if you can at least suggest something they might read or someone they could talk to.[38] Also, if you suspect it will take a long time before you respond, let them know it may be a while so they do not think you have forgotten about them. Either way, it is very important to follow through and not leave them hanging.

If these questions emerge in a Sunday school class or group setting, consider inviting a trusted pastor, Bible professor, or religiously educated layperson to come and speak on the topic. This is a nice alternative since it takes some pressure off you. If you do go this route, I would recommend having a conversation with the person you plan to invite to be sure you are comfortable with what they are going to say. If you find out they are going to respond in unhelpful ways or take the conversation in a direction you do not want it to go, invite someone else.

A FINAL WORD TO THOSE
WHO TEACH CHILDREN

If you are involved in teaching the Bible to children, you have a high and holy calling. What you do really matters—to God, to the world, and, of course, to the children you teach. While I hope the church you attend will equip you for the task,[39] here are a few things you can do on your own to prepare yourself.

First, familiarize yourself with violent Old Testament stories, particularly the ones you anticipate will be part of what you teach. Read and reflect on these stories. What do you personally find most helpful about them? What is most challenging? If you find journaling helpful, write out your responses to these questions.

Second, try to anticipate some of the questions children might ask about these stories. What will intrigue them? What will bother them? Who do you think they will identify with in the story? Then, having anticipated some of their questions, think about how you could respond.

Third, as you prepare to teach, ask yourself what your students are likely to take away from the passage. Will they leave thinking God is cruel, heartless, and ultimately unfair, helping some while hurting others? If so, what can you do to guide them toward a more accurate view of God? Will they be tempted to see violence as "virtuous" because the text presents it that way? If so, how can you problematize violence? How can you help them develop compassion for the victims in the story, and what will you say to emphasize that violence is inconsistent with Christian ethics? We certainly do not want children to leave church with the impression that it's OK to harm others or that violence is a Christian virtue.

Finally, as you prepare to teach, always keep in mind the two greatest commandments: love for God and others. Ask yourself this simple question: Will the way I teach this class increase my students' love for God and others? If so, you are surely on the right track.

A NOTE FOR THOSE WHO TEACH ADULT SUNDAY SCHOOL

While this chapter has focused on teaching violent biblical texts to children and youth, a number of principles discussed here also apply when teaching these challenging texts to adults (e.g., talking honestly about the violence, refusing to valorize violent men and women in the Bible, helping people imagine nonviolent versions of violent stories). Likewise, many of the suggestions offered in chapter 6, though it is devoted to preaching, are easily adaptable for use in an adult Sunday school class or a similar context (e.g., using violent texts to talk about violence in the world today, developing compassion for victims, critiquing "virtuous" violence in the Old Testament). Thus, even though this book does not have a chapter devoted to teaching adults, a considerable amount of material here is directly relevant to that task.

CONCLUSION

There is a desperate need to do something constructive with violent biblical texts in church. One thing we can do—and should do—is teach these stories honestly and responsibly to children. Throughout this chapter, I have offered numerous suggestions to help in this regard. See the quick reference guide at www.wjkbooks.com/RedeemingViolentVerses to remind yourself of these suggestions. I am hopeful these ideas and techniques will help decrease your anxiety and enable you to feel more confident about teaching violent Old Testament stories to children. Young people need to know how to read, interpret, and apply these stories in ways that discourage the use of violence and promote a healthy view of God. This will happen if we do our job faithfully, teaching these texts in ways that do no harm and that foster a love of God and others.

5

Using Violent Verses in Worship

*Dos and Don'ts for Songs, Scripture
Readings, Prayers, and Liturgies*

> Many of us—liturgists, worship leaders, pastors, song writers, and
> lay people—have been uncomfortable with biblical violence for years
> and have been designing services and prayers that discretely avoid the
> more blatant of these images.
> —Bret Hesla, *Worship in the Spirit of Jesus*[1]

Imagine, for a moment, that you have recently moved and are in the process
of looking for a new church to attend. You have already visited a number of
well-known churches in the area, and this week have decided to pick one at
random from an online search you did late last night. You arrive just in time
to grab a cup of coffee, shake hands with an overly friendly greeter, and settle
into a vacant pew near the back of the sanctuary. Within moments, the service
begins.

After a warm welcome from the pastor and a few praise choruses, a well-
dressed man steps up to the podium and reverently opens his leather-bound
Bible. After clearing his throat, he announces the Scripture reading for the
morning. "A reading from the book of Deuteronomy, chapter twenty-eight,
verses twenty-five through twenty-nine." He then begins to read the passage
with great authority and deliberation, pausing repeatedly for dramatic effect.

Leader: The LORD will cause you to be defeated before your enemies;
        you shall go out against them one way and flee before them seven ways.

You shall become an object of horror to all the kingdoms
of the earth.

Your corpses shall be food for every bird of the air and animal
of the earth,
and there shall be no one to frighten them away.

The LORD will afflict you with the boils of Egypt,
with ulcers, scurvy, and itch, of which you cannot be healed.

The LORD will afflict you with madness, blindness, and confusion
of mind;

you shall grope about at noon as blind people grope in darkness,
but you shall be unable to find your way;
and you shall be continually abused and robbed,
without anyone to help.

The word of God for the people of God!

People: Thanks be to God!

You frantically scan the sanctuary for the nearest exit. You want to get out as fast as possible before they start serving the Kool-Aid!

Admittedly, this scenario is far-fetched. It is highly unlikely you will ever hear these disturbing verses read aloud at church. Passages like Deuteronomy 28:25–29 are not welcome in Sunday morning services. They are typically not part of the liturgy, and they rarely appear in hymns, pastoral prayers, or responsive readings. Yet, if we believe all Scripture is "useful," how can passages like this—and other violent biblical texts—be used effectively in Sunday morning worship services? Are certain aspects of the worship service more conducive to employing violent verses than others? Are there some parts of a service where it would be ill-advised to use a passage like this?

This chapter will attempt to answer these questions, offering numerous suggestions designed to help pastors and worship leaders use violent biblical texts responsibly when planning and facilitating worship services. Specifically, we will consider constructive and spiritually edifying ways to use violent verses in songs, prayers, and readings. And we will discuss some instances when it is probably best to avoid using them at all unless special care is taken. Since sermons occupy such a prominent place in many worship services, and since they pose their own unique set of challenges and opportunities, we will devote the next chapter to discussing how to use violent biblical texts for preaching.

THE CALL TO WORSHIP

Many church services begin with a call to worship inviting the gathered community to focus on God and to be open to what God might want to do among them. While this part of the service can take various forms, it is common for ministers to read a portion of Scripture as a way of centering the congregation and ushering them into the presence of God. Pastors and worship leaders regularly turn to the Psalter (the book of Psalms) to find material suitable for this purpose. There is a lot to choose from.

> Make a joyful noise to the LORD, all the earth.
>> Worship the LORD with gladness;
>> come into his presence with singing.
>>>> Ps. 100:1–2

> Praise the LORD!
>> Praise the name of the LORD;
>> give praise, O servants of the LORD,
> you that stand in the house of the LORD,
>> in the courts of the house of our God.
>>>> Ps. 135:1–2

Examples like these abound in the book of Psalms.

But not everything in the Psalter is suitable as a call to worship, especially not many of the violent verses found there. Reading verses that speak about God harming, destroying, or killing people is not a particularly helpful way to invite people into God's presence or lead them into worship.

> Rise up, O LORD!
>> Deliver me, O my God!
> For you strike all my enemies on the cheek;
>> you break the teeth of the wicked.
>>>> Ps. 3:7

> O LORD, you God of vengeance,
>> you God of vengeance, shine forth!
>>>> Ps. 94:1

> He will repay them for their iniquity
>> and wipe them out for their wickedness;
>> the LORD our God will wipe them out.
>>>> Ps. 94:23

> O that you would kill the wicked, O God.
> Ps. 139:19

> The LORD watches over all who love him,
> but all the wicked he will destroy.
> Ps. 145:20

> The LORD lifts up the downtrodden;
> he casts the wicked to the ground.
> Ps. 147:6

While most ministers would never think of using violent verses like these *alone*, they sometimes do appear as a portion of the call to worship because they are embedded in larger passages used for that purpose. Bible verses that talk about God casting down, destroying, and wiping out the wicked—not to mention smacking cheeks and breaking teeth—are not appropriate as a call to worship.

Part of the problem with including violent verses in the call to worship is that this aspect of the service usually takes place without comment or explanation. Including such verses, even as part of a larger text, has the unfortunate effect of reinforcing violent views of God, and it may lead people to assume the church actually believes this is what God is really like. If we believe God is a loving redeemer working to save sinners rather than exterminate them, it seems unwise to use verses that suggest otherwise when they are left to speak for themselves. Given the potential for confusion, ministers should steer clear of such texts when planning this part of the worship service.

I realize it may seem like I am reversing course here, given my earlier criticism of the church's tendency to avoid using violent verses. I am not. I firmly believe it is unwise to ignore unseemly verses in the regular rhythms of church life, and I stand by the argument I made to that effect in chapter 2. But I am *not* advocating the church should use violence verses always and everywhere. There are special circumstances when it *is* prudent to avoid using certain kinds of biblical texts. This is one of them.

RESPONSIVE READINGS

Responsive readings are another standard element of many worship services. They are read aloud during the service and usually alternate between words spoken by the minister (leader) and words spoken by the congregation (people). For the same reasons noted above, I do not think it is wise to use verses that sanction violence, or that portray God behaving violently, as part of responsive readings since these passages are presented without additional interpretation. Doing so runs the risk of reinforcing a positive view of violence, something the church should assiduously avoid.

That said, I do believe there are ways to use certain kinds of violent verses in responsive readings. For example, I think it is entirely appropriate to use verses that demonstrate how people *responded* to violence in ways that reduced hostilities and deescalated tense situations. To illustrate what this might look like, consider the following responsive reading that highlights three incidents in the Old Testament where violence could have been used but wasn't: Joseph's treatment of his miscreant brothers, Israel's altercation over an altar, and Abigail's actions in the face of a retaliatory assault.

A Reading to Help Us Find Alternatives to Violence

Leader: When people have wronged us and we find ourselves in a position to exact revenge,

People: let us be like Joseph, who forgave his brothers for the wrongs they committed against him many years prior.

Leader: When we hear the drumbeats of war and see people lining up to march into battle,

People: let us be like the tribes of Israel who avoided going to war by engaging in a conversation about a dispute over an altar.

Leader: When we encounter people who are bound and determined to do us harm,

People: let us be like Abigail, a courageous woman who prevented a massacre by her quick thinking, generous gifts, and wise words.

All: **Let us be inspired by these women and men to find alternatives to violence when conflict comes our way so that we might live at peace with all people, insofar as that is possible. Amen.[2]**

This short responsive reading has the advantage of drawing people's attention to stories in the Old Testament that contain violence, or the threat of violence, but do not encourage that kind of behavior. Rather than promoting violence, this reading demonstrates how people *prevented* it by choosing to forgive, engaging in conversation, and offering hospitality.

Violent verses can also be used effectively in responsive readings designed to facilitate confession. Old Testament stories that describe people behaving violently, and suffering the consequences for doing so, work particularly well in this regard. Ministers can use these passages to help people reflect on their own attitudes and actions toward others as they prepare to confess their sins.

A Reading to Confess the Violence in Our Hearts and the Blood on Our Hands

(This, or something similar, could be said by the leader before beginning this reading:)

Leader: The Old Testament contains numerous stories of men and woman who participated in terrible acts of violence and cruelty toward others. As we recall some of these troubling texts, let us use them to confess the hatred, violence, and murder that lurk within our own hearts.

Leader: Like Cain who killed his brother Abel, sometimes we do the most harm to those closest to us.

People: Forgive us, God, for the ways we have mistreated people in our family this week. For our unkind words, our impatience, our selfishness, and our disrespect, forgive us and "put a new and right spirit" within us.

Leader: Like David, who had Bathsheba's husband Uriah killed in a desperate attempt to cover up his sexual transgressions, sometimes we too hurt others in a futile effort to hide our own sins.

People: You know the sins we are hiding, O God. And you know the lengths to which we have gone to conceal them. Forgive us for hiding our sins rather than confessing them, and for hurting others in the process.

Leader: Like Queen Jezebel, who devised a ruthless and deceitful scheme to kill an innocent man so her husband could have his vineyard, we too are sometimes guilty of abusing the power we have to get what we want.

People: Forgive us for the ways we have misused our power and taken advantage of others—at home, at school, in church. Forgive us for the violence we have done to others, whether physical, emotional, or verbal, in spaces both public and private.

Leader: Thank you for hearing our prayers. Thank you for forgiving our sins. Give us the strength, courage, and conviction to go now and sin no more. Amen.[3]

Obviously, both of these responsive readings could be developed and expanded in lots of directions, but hopefully this helps demonstrate how violent texts can be used in liturgically responsible ways.

I am aware that many ministers and worship leaders do not create their own liturgical materials but use what others have produced. There is certainly nothing wrong with this. In fact, many liturgical resources are produced for this very purpose. Still, if you are borrowing a responsive reading or liturgical resource from somewhere else, it is important to pay close attention to its content. What—if anything—does it say about violence? Does that align with the message you want to convey to the congregation? If not, try modifying it in ways that challenge any views of "virtuous" violence it might contain. If that is not viable, simply choose a different reading or try creating one of your own.

SCRIPTURE READINGS

Most churches include at least one Scripture reading as part of their corporate worship experience. Passages containing "wrongful" violence, violence that is critiqued in the text, are generally fine as Scripture readings, provided appropriate trigger warnings have been issued if the passage is particularly graphic or disturbing. It is very unlikely anyone would decide to "go and do likewise" when they hear a Scripture reading about behavior that is *condemned* in the Old Testament. After hearing the story of Cain and Abel in Genesis 4, no reasonable person is going to say, "I should kill my brother just like Cain did!" Nor is someone likely to hear a reading from 2 Samuel 11–12, which describes David's predatory behavior with Bathsheba and his treachery with Uriah, and then conclude, "I should have sex with my neighbor's wife—and then kill my neighbor." Texts like these *discourage* violent behavior because they clearly demonstrate the negative consequences that follow. Cain becomes an outcast who fears for his life; David suffers the death of his child and eventually loses control of his kingdom.[4]

But what happens when people encounter biblical texts that *condone* violence rather than *condemn* it? Is it appropriate to read texts like these in public without commenting on them?

To explore this question, it is interesting to see how Jesus handles a violent passage of Scripture at the beginning of his public ministry. While attending a Sabbath day service at his hometown synagogue of Nazareth, Jesus is given the opportunity to read Scripture publicly. After standing and being handed the scroll of Isaiah, Jesus reads the following passage:

> The Spirit of the Lord is upon me,
>   because he has anointed me
> to bring good news to the poor.

> He has sent me to proclaim release to the captives
> 　　and recovery of sight to the blind,
> to let the oppressed go free,
> to proclaim the year of the Lord's favor.
> 　　　　　　　　　　　　　　　　Luke 4:18–19

With that, we are told that Jesus "rolled up the scroll, gave it back to the attendant, and sat down" (v. 20).

What's intriguing about this story is *where* Jesus stops reading. He ends right in the middle of a verse, just before it mentions "the day of vengeance of our God."[5] This "day of vengeance" was thought to be a time when God would punish evildoers, particularly Israel's enemies. It was a day eagerly anticipated by many of Jesus' listeners, a day when they believed God would overthrow the wicked and free the people of Israel from foreign tyranny and oppression. For Jews living under Roman domination, such a day could not come soon enough.

Yet Jesus chose not to read these violent words. Why? It is impossible to know for sure, but it could have something to do with his view of God.[6] Jesus understood God to be "kind to the ungrateful and the wicked" (Luke 6:35), not one poised to unleash a payload of divine wrath against evildoers, which might be how his listeners would have interpreted Isaiah's reference to the day of vengeance.

In any case, Jesus' more gracious and inclusive view of God is clearly evident in what happens next. After Jesus finishes reading from Isaiah, he refers to two additional stories from the Hebrew Scriptures that both emphasize God's care for outsiders. Jesus first mentions a story about the prophet Elijah being sent to care only for a *foreign* widow in Sidon despite the fact there were many widows in Israel (1 Kgs. 17). Then Jesus cites the story of Naaman, a Syrian army commander who was the only person healed of a skin disease during the days of Elisha even though many in Israel suffered from this ailment at the time (2 Kgs. 5).

While I do not think Jesus was trying to minimize God's care and concern for the people of Israel, I do believe he was trying to expand their vision of who God cares about. By referencing these stories, Jesus was emphasizing that God had a history of extending mercy to the very kind of people many in the crowd were eager to see destroyed. Since Jesus had a more expansive view of God than certain interpretations of Isaiah's words about the "day of vengeance" would allow, that may explain why Jesus chose not to read them.

If so, we do well to follow Jesus' example when it comes to the *public* reading of Scripture. Since we do not want to leave people with the impression that God is violent, or that God sanctions violent behavior, Scripture readings that speak approvingly of violence should be used in worship only if one of two things happen: (1) the issue is addressed responsibly elsewhere in the service, such as during the sermon, or (2) some kind of caveat, qualification, or contextual remark is made before reading the passage. Since the next chapter is devoted to using violent Scripture passages as sermon texts, I will limit my comments here to the second point.

Let's suppose you decide to use Psalm 145 as a Scripture reading in worship. It is a beautiful passage that emphasizes many key attributes of God: goodness, mercy, compassion, faithfulness, and so forth. But in verse 20 it also claims God will destroy the wicked:

> The LORD watches over all who love him,
>   but all the wicked he will destroy.

To avoid perpetuating an image of God as one who destroys the wicked, you could perform a "psalmectomy" and simply omit verse 20 when reading the psalm.[7] If you choose to do this, I think it is important to be transparent about what you are doing. You should clearly indicate in the bulletin (or on the screen) that you are reading Psalm 145:1–19, 21. This is more honest than just sort of skipping over the offending verse. Alternately, you might simply decide to limit the reading to verses 1–19. That way, you do not need to skip a verse. You just stop before you arrive at it. And just to be clear here, I am *not* suggesting verse 20 (and others like it) have no place on Sunday morning. I am simply saying this part of the service might not be the *best* place to introduce a verse like this, since it does not allow space for further exploration and qualification.

But let's suppose you prefer to read the entire psalm as is, without omitting verse 20. In that case, I would encourage you to consider prefacing the reading with a brief word of explanation. You could say something like this:

> Psalm 145 is a wonderful passage of Scripture that makes many lofty claims about the character of God. While Christians today affirm most of these claims, some would disagree with the portrayal of God as one who destroys the wicked. Instead, they see God as one who is always striving to redeem, lovingly pursuing even the most obstinate sinners in the hopes of reconciliation and relationship. Hear now these words from the psalmist.

This strikes me as a very gentle way to raise people's awareness that some of what they are about to hear may not be the gospel truth. And it does so without committing the church to any particular position on the matter. People in the pew are simply informed that not all Christians today embrace the notion that God destroys the wicked. This approach is especially beneficial in theologically conservative churches, and even more moderate ones, where people are often reticent to engage in a critique of Scripture, especially when it comes to the Bible's portrayal of God.

Churches wanting to make a more forceful statement about this can easily do so by slightly modifying the explanation given above. Instead of "some would disagree," they can say, "*we* disagree." And instead of "they see God as a redeemer," the church can say, "*we* see God as a redeemer."

If you are concerned that making a statement like this might disrupt the flow of worship, consider placing it in the bulletin or projecting it on the screen if your church has this capability. That way, people can read it on their own and those leading worship can continue unhindered.

Let's take another example. Suppose your church has a sermon series titled "Pivotal Moments in the History of Israel," and you are asked to include 2 Kings 17:1–20 as a Scripture reading. This passage recounts the Assyrian conquest of the northern kingdom of Israel and offers a theological explanation of why it happened:

> This occurred because the people of Israel had sinned against the LORD their God, who had brought them up out of the land of Egypt from under the hand of Pharaoh king of Egypt. (v. 7)

The passage goes on to describe numerous sins the people committed, and it emphasizes the idea that their violent removal from the land was orchestrated by God.

> Therefore the LORD was very angry with Israel and removed them out of his sight; none was left but the tribe of Judah alone.
> Judah also did not keep the commandments of the LORD their God but walked in the customs that Israel had introduced. The LORD rejected all the descendants of Israel; he punished them and gave them into the hand of plunderers, until he had banished them from his presence. (vv. 18–20)

When you talk with the senior pastor about this passage prior to the service, you learn the focus of her sermon will be on the way tragedy can upend our lives and precipitate a faith crisis. She asks if you would preface the reading with a contextual statement that mitigates its violent view of God. You are happy to comply and craft the following statement to be read immediately prior to the Scripture reading:

> One of the most common beliefs in the ancient world was that God (or the gods) punished people who sinned and rewarded people who obeyed. Punishments could come in the form of illness, crop-destroying

natural disasters, and military conquest, while rewards might include physical health, a good harvest, and national peace and security.

The passage I am about to read works on this assumption, though it is important to note that not everyone in Israel thought this way. The notion that God blesses the righteous and punishes the wicked is strongly challenged in the book of Job and is even contested by Jesus himself. Therefore, as you hear these words, keep in mind they reflect a view of God that many people today take exception to.

Including a brief contextual statement like this helps people understand that they do not need to believe God behaved violently just because an ancient Israelite scribe did.

I realize there is only so much "educating" you can do in a short statement made before a Scripture reading. Still, we should not underestimate the power and importance of making contextual statements like these. Even brief words of explanation will, over time, do their good work, equipping churchgoers to read and understand these violent verses more responsibly.

PASTORAL PRAYERS (AND IMPRECATORY PSALMS)

While I am sure there are exceptions, most pastoral prayers offered on Sunday morning include very little Scripture from either the Old or New Testament. Even positive and uplifting Bible verses that would presumably pose no problems for ministers or congregants rarely find their way into the "prayers of the people." And if *congenial* verses are unlikely to appear in pastoral prayers, how much less *contentious* ones!

Obviously, this is not all bad. It would be extremely disturbing to hear a minister offer a prayer like this:

> We praise you, O God, for your holy violence and righteous vengeance.
>
> Thank you for killing every firstborn child in Egypt, causing such grief and pain among the Egyptians that Pharaoh had no choice but to let the Hebrew people go. We worship you as the almighty God for drowning the entire Egyptian army in the Red Sea and creating untold numbers of widows and orphans in the process so that your people could be free.
>
> We acknowledge your justice in ordering Israelites to slaughter Canaanites without mercy. And we praise you for commanding the people of Israel to utterly annihilate every last Amalekite—babies and

all! Thank you, O God, for your lethal judgments, for punishing your enemies with death and destruction. Truly you are good in all your ways, and praiseworthy in all your deadly deeds. Amen.

(And now for a song from the children's choir about God's love . . .)

Praying like this would undoubtedly get people's attention! And it would be "accurate" based on a literal reading and understanding of various Old Testament passages. But it would be terribly misguided and highly inappropriate.

So how can we use violent verses responsibly in prayer? One possibility involves using a particular *type* of violence in the Bible as a focal point of the prayer. To illustrate this, let's take an issue like human trafficking. Since January is Human Trafficking Awareness Month, you might consider praying about this form of violence during one of the first few worship services of the year. As part of your prayer, you could recall what happens to Joseph in the Old Testament. When just a teenager, Joseph is trafficked by his brothers, sold to Midianite traders for twenty pieces of silver (Gen. 37:28). You could also mention the story of an unnamed Israelite girl recorded in 2 Kings 5. She too is a victim of human trafficking. She is kidnapped by Aramean raiders from the north and is ripped away from all that is familiar: her country, her family, and the life she knew. Taken to a foreign land, she is enslaved and forced to serve the wife of Naaman, the commander of the king's army (v. 2). Her story, along with Joseph's, could be incorporated into a prayer for victims of human trafficking today, those we know by name, and those we do not. Your prayer could emphasize the church's commitment to work for healthy human relationships that honor and respect the personhood of each individual. And you might use this prayer to issue a call to action, inviting people to be open to the ways God may be prompting them to take concrete steps to reduce and prevent this form of evil.[8]

Some of the most violent verses in the Old Testament are actually contained in Israel's prayers—prayers for their enemies, that is. These prayers, found in the Psalter, are known as imprecatory psalms. In these prayers, the psalmist asks God to do terrible things to their enemies. Consider these harsh words from Psalm 109:[9]

> Appoint a wicked man against him;
>   let an accuser stand on his right.
> When he is tried, let him be found guilty;
>   let his prayer be counted as sin.
> May his days be few;
>   may another seize his position.
> May his children be orphans,
>   and his wife a widow.

May his children wander about and beg;
    may they be driven out of the ruins they inhabit.
May the creditor seize all that he has;
    may strangers plunder the fruits of his toil.
May there be no one to do him a kindness,
    nor anyone to pity his orphaned children.
May his posterity be cut off;
    may his name be blotted out in the second generation.
May the iniquity of his father be remembered before the LORD,
    and do not let the sin of his mother be blotted out.
Let them be before the LORD continually,
    and may his memory be cut off from the earth.
For he did not remember to show kindness,
    but pursued the poor and needy
    and the brokenhearted to their death.
He loved to curse; let curses come on him.
    He did not like blessing; may it be far from him.
He clothed himself with cursing as his coat,
    may it soak into his body like water,
    like oil into his bones.
May it be like a garment that he wraps around himself,
    like a belt that he wears every day.
May that be the reward of my accusers from the LORD,
    of those who speak evil against my life

vv. 6–20

There is considerable debate among Christians about whether it is appropriate to pray these kinds of prayers. Some, like Pastor Wiley Drake, believe it is completely fine.

> Several years ago, radio host Alan Colmes conducted an interview of Wiley Drake, a pastor of a Southern Baptist mega-church and former vice president of the Southern Baptist Convention. At one point in this interview, Drake admitted that he regularly prayed for the death of President Obama, whom he referred to as "the usurper that is in the White House." Shocked by this admission, Colmes inquired how a Christian pastor could pray such a hateful thing. Wiley proudly responded that it is because he "believes the whole Bible," including its imprecatory prayers, which include a number of vengeful prayers for enemies to die.[10]

Likewise, certain biblical scholars, like John Day, affirm the use of these prayers. In his book *Crying for Justice: What the Psalms Teach Us about Mercy and Vengeance in an Age of Terrorism*, Day addresses the issue at length and concludes:

> The imprecatory psalms retain an appropriate place in the life of the Christian church. *It is legitimate at times for God's present people to utter prayers of imprecation or pleas for divine vengeance—like those in the psalms—against the recalcitrant enemies of God and his people.*[11]

I am not convinced.

While a fully adequate response to this issue is beyond the scope of this book, suffice it to say it is difficult to reconcile these violent, vengeful prayers with the life and teachings of Jesus. Jesus calls us to *love* enemies and to pray *for* persecutors (Matt. 5:44). Rather than beseeching God to send terrible evil upon those who have harmed us, Jesus says we must forgive them (6:12–15). And the apostle Paul instructs us to show kindness to our enemies by meeting their physical needs as we strive to "overcome evil with good" (Rom. 12:17–21). Imprecatory psalms certainly seem to stand at odds with the nonviolent way of Jesus and the nonviolent nature of Christian discipleship.[12]

So how should we deal with these violent verses in church? How can they be redeemed?

One option—and this would need to be done carefully—is to help people see that these hate-filled prayers are valuable because they remind us that we can be totally honest with God when we pray. Imprecatory psalms remind us that God can "handle" all of our emotions. When we have been profoundly hurt by others, we can tell God exactly how we feel. We can share all of our rage, fear, and bitterness. We can even express our *desire* for revenge against those who have harmed us and caused us pain.

Still—and this is very important—we can do all that *without* asking God to do terrible things to those who have wronged us. That's the difference. We can share our strongest emotions with God, and can tell God precisely what we are thinking and feeling, without asking God to harm our enemies. Telling God, "I am so angry at my spouse for cheating on me that I wish he was dead," is different from praying, "God, I want you to kill my unfaithful spouse in a car crash on their way home from work today."

Some people might find the words used by these ancient worshipers to be helpful in processing their own pain. Trauma survivors and others who have been deeply wounded might resonate with the words of these ancient worshipers who long for justice. These words may enable them to give voice to feelings and emotions that are otherwise hard to express.

For a different way to use these violent prayers, you could try an intriguing possibility suggested by Ellen Davis. Rather than thinking about the people we might be tempted to target with words of imprecation, Davis invites us to consider who might be inclined to use words like these against *us* due to pain or trauma we have caused them—directly or indirectly, intentionally or inadvertently. She writes, "Try turning the psalm a full 180 degrees, until it is directed at yourself, and ask: *Is there anyone in the community of God's people who might want to say this to God about me—or maybe, about us?*"[13] Doing this puts imprecatory psalms in a completely different light. Applying this approach to Psalm 109, Davis offers the following reflection:

> I am materially privileged beyond most people who are alive at this time, who have previously lived on the earth, or who will live in future generations. By social location, income, and personal habit, I am an active participant in a rapacious industrial economy, regularly consuming far more than I need of the world's goods. I have largely failed to moderate my lifestyle in accordance with what I can reasonably expect will be the needs of my great-grandchildren's generation, to say nothing of the present needs of those living in the Two-Thirds World. Yes, there are those who might cry out to God this night or fifty years hence:
>
> > Let [her] memory be cut off from the earth,
> > Because [she] did not remember to act in
> >   covenant faith
> > but hounded a person poor and needy,
> > crushed in heart, even to death. (109:16)[14]

By considering who might direct prayers like these toward us, we are invited to do some deep soul-searching as we reexamine our own values, priorities, and actions.[15]

Following Davis's lead, Matthew Schlimm uses a similar approach to reflect on one of the most notoriously troubling examples of imprecation in the entire Psalter, the final verse of Psalm 137: "Happy shall they be who take your little ones and dash them against the rock" (v. 9). Some context helps here. In the early sixth century BCE, the Babylonians conquered Jerusalem, burnt the temple to the ground, and killed or exiled many people living in Judah. As a result, the people of Judah wanted the Babylonians to suffer for all the terrible things they had done. This verse clearly expresses that desire for revenge.

But Schlimm turns this psalm around. Rather than using Psalm 137 to think about people who have wronged him, he uses it to consider who might feel wronged *by* him. Schlimm writes:

> I am reminded of military action my country has taken that has left countless children dead. I think not only of the horrors of Hiroshima and Nagasaki, but also of more recent wars in Iraq and Afghanistan that have made it so mothers and fathers will never again see life in

their own infants, toddlers, and children. I am made deeply concerned and ashamed about my country resorting to military action under any circumstances. *Strikingly, a text that initially seems morally repulsive actually causes me to face the horrors of war and oppose violence under any conditions.*[16]

Using imprecatory psalms this way seems very promising and is easily adaptable for use in public worship. Ministers could read an imprecatory psalm and then invite the congregation to reflect on the question Davis posed above: "Is there anyone in the community of God's people who might want to say this to God about me—or maybe, about us?"[17] You could prime the pump by offering suggestions:

> Maybe it's a family member you mistreated.
> Perhaps it is an employee you took advantage of.
> Maybe it's a classmate you bullied in school.
> Perhaps it's someone from a marginalized population who experienced discrimination rather than inclusion in the church
> Or maybe it's someone living in crippling poverty who is furious with people who say they love God but never provide any material support to those in need.

Time could then be given for silent reflection and confession.

Using imprecatory psalms for self-examination and critical reflection, rather than as a means to perpetuate hatred or the desire for vengeance, enables the church to redeem these texts by using them in ways that are both creative and constructive.[18]

PRAYER OF CONFESSION

Another way to include violent verses in public worship—and this is related to what has just been said—is to use them to construct a prayer of confession. These confessional prayers are relatively easy to create. All you need to do is (1) select someone who behaves violently in the Old Testament, (2) reflect on the problematic nature of their behavior, and (3) use this as a means to invite congregants to confess similar failings of their own. Before leading this prayer of confession, it might be helpful to provide some context for the passage you have based the prayer upon, since it works better if people have some knowledge of the story you are using.

To illustrate how this works, I have created a confessional prayer related to the story of Haman and his treacherous plans.

Contextual Statement (Spoken by the Minister before the Prayer of Confession)

In the book of Esther, we meet a powerful royal official named Haman. He is a textbook narcissist who expects everyone around him to recognize his "greatness." When a single Jew named Mordecai refuses to do so, Haman is outraged. In response, he devises a plan to eliminate not only Mordecai, but every last Jew in the kingdom (Esth. 3:1–6). Haman's plan would likely have succeeded were it not for the combined efforts of Mordecai and his cousin, the courageous Queen Esther (Esth. 4–6). Please join me in this prayer of confession *(read in unison with the congregation or spoken alone by the minister)*:

Prayer of Confession

Lord, forgive us for the times we act like Haman.
Forgive us for our pride, arrogance, and self-importance.
Forgive us for thinking more highly of ourselves than we ought
    to think.
When we become self-consumed with our own accomplishments,
        awards, and accolades,
    remind us of what true greatness really means.
You said that the greatest is the one who serves.
So teach us how to serve,
    and keep us from becoming like Haman who lived only to *be* served.

Lord, forgive our violent inclinations toward those who refuse to
    honor us the way we think we deserve.
It is all too easy to behave like Haman, to have one or two disagreeable
    encounters with someone from a different race,
    religion, ethnicity, or nationality,
    and then to stereotype the entire group negatively.
Forgive us for our prejudice.
Forgive us for our racism and bigotry.
Forgive us for our hatred and violence.
Help us to see people as you see them and love them as you
    love them.

Thank you for hearing our prayer.
Thank you for forgiving our sins.
By the power of your Spirit, help us to go from here and sin no more.
Amen.[19]

Using violent Old Testament texts for confession in this way is yet another example of how beneficial these passages can be for people of faith. When ministers use violent verses this way in confessional prayers, they provide churchgoers with opportunities to reflect on their own violent inclinations, to confess these to God, and to find forgiveness and release.

HYMNS AND WORSHIP SONGS

Before bringing this chapter to a close, a few words about hymns and worship songs are in order. Singing is a crucial and powerful part of most public worship gatherings. The music stays with us long after the service ends and sometimes influences us in profound ways. It behooves ministers, music leaders, and vocalists to be judicious about what songs they choose to sing in worship. Songs that celebrate acts of violence in Scripture should be avoided, *even if those acts are celebrated in the biblical text.*

Back in the 1980s, when contemporary Christian music was still in its infancy, I recall attending an outdoor Christian music festival. I was young and cannot remember very much about the day, but I distinctly remember hearing a song I had never encountered before. It was a song by Kemper Crabb aptly titled "Warrior."[20] The opening lyrics of this catchy tune speak of the Lord being a "warrior" and "mighty in battle" and come directly from Exodus 15:3 and Psalm 24:8. What's especially interesting is that Exodus 15:1–18 is itself a song in the Old Testament, sometimes referred to as the Song of the Sea. It is a song that praises God for delivering the Hebrew people from bondage and destroying their enemies in the Red Sea.

But Israel's deliverance comes at a steep price. To deliver Israel, God drowns the entire Egyptian army: "horse and rider he has thrown into the sea" (Exod. 15:1). Then, while the bodies of dead Egyptian soldiers wash up on the beach (14:30), the Israelites stand on the shoreline praising God for their deliverance. While it is easy to understand Israel's palpable relief at finally being beyond Pharaoh's grasp, and their desire to praise God for their liberation from oppression, we should avoid singing songs that celebrate the death of others. When we remember that every human being is created in God's image (Gen. 1:27), we realize just how precious life truly is. According to one Jewish tradition, when the angels witnessed the events at the Red Sea and wanted to join in singing, God stopped them, saying, "My own creatures are drowning in the sea, and yet you would sing?"[21]

Thankfully, most worship songs do not draw upon violent biblical texts for their inspiration. But some clearly do. Children's songs are especially notorious in this regard.[22] A quick internet search yields a plethora of songs celebrating the violent deeds of Old Testament characters such as Joshua, David, and Samson. These should be avoided. While it is fine to sing songs about these individuals, those songs should not praise them for their violent behavior. It is important for the church to send a clear and consistent message on this point: the use of violence is incongruent with the teachings of Jesus and has no place in the life of his followers.

That said, I do believe it is possible to use violent biblical texts in worship songs as long as it is done with a great deal of care. For example, it would be appropriate to use songs that critique brutality in the Bible or that lament those victimized by it. Songs that express sorrow for the Egyptians killed by the plagues or in the Red Sea, for example, would be acceptable, as would songs mourning the sexual assault of women like Dinah and Tamar. Similarly, it would be appropriate to use songs that accurately retell violent biblical stories without sanitizing them or celebrating the violence they contain. Ultimately, whatever songs are used in worship, they should always promote peace and justice and should reflect the nonviolent love of God.[23]

CONCLUSION

As I have tried to demonstrate, there are many ways to use violent verses in liturgically responsible ways. Doing this enhances our worship experience *and* models constructive ways to use these texts. It also enables people to recognize how valuable these verses can be for spiritual growth and reflection.

While violent verses may not be appropriate for *every* part of the liturgy, there are numerous ways they can be used effectively and responsibly in worship. Worship leaders, liturgists, and ministers should incorporate them into worship services on a regular basis. This will require careful thought and intentionality, but it is well worth the effort. Though I am not suggesting *every* worship service must include either a passage of Scripture or responsive reading or prayer that makes reference to violence in the Old Testament, some of them certainly should.

In the next chapter, we narrow our focus to one specific component of worship services that often takes pride of place: the Sunday morning sermon. There we explore how violent biblical texts can be used for preaching in church and for speaking in various ministry contexts.

6

Preaching from Violent Passages

Strategies for Crafting Sermons from Troublesome Texts

Let churches pledge themselves for a set period—say, several months—to using the severest and most nightmarish texts for their Bible study and preaching, the hardest of hard sayings. They should read and preach on the texts of terror, to understand them and their place in the larger pattern of scripture and of the faith as a whole.
—Philip Jenkins, *Laying Down the Sword*[1]

Renowned preacher Barbara Brown Taylor recalls a time she offered a course titled Preaching Difficult Texts at McAfee School of Theology.[2] On the first day of class, she allowed the students to determine the type of passages they found most difficult. Biblical texts containing divinely sanctioned violence were near the top of their lists, second only to miracle stories. According to Rev. Taylor, no one was eager to preach a series on Joshua or Judges, or "to proclaim the good news of Elijah's slaughter of the prophets of Baal."[3]

While requiring students to preach from such undesirable passages might seem like a recipe for disaster, that was not the case. Instead, something wonderful happened. Both Taylor and her students were astonished to discover that these were "some of the freshest sermons any of us had heard in ages."[4] Preaching from difficult texts has its advantages! It can help people get more engaged with the sermon and can enhance their interest in the Bible as they see relevance and value in some of its most notoriously troubling texts.

THE BENEFITS OF PREACHING
FROM VIOLENT VERSES

Many ministers are (understandably) hesitant to preach from violent biblical texts. In light of that, it may be helpful to say more about some of the benefits of doing so before offering some strategies for tackling troublesome texts in the pulpit.

It Increases Biblical Literacy

One thing preaching from these texts will almost certainly do is increase biblical literacy. Since many of the seventeen hundred Old Testament passages containing violence are not well known, ministers who preach from them render a real service to their listeners. While it is impractical for any minister to preach from every single passage of Scripture during her or his tenure at a church, preachers should utilize a representative sampling of the diverse range of material in the Bible. Preaching from *violent* biblical texts, especially those that are less familiar, gives people greater knowledge and understanding of what the Bible actually contains.

It Promotes Attentive Listening and Receptivity

Preaching from lesser-known biblical texts also encourages churchgoers to listen carefully to what is being said. When people are unfamiliar with a violent passage of Scripture, it is less likely they will zone out during the sermon, since they cannot automatically assume they know what the text means or what they are supposed to "take away" from it. This requires them to listen more closely to what you have to say. As Joseph Jeter observes with reference to Judges, a book that contains many violent verses:

> Since most of our people are unfamiliar with these stories, they do not carry with them any preconceived baggage about the text. When the scripture is announced, people do not groan inwardly, "Oh, no, not again," because they have never been there. With the exception of Samson and Delilah, and possibly Deborah and Gideon, most of our people could not name a single character upon the stage of Judges' action. This gives us the chance to preach some very contemporary messages based on some very old and yet new stories.[5]

When people do not already *think* they know what the story is about, or what "lesson" it teaches (as though stories are prepackaged moral tales with a single meaning), they are likely to be more attentive—and possibly more receptive—to what you are saying. Also, there is no need for them to unlearn mistaken notions they have gathered about the passage over the years, for one simple reason: they probably do not have any! Since the text is new to them, you have the opportunity to help them make first contact with it. That is exciting and deeply satisfying work. You have the privilege of introducing them to part of the Bible they have little (if any) knowledge about, and you can help them encounter it in positive ways.

It Removes Barriers to Faith

As noted earlier, violent biblical texts create formidable barriers to faith. Preaching from these passages can help remove some of these. Ministers who use violent verses creatively and constructively will help people realize there is real value in these texts. The presence of these passages in Scripture does not render Christian faith impossibly problematic or untenable and need not be a deal-breaker. On the contrary, when used responsibly, violent texts can be a valuable resource for the life of faith. Realizing this can make Christianity—and Bible reading—much more appealing.

It Communicates Willingness to Address Difficult Topics

Preaching regularly and responsibly from violent biblical passages demonstrates the church's commitment to deal honestly with the Bible. Pastors signal they are willing to be honest with the Bible and ready to talk about difficult topics. Young people are especially hungry for this kind of openness and authenticity in the church. Both spiritual seekers and longtime Christians are likely to appreciate a church that is willing to engage in conversations like these, making it easier for them to commit to the church and its mission.

It Encourages Churchgoers to Explore Violent Texts

Finally, preaching from violent verses is good modeling. It can inspire people to stop avoiding and start exploring these oft-neglected passages. When preachers demonstrate how valuable these passages can be, churchgoers will be encouraged to investigate them on their own. And, having heard sermons on these kinds of passages, they will have acquired strategies and tools for doing so effectively.

A GENERAL RULE: TALK DIRECTLY ABOUT THE VIOLENCE

As a general rule, whenever you preach from violent biblical texts it is important to acknowledge the violence contained in them. In one way or another, these elements should be named and addressed in sermons, homilies, and meditations. To preach from one of these texts without acknowledging the violence it contains is sort of like describing a baseball game without ever discussing the game itself. While it is fine to pontificate on how great the concessions are, how beautiful the stadium looks, and how visually stunning the scoreboard is, to do that without saying a word about the players on the field, or the game being played, would be very odd indeed.

Yet that is what often happens with violent biblical texts.[6] Preachers talk *around* the violence in the text without ever talking *about* it. Consider the way the exodus story is typically handled in sermons. Most preachers tend to focus on God's dramatic deliverance of Israel from Egyptian slavery, holding up the story as a wonderful example of God's care for oppressed Israelites. While that is certainly true, it is only part of the story. The exodus narrative is not just about Israel's deliverance; it is also about Egypt's destruction. Israel's freedom comes at an exceedingly high price. Egypt's waterways, crops, and animals are decimated, every firstborn is killed, and the entire army is destroyed. It is both a dramatic story of deliverance *and* a disturbing story of divine violence. The two are inseparable. Yet, many preachers seem content to focus on Israel's triumph with nary a word about Egypt's tragedy.

This sort of lopsided preaching happens all the time. It happens when sermons focus on God's deliverance of Noah and his family without acknowledging the countless men, women, and children drowning outside the ark. It happens when preachers celebrate Israel's conquest of Canaan without agonizing over the moral atrocities they commit against the indigenous population. If preachers want to deal responsibly with violent biblical texts, they need to find ways to talk directly about the violence.

SUGGESTIONS FOR PREACHING FROM VIOLENT TEXTS

This section offers five options for preaching from violent biblical texts. All of these acknowledge the violence in the text and demonstrate various ways to use these passages responsibly.

Since there are many similarities between preaching and teaching, a number of the ideas introduced in chapter 4 will be revisited here. This reiterates their usefulness as strategies for dealing with violent verses, not just with young people but also with adults, and provides an opportunity for us to explore them in greater depth as we consider how they apply specifically to the important task of preaching.

Describe How Violent Verses Have Been Used to Harm Others

For centuries, people have appealed to the Bible to justify warfare and genocide, violence against women, child abuse, religious intolerance, capital punishment, slavery, racism, and other terrible acts.[7] Preachers should readily acknowledge this troubling legacy, especially when preaching from verses that have been used this way. It is important for churchgoers to be aware of various ways Christians have weaponized the Bible to inspire and justify acts of violence.

If you decide to preach a sermon on the conquest narrative (Josh. 6–11), for example, you could devote some time to talking about the way this narrative has been used to justify colonialism and its attendant evils of warfare, killing, theft, and dispossession.[8] Or if you happen to be preaching from verses in Proverbs that talk about physically disciplining children, it would be important to give some attention to how these verses have been used to abuse children.[9]

There is much to be gained by using violent biblical texts to discuss how Scripture has been used against others. Preachers can educate people by giving specific examples of the way these verses have been—and sometimes continue to be—misused. This will help people realize how unacceptable it is to use biblical texts to oppress, marginalize, and dehumanize others. Anyone who uses the Bible to cause physical, emotional, or spiritual harm is guilty of religious malpractice. By talking about the way violent verses have been used wrongly, ministers can state clearly and unequivocally that the Bible should never be used to harm others.

Sermons that focus on the way violent biblical texts have been used against others also provide opportunities for confession and action. Churchgoers can be encouraged to confess the ways they themselves may have wielded Scripture against others. More broadly, they can be invited to take action in an effort to undo some of the damage done by such terrible readings and interpretations of these texts over the years.

Understandably, some ministers may not wish to devote an entire sermon to discussing how a particular biblical text has been misused over the centuries. There are other things to be said, and they might choose to devote the majority of their time and attention elsewhere. Still, in my opinion, it would be a missed opportunity to preach a sermon about the Battle of Jericho in Joshua 6 (a passage that is part of a narrative that has been used to support colonialism) or the annihilation of the Amalekites in 1 Samuel 15 (a passage that has been used to demonize others) without saying something about the long and shameful history of interpretation that accompanies brutal passages like these.[10]

Preachers who are unaware of how violent verses have been used to harm others should take some time to learn about it. A number of resources in the notes to this section are very helpful in this regard (see notes 7, 8, and 10 on page 160).

Although exploring the church's violent use of Scripture does not make for easy reading, it is important for ministers to be educated on this point, because people sometimes still misuse the Bible this way. Preachers who devote time and attention to this issue in the pulpit can steer people away from this kind of abuse. They can remind their listeners that the Bible should never be used to harm others or to justify that harm, and they can alert them to the need to handle violent verses very, very carefully.

Use Violent Texts to Discuss Violence Today

An especially helpful way to use these texts is to make them the basis for sermons that address various forms of violence in the world today. This offers a convenient entry point into subject matter that is rarely discussed in many churches. For example, one way the church could model an openness to talk about the problem of violence against women is to preach responsibly from passages related to it. A preacher could use the opening chapters of the story of Esther to reflect on "the sexual exploitation of young girls," something that still happens with alarming frequency.[11] "If we become more aware of the inherent violence of such biblical texts [like Esther 2] and start to contest it," writes Cheryl Anderson, "we will be better able, as people of faith, to confront and contest sexual violence today."[12]

Numerous Old Testament texts also lend themselves quite naturally to discussions about domestic violence, which disproportionately affects women.[13] In her study of Ezekiel 16, Linda Day discusses the typical pattern of abuse that battered women experience ("tension building," "the acute violent incident," and "kindness and contrite behavior") and then demonstrates how God is portrayed behaving this way toward Jerusalem.[14] Similar observations have been made about the way God treats Gomer in the book of Hosea.[15] Even though these texts do not censure the abuser (God!), when they are read critically they provide natural opportunities to talk about the problem of domestic violence and the destructive patterns of abuse that are all too common around us.[16]

Regrettably, many biblical passages condone violence against women or pass over gender-based violence without comment. When preaching from passages like these, ministers can offer a different perspective, one that clearly disapproves of such behavior. This also sends strong signals about the church's position on how women should be treated.

Obviously, violence against women is just one of many topics that could be addressed by preaching from violent texts. A number of biblical texts would also serve as an excellent starting point for sermons dealing with topics such as suicide (Judg. 9:50–54; 16:23–31; 1 Sam. 31:1–5; 2 Sam. 16:15–17:23; 1 Kgs. 16:15–20; Matt. 27:3–5; Acts 1:15–18), capital punishment (Lev. 24:10–23; Num. 15:32–36; Josh. 7), child abuse (Gen. 22:1–19; Judg. 11:29–40; Prov. 13:24; 22:15; 23:13–14), and other matters.

Given the sensitive and controversial nature of many of these topics, ministers will want to be well informed when addressing them from the pulpit.

Thankfully, many quality resources are available to those who decide to preach about issues like these.[17] By consulting these materials, ministers will be equipped to speak more accurately and responsibly about these crucial topics which desperately need to be addressed.

Encourage Compassion toward Victims of Violence

Violent biblical texts provide limitless opportunities to cultivate compassion for victims, and sermons can be one of the most powerful means to help people do so. Although many violent verses focus almost exclusively on the perpetrators, preachers should consider using these texts to remember the people who are victimized, those who suffer, bleed, and die in these stories.

Millions are slain in the Old Testament, yet the vast majority of these individuals remain nameless and faceless. We know nothing, or next to nothing, about them.

> So they killed him [King Og], his sons, and all his people, until there was no survivor left; and they took possession of his land. (Num. 21:35)

> Then they devoted to destruction by the edge of the sword all in the city, both men and women, young and old, oxen, sheep, and donkeys. (Josh. 6:21)

> Forty-two thousand of the Ephraimites fell at that time. (Judg. 12:6)

Because we are rarely introduced to an *individual* Ephraimite or a *particular* Canaanite, we never really get to know these people. As a result, most of us have not been taught to care very much about them. Their anonymity makes it easy to read over their tragic stories without even giving them a second thought. But doing so desensitizes us to the horror of warfare and killing and hardens us toward the pain and suffering these people experience.

This happens all the time in our world today. We rarely know the names or stories of untold thousands who die through acts of war and violence each year. This makes it much more difficult to feel empathy toward them or to care deeply about their plight. Likewise, many people who oppose things like abortion, gay marriage, or transgender rights on religious grounds are often not personally connected with the individuals most directly affected. They have not often journeyed with women who face the very personal and often agonizing decision of whether to continue a pregnancy. Nor have they typically developed deep friendships with people who are queer or trans. But once they move beyond anonymity and really get to know people, it invariably changes how they view things. These are not just issues to discuss or ideas to debate. Real people's lives are at stake. And that insight generates compassion.

Unfortunately, rather than feeling compassion toward victims of violence in the Bible, we often celebrate their destruction, especially when they are Israel's enemies.[18] As a case in point, consider your own feelings toward Philistines. If you are like most readers, you probably classify Philistines as "the enemy." Since the Philistines routinely fought against Israel (God's "chosen" people), and since they occupied land God ostensibly promised to Israelites, they seem to be on the wrong side of history. Through popular stories like David and Goliath, we are conditioned to see Philistines as the "bad guys," and we generally feel little, if any, compunction about them being killed. In fact, I suspect many people feel no more regret over the death of a Philistine in the Bible than they do over the death of an orc in J. R. R. Tolkien's *The Lord of the Rings*. But if that is true, then something is surely wrong with how we read the Bible (and perhaps also how we read *The Lord of the Rings*).[19]

Reading with that level of unconcern for Philistines—or anyone else, for that matter—is extremely dangerous. It perpetuates stereotypes, reinforces prejudice, and encourages violence against others. After all, if we believe certain kinds of people of the Bible are worthy of destruction, what is to keep us from thinking the same is true today? To reiterate a point made earlier, the way we view people in the Bible directly influences the way we view people in the world around us, for better or for worse. That is why it is so important to preach from violent biblical texts in ways that cultivate compassion for the victims in these stories, emphasizing that *all* life is sacred and should be revered, and that each person reflects God's image.

One way to do this homiletically is to create first-person accounts from the perspective of the victims. Tell the story of an Egyptian father or mother devastated by the loss of their firstborn child (Exod. 12). Listen to an Amalekite teen describe the brutal slaughter of her family at the hands of Saul and his soldiers (1 Sam. 15). Give voice to the women of Shiloh who are kidnapped and forced to marry men from the tribe of Benjamin (Judg. 21:15–24). Feel free to supply names for individuals who are unnamed, and create a backstory that will humanize them and help congregants see them as real people. This takes some creativity and imagination, but it is well worth the effort.

In some instances, it might be very impactful to use a first-person account for just part of the sermon. Other times, preachers might decide to stay in character throughout the entire message. Either way, given the unconventional nature of first-person preaching, it is probably best to use this approach strategically and sparingly. I would not envision many sermons in the course of a year taking this first-person form. But I do think that preaching sermons like this from time to time can be very effective. It helps people develop compassion for victims of violence as they experience the story through their eyes.

Many resources are available for preachers who want some practical advice for crafting first-person narratives like these, including books like Daniel Buttry's *First-Person Preaching* and J. Kent Edwards's *Effective First-Person Biblical Preaching*.[20] These books take pastors step-by-step through the process of writing this kind of sermon, and they provide sample sermons as well.

Examples of fictional first-person narratives already exist, and some of these could easily be adapted for use in sermons. One powerful illustration of this kind of writing is "The Jericho Woman," a relatively brief story by Ulrike Bechmann. Bechmann tells the story of a woman inside Jericho just before the walls fall down and the Israelites slaughter everyone inside.

> Hello. You don't know me, but we met already in the story. I'm a woman of Jericho. You don't know me by name—by the way, my name is Nachla—I'm one of the forgotten ones.
>
> But I'm there in the text, in the last verse you just heard: ". . . men and women, oxen, sheep and donkeys." You see—I'm one of these women. I want to meet you. You are going with Joshua?
>
> Well, still the wall of Jericho is there and the gate is open. I'll show you around a bit if you like. You know, we live in a nice city. There is a spring that never dries up, not even in the summer. This spring is important, because Jericho can be hot, especially in summer. Because of the water we have all this greenery here! You can see a lot of fruit trees all around the city. And palms; there are plenty of them. Some call Jericho the "City of Palm Trees."
>
> Look at the wall and the big gate. It is necessary to have it and to protect it well. We are a rich city! Many travelers and merchants are coming to our city. And sometimes also enemies.
>
> Come with me down our main street; I'll show you our temple. Isn't it a fabulous building? Perhaps you can get a glimpse through the open door of all the silver and gold vessels that are in there! We are really very thankful to our goddesses and gods to live in such a good place.
>
> But come to my house. You must be thirsty. I can offer some milk and some fruits. Here is my house.
>
> Look, these are my children. I have three of them. Here, my daughter is twelve years old. Isn't she a beauty? And I can tell she is bright, too! I really have to find a good man for her who likes her. Oh, here comes my youngest child. He is three years old. He likes to play around with our donkey. And you know, we sometimes think that the donkey likes him best too.
>
> But look at the sun; time is running out. You have to hurry to join Joshua again. You must leave before the gate is closed. If the gate is closed, nobody can go out or in. So hurry up to go back.
>
> Tomorrow, when the sun rises, the wall will fall down. The city will be burnt. Joshua will take all the silver and gold for his God. You

know, the God of Joshua has no mercy at all, not even for the old ones
or the children.

So go now, and tomorrow, when the walls come down, we will
meet again—and then you will kill me.[21]

Getting to know Nachla and her three children makes it well-nigh impossible to ever hear the story of Jericho the same way again. Churchgoers who
contemplate the personal tragedy of those who suffer and die in the Bible are
likely to critique misguided notions of "virtuous" violence in Scripture as they
cultivate compassion toward those harmed within its pages.[22]

Critique Examples of "Virtuous" Violence

The most forceful way to deconstruct the notion of "virtuous" violence in the
Old Testament is to critique it directly. This may initially feel difficult and
uncomfortable. Some preachers worry that critiquing "virtuous" violence in
the Old Testament indicates a lack of respect for Scripture and undermines
its authority. Yet Carol Hess reminds us that "resistance . . . can be a sign of
a deep piety."[23] As Hess sees it, "To understand the Bible as the word of God
means that we converse with it. We listen to it, we try to understand it, we
allow ourselves to be challenged; *and also we talk back to it, we argue with it, we
critique it.*"[24]

Actually, when you stop to think about it, we do this all the time.[25] Although
biblical writers sanction slavery, Christians today do not. And while numerous passages in the Bible approve of having sex with multiple partners, most
churchgoers beg to differ. Whether we are aware of it or not, we routinely
critique certain beliefs and practices in Scripture. To reiterate a point made
earlier, there is no need to agree with everything in the Bible.[26] Preachers can
play a huge role in helping people realize this and can provide interpretive
guidelines that enable people to discern what to embrace and what to challenge. For example, "three key commitments" that can help readers engage
in an ethically responsible critique of the biblical text are "the rule of love, a
commitment to justice, and a consistent ethic of life."[27]

Ministers have a responsibility to contest values in the biblical text that conflict with their most fundamental Christian convictions and commitments.[28]
Rather than remaining silent about "virtuous" violence—or worse, justifying
it and giving hearty assent to it—preachers should challenge all forms of violence in the text. They should be willing to say violence is wrong, *even if* the
text says it is right.

Critiquing positive portrayals of violence in Scripture is not an attack on
the Bible, nor is it meant to disparage the Bible. On the contrary, it represents
an effort to use the Bible in ways that are consistent with faithful Christian discipleship. Jesus himself rejected violence at every turn.[29] He preached, taught,

and modeled nonviolence and called his followers to do likewise.[30] Since the notion of "virtuous" violence is inconsistent with the teachings of Jesus, and since we are to be obedient to the teachings of Jesus, this critique is a principled one, not merely one rooted in personal opinions.[31] Therefore, when we preach from texts that praise violence, we should raise our voices in protest, critiquing the violent behavior rather than celebrating it.

So let's imagine you decide to preach a sermon about David and Goliath. Whatever else you may say, it is important to let people know you do not believe that God desires one person to kill another (1 Sam. 17:45–47) or that killing is praiseworthy (18:6–7). As discussed in chapter 4, the church needs to avoid valorizing men and women in the Bible for committing acts of violence, even if these individuals are popularly regarded as heroes of the faith.

Likewise, if you preach about Joshua and the Battle of Jericho—a story more accurately titled "Joshua and the *Massacre* at Jericho"—you should make it absolutely clear you do not condone the killing of "men and women, young and old, oxen, sheep, and donkeys" (Josh. 6:21). Rather than attempting to "explain" why Canaanites *deserved* to be killed (who ever *deserves* to be terrorized?), preachers should clearly and unequivocally declare that slaying women and children—Canaanite or otherwise—and slaughtering the elderly and infirm is a moral atrocity. Today we would classify such barbaric acts as war crimes and would bring those responsible before the International Criminal Court in The Hague. Indiscriminate killing is *never* justifiable, and ministers should have the courage to say so.

Making this point does not need to be the main focus of the sermon. Nor does it need to take a disproportionate amount of time away from other things you might wish to say. Unless you want to devote the entire sermon to the problem of "virtuous" violence in the Bible, a few minutes should be enough to critique the violence and move on to other things.

Ministers who fail to critique "virtuous" violence, and subtly (or not so subtly) reinforce it, send terribly confusing messages about how Christians are to feel about violence.[32] After all, what are people to think when one week we implore them to love their enemies, and the next week praise David for killing his? Why should we expect them to believe our bold proclamation that God loves all people when, in the same breath, we affirm that God commanded the slaughter of every last Canaanite? If ministers intend to teach people that violence and killing are wrong, they must critique "virtuous" violence rather than condone it.

In doing so, it is important to keep in mind that the *primary* purpose of this critique is *not* to pass judgment on ancient Israelites for *their* beliefs, values, or practices.[33] While it is true that we are judging and evaluating certain ideas embedded in these texts, we are not doing this so we can say,

"Look how bad those ancient Israelites were and how good and enlightened we are!" That would be both arrogant and naive. Instead, our evaluation of the text is designed to raise questions about the extent to which
the ethics inscribed in various Old Testament texts can—or should—
inform our own. Rather than condemning people for choices made in
the distant past, this critique is intended to help modern readers use the
Bible responsibly and make wise decisions about how to apply these texts
faithfully today.

As we do, we should be ever mindful that critique is a two-way street. As
we critique the Bible, we are also critiqued by it. Frances Taylor Gench recalls
the late biblical scholar Walter Wink saying something to this effect: "I yell at
the Bible about its sexism, its violence, its homophobia—it yells back at me
about my attachment to wealth, my neglect of the poor."[34] The Old Testament often stands in judgment over us when it comes to things like the importance of community, caring for the most vulnerable, and doing justice. We
must constantly be aware of how much we have to learn from our Israelite
forebears as we do this work.

Do Something Positive with Violent Texts

While critique is important, as just discussed, preachers should not only critique. They should also construct. It's not enough to state what's wrong with
the text. Ministers need to help people see what's right with it as well. Not
every sermon based on a violent biblical text needs to be devoted to an extensive discussion of the problem of divine violence. Nor does it need to provide
parishioners with three easy ways to subvert "virtuous" violence. While there
is a time and place for sermons like these, it is sometimes desirable to set these
issues aside so other issues can be explored.

To illustrate this, I have included a small portion of a sermon I preached
from Genesis 22, a disturbing passage that describes the near sacrifice of Isaac.
What follows is an edited version of the beginning of that message.

> If I were to ask you, "What is the most valuable thing you possess?"
> how would you respond? Of everything you have, what is it that you
> value the most? A priceless family heirloom? Your 1972 Chevy Nova
> with mag wheels, dual exhaust, and 307 engine under the hood? Your
> home? Whatever it is, how would you feel if someone asked you to
> give it up or give it away?
>   It is precisely this situation in which Abraham finds himself in Gen-
> esis 22. Only in Abraham's case, the stakes are even higher. What
> Abraham is asked to give up is not some inanimate object, it's his son
> Isaac! To be more precise, God asks Abraham to *offer up* Isaac as a
> burnt offering, to sacrifice his son.

For many readers, this is a terribly troubling story. Before we even get past the second verse we are faced with a nasty moral dilemma. God is portrayed as ordering human sacrifice. Numerous scholars have reflected on the problematic dimensions of this text. James Crenshaw believes "one labors in vain . . . to discover the slightest hint of divine compassion in the dreadful story."[35] Terence Fretheim warns against simply glossing over the problems this passage, and others like it, raise: "To continue to exalt such texts as the sacrifice of Isaac (Genesis 22), and not to recognize that . . . it can be read as a case of divine child abuse, is to contribute to an atmosphere that in subtle, but insidious, ways justifies the abuse of children. . . . Lives are at stake."[36]

Whether or not you fully agree with these sentiments, they do raise an important point. This text is difficult and potentially dangerous. It needs to be handled with care.

In light of that, let me be as clear as possible here. God does not want human sacrifice. God never has and never will. If you ever think you hear a divine voice commanding you to offer your child as a burnt offering, you have not heard the voice of God. Children are of enormous worth and importance to God and must never be neglected or abused. Whatever we take away from this passage, it should not be a message suggesting that kids are disposable.

Obviously, simply saying that does not resolve all the difficulties this passage raises. We are still left with a problematic portrait of God. But that issue must be left for another time and a different conversation since I want to focus on some other dimensions of the text. Even disturbing passages of Scripture can be read in constructive ways, and that is what I would like to do this morning. So without denying the problems a passage like this raises, I would like to offer a positive reading of this text, one that I think has profound implications for us today.[37]

At this point in the sermon, I discontinued my critique and turned my attention to a positive reading of Abraham's actions in the narrative.[38] I stressed the uniqueness of Isaac and how Abraham's willingness to give him up indicated Abraham's total commitment to God. I suggested God wants us to come to the same place as Abraham, to the place where we are totally committed to God and will withhold nothing from God.[39] (Hopefully, given the way I started the sermon, nobody would think I was suggesting we should give our children away, much less kill them!) This was the primary focus of my message, and most of the sermon was devoted to developing this idea.

As this example demonstrates, not every sermon based on a violent biblical text needs to focus exclusively—or even extensively—on the violence embedded in the text. While some sermons should make this a primary focus, others can acknowledge the violence more briefly and then proceed to other matters. In my sermon about Abraham and Isaac, I voiced some concerns about the problematic nature of God's terrifying command to kill Isaac but then turned my attention elsewhere. While I certainly could have used this passage to address the problem of divinely sanctioned violence, my interests lay elsewhere. I wanted to encourage the congregation to be fully committed to God—albeit a God who looks different from the one portrayed in the text at hand in many ways—and therefore chose not to make the issue of divine violence the focus of my message.

TWO PASTORAL CONSIDERATIONS

There are two pastoral considerations to discuss before bringing this chapter to a close. One has to do with issuing trigger warnings, and the other with providing opportunities for continued conversation.

Provide Trigger Warnings

Like teachers, preachers should warn people before using biblical texts that contain particularly graphic material or that deal with sensitive topics like suicide or sexual assault. This is especially true if there are young children in the congregation. Some biblical content—like the gang rape of the Levite's concubine and her subsequent dismemberment—is not appropriate for all ages.[40] If you plan to talk candidly about some of the most disturbingly violent dimensions of these texts, it would be good to provide child care or alternative programming for children and to give families a heads-up with enough lead time to make whatever arrangements they feel are best.

But warnings like these are not just for children. They are important for anyone who has a history of trauma. Some adults will find a discussion of certain violent biblical texts triggering for various reasons, and it is wise to let people know what's coming well in advance so they can make an informed decision about whether it is healthy for them to attend.

Church should be a safe space for people of all ages and all walks of life. One of the ways preachers can help the church be a safe space is by providing appropriate warnings prior to preaching about topics that might trigger a trauma response. While not every sermon that uses a violent biblical text needs a trigger warning, some will. The decision whether to give advance notice will likely depend on how the text in question is going to be used in the sermon. If you decide to preach a sermon about David and Bathsheba (2 Sam. 11) and plan to devote a significant amount of time talking about the sexual trauma Bathsheba experienced, it would be prudent to provide some advance notice. On the other hand, if you preach a sermon about the Assyrian conquest of the northern kingdom of Israel in 2 Kings 17:1–23, it is probably not necessary to issue a trigger warning unless you intend to draw upon other sources to talk explicitly about some of the terrible ways Assyrians treated conquered peoples.[41] Obviously, ministers know their own congregations best and will need to decide when it is most helpful to issue warnings like these, though it is never wrong to err on the side of caution.

Ideally, trigger warnings should be communicated days in advance so people can plan accordingly. This could be done by making an announcement in church or placing a notice in the bulletin a week before the sermon in question. It could also be communicated through emails, text messages, and the church's website. At the very least, a word of warning should be communicated at the beginning of the service and again just before the start of the sermon. People should be assured they are welcome to leave at any time if they find the topic triggering or feel it would be unsuitable for children in their care. One drawback of waiting until the day of the sermon to make this announcement is that some people who probably *should* remove themselves might not because they feel embarrassed to walk out.

In all likelihood, most people will stay after being informed about what is to come. The majority of congregants will not be triggered by sermons based on violent biblical texts. While they may not feel entirely comfortable with the topic at hand, it will not induce a trauma response for them. Still, it is important to let the congregation know what is coming. People will be grateful for your pastoral sensitivity so they can decide what is best for them and their family.

Offer to Continue the Conversation

Sermons that deal with violent biblical texts are likely to raise theological questions and concerns for many churchgoers. This is especially true of sermons that critique "virtuous" violence in Scripture. People tend to be uncomfortable when objections are raised about God's behavior in the Bible—even if they themselves find that behavior objectionable. This discomfort is particularly prevalent among people of faith who have never heard any critique of the Bible whatsoever. It is natural for them to have questions. They are not going to flip a switch that immediately allows them to shift from believing that the Bible is perfect to acknowledging that it contains (and promotes) some ideas that are extremely harmful. Because it takes time to process this new information, it is important to provide opportunities to do so.

Depending upon the nature of your congregation, it might be helpful to preface your sermon with an invitation to have further conversation. Let people know that you are going to be dealing with some difficult issues that cannot be fully explored in twenty minutes. Express your willingness and *eagerness* to keep talking with them, especially with those who might find the message upsetting or confusing. Let people know you are willing to meet with them in your office or over coffee to talk more about their questions and concerns. Tell them your door is open. Let them know you are eager to journey with them as they process these challenging issues.

You might consider having a talkback session after a particularly challenging sermon, and you could offer a Sunday school class that covers some of the same issues but allows space for more conversation and dialogue. You could also include a list of resources in the bulletin and make books and other materials available in the church library, the lobby, or elsewhere. Doing these kinds of things keeps the sermon from feeling like a "hit-and-run" and gives people additional opportunities to wrestle honestly with some very violent—and very difficult—biblical texts.

SOME FINAL WORDS OF ADVICE TO PREACHERS

Although preaching from violent Old Testament texts is likely to take more time and energy than usual, it is well worth the effort. To encourage you to stay the course, you might find it helpful to set some goals for preaching from these troubling texts. Maybe your goal for the coming year will be to preach one sermon from a violent passage you have never previously used in church. The following year you might decide to preach more frequently from such texts. You could plan to preach a "violent verse" sermon each quarter, alternating between familiar stories like David and Goliath (1 Sam. 17) and less familiar ones like the boys who are mauled after taunting the prophet Elisha (2 Kgs. 2:23–25). Perhaps the year after that you might choose to preach a brief summer sermon series on Old Testament texts that address sexual violence and assault. Again, these are just suggestions. You know what will work best for you and for your congregation. Whatever you decide, having some kind of plan in place will give you something to aim for and will provide a means of accountability.

As you begin to craft sermons like these, I would encourage you to run your sermons by others before preaching them.[42] This is always a good practice, especially when preaching on topics that are potentially controversial. When preparing to preach from a violent biblical text, find another minister (or group of ministers) and share your sermon with them. "Preach" it to your spouse or some close friends. Ask for their honest feedback. What kinds of questions does the text raise for them, and to what extent does your message address these? What would they suggest clarifying or revising? Did they find your approach helpful, and was anything in your sermon triggering for them?

Obviously, receiving this kind of input from others takes time and planning. But it is worth it. Getting feedback like this is invaluable. It has the potential to strengthen and improve your sermons considerably, which will enrich your congregation as you learn to reckon with violence in Scripture together. I have done this with sermons I have preached, and I do something similar with my writing. Before I publish a book, I invite a select group of individuals to read and comment on the manuscript. I then use this feedback to help me revise my work. The result is a much better final product.

CONCLUSION

Preachers have the unique privilege and responsibility to help people learn how to use violent biblical texts responsibly, in ways that do no harm. Hopefully, the suggestions offered in this chapter will help you engage in this important task more frequently and more effectively. The church needs to hear good, solid preaching from problematic passages too long neglected. You are the one who can provide it, so let the sermons begin!

PART III

Exploring Sample Texts and Talking about Violent Portrayals of God

7

Exploring Selected Passages
for Use in Church

Applying What We Have Learned

All scripture is inspired by God and is useful for teaching, for reproof, for correction, and for training in righteousness, so that everyone who belongs to God may be proficient, equipped for every good work.

—2 Tim. 3:16–17

While the previous three chapters offered numerous suggestions for using violent verses responsibly in church—particularly in the context of Christian education, worship, and preaching—there was limited space to demonstrate how these suggestions could be applied to specific biblical texts. This chapter seeks to provide that by focusing on three Old Testament passages and illustrating various ways pastors and lay leaders could use them in church.

In the pages that follow, we will explore the stories of Sodom and Gomorrah (Gen. 19), Naboth's vineyard (1 Kgs. 21), and Daniel and the lions' den (Dan. 6). My choice of these particular passages is not meant to suggest they are "special" or that they represent the most important violent texts to use in church. I could have chosen any violent biblical passage for the purpose of this chapter. Still, these three work especially well because they enable us to explore texts from different parts of the Old Testament that include various forms of violence. That, plus the fact that some of these stories are more familiar than others, makes them useful for illustrative purposes.

THE SEVEN APPROACHES REVISITED

In chapter 3 we explored seven ways to use violent biblical texts constructively:

1. To demonstrate why violence is so harmful
2. To consider ways to respond to violence
3. To develop compassion for victims of violence
4. To talk about difficult topics
5. To raise awareness of violence and act to stop it
6. To warn against using violent texts to do harm
7. To make personal connections and applications

In this chapter, we will have the opportunity to see many of these approaches in action as they are applied to Genesis 19, 1 Kings 21, and Daniel 6. This will demonstrate how violent Old Testament texts like these can be used creatively and constructively for preaching, teaching, and worship. Hopefully, it will also encourage you to try some of these approaches yourself when using violent verses in church.

In an effort to be clear about which approach is being utilized, I will identify these along the way with a parenthetical notation: (option 1), (option 2), etc. These correspond to the seven numbered approaches listed above.

SORTING OUT THE STORY OF SODOM (GEN. 19)

The destruction of Sodom and Gomorrah is often regarded as the paradigmatic act of divine destruction in the Old Testament.[1] The Lord rains down "sulfur and fire" on these cities in a conflagration that leaves only four survivors. Though the specific number of casualties is not reported, one assumes countless men, women, and children perish in this terrifying calamity. Yet this horrific act of divine destruction is only part of the story. Violence surrounds and permeates this troubling tale.

The destruction of Sodom and Gomorrah is bracketed by two stories of sexual violence. One precedes the destruction of these cities (Gen. 19:1–11), and one follows (vv. 30–38). The narrative begins with two men (angels) coming into the city of Sodom. Abraham's nephew Lot offers them food and shelter for the night. They initially refuse, but Lot eventually persuades them to lodge with him. The two visitors enter his house and eat an elaborate meal Lot prepares for them. After they finish, things get ugly.

A large crowd of men has gathered outside Lot's door. They order Lot to hand over his two guests so they can rape them.[2] Lot is unwilling to comply.

Permitting his guests to be sexually assaulted would constitute a gross breach of hospitality. So Lot proposes an alternative plan, one he hopes will pacify this menacing crowd. It is a plan that is at once both horrible and horrifying. Instead of sending out his guests, Lot offers to give this unruly mob his two virgin daughters. The men of Sodom are not interested and are just about to break into Lot's house when his guests strike them with blindness, making it impossible for them to find their way to the door.

The next morning, Lot, along with his wife and two daughters, leaves the city just moments before it is destroyed. There are no other survivors. Soon after leaving the city, Lot's wife is also killed because she disobeys orders by looking back (v. 26; cf. v. 17).

After escaping to Zoar, Lot and his two daughters head for the hills. His daughters are concerned about progeny and are worried there is nobody around who would be willing to have sex with them (v. 31). Therefore, *they* devise and carry out a desperate plan.[3] On two consecutive nights, they get their father drunk and lie down with him: the oldest daughter first, and the youngest daughter second (vv. 33–35). Both become pregnant—their stated agenda—and thus are born Moab, the eponymous ancestor of the Moabites, and Ben-ammi, the eponymous ancestor of the Ammonites (vv. 36–38).

The story of Sodom and Gomorrah rarely appears in church. It is not part of the Revised Common Lectionary, and few ministers teach or preach from it. Although I grew up in the church and have heard hundreds of sermons over my lifetime, I do not recall ever hearing one about this passage.

So how might a story like this be used in a sermon or Sunday school class? One possibility would be to describe the way Genesis 19 has been *mis*used by Christians to condemn "homosexuality" (option 6).[4] Many people assume this passage condemns same-sex relationships.[5] Matthew Vines, a gay Christian and the executive director of the Reformation Project, was confronted by this perspective when he was a teenager. "I was in high school," writes Vines, "and I had just asked my dad why Christians oppose gay rights. He said it had to do with God's reaction to the men of Sodom. They wanted to have sex with other men, so God destroyed them."[6] This interpretation of Genesis 19 is quite common and has resulted in enormous harm to members of the LGBTQIA+ community. But this interpretation is clearly flawed.

Christians who cite the story of Sodom to declare that "God is against homosexuality" or to argue that "God opposes same-sex relationships" wittingly or unwittingly misappropriate this text in harmful ways. They perpetuate violent readings of the story that fundamentally misunderstand the nature and purpose of Genesis 19. Religious leaders can—and should—critique these problematic interpretations. This is necessary and important work, given the harm this passage has caused the LGBTQIA+ community. By preaching and teaching responsibly from this passage, pastors can lead people to a more appropriate understanding of the story of Sodom.

To correct the "God punishes Sodom because they are having 'gay sex'" interpretation, ministers could emphasize a number of points. First, Genesis 19 is about a breach of hospitality, and this is what ancient readers would have found especially troubling. As it happens, this breach of hospitality was predicated upon sexual violence and domination. The men of Sodom wanted to rape the two men who were lodging with Lot. Any morally astute reader—gay or straight—should categorically condemn this form of sexual violence.

Second, preachers and lay leaders would do well to emphasize that this passage is *not* addressing same-sex attraction, same-sex relationships, or same-sex marriage. Ancient Israelites had no knowledge of the fact that people have a sexual orientation. Nor did they realize that our sexual orientation is hardwired. This understanding of human sexuality has only been discovered more recently. Therefore, it is inappropriate to use a passage like Genesis 19 to say God is against people who are gay or people who engage in same-sex relationships. As Yale professor John Collins rightly observes, "the story says nothing about the permissibility of consensual sex between males."[7] It simply is not addressing that question. Whatever Genesis 19 is about, it is not about the morality of sex between consenting adults who are same-sex attracted.

Third, when this story is mentioned in the Prophets, the destruction of Sodom is not associated with the sexual behavior of the general population or the sexual violence expressed by the men at Lot's door.[8] Instead we read:

> As I live, says the Lord GOD, . . . This was the guilt of your sister Sodom: she and her daughters had pride, excess of food, and prosperous ease, but did not aid the poor and needy. They were haughty, and did abominable things before me; therefore I removed them when I saw it. (Ezek. 16:48–50)

As this passage suggests, it is simplistic and inaccurate to say the sin of Sodom was "homosexuality."[9] Clearly it was not. The inhabitants of Sodom are condemned for their luxurious living and lack of concern for those in need. And while their desire to sexually assault the visitors to their city is reprehensible, suggesting that God destroyed Sodom because the people there were engaging in "homosexual behavior" is not warranted by the text.[10]

Christians who use Genesis 19 to condemn people who are same-sex attracted, or who engage in same-sex relations, misuse the Bible and do enormous harm to members of the LGBTQIA+ community. The same could be said about those who misuse other Old Testament texts, like Leviticus 18:22 and 20:13, to discriminate against this population.[11] Ministers should warn people against oppressive interpretations like these and should remind congregants that biblical texts should never be used to harm others.

Emphasizing the way Genesis 19 is often *mis*used will naturally lead to conversations about the church's view on same-sex relationships and about human sexuality more broadly.[12] Used responsibly, Genesis 19 can serve as a springboard to launch into these crucial conversations (option 4). The church desperately needs to find ways to talk about sexual orientation and same-sex attraction that move toward full inclusion.[13] Discussing this passage allows Christian leaders to explore a wide range of important questions: How should the Bible inform our thinking about same-sex attraction? What biblical passages are relevant in this conversation? What additional resources are needed to have a more fully informed conversation?

Since opinions about same-sex marriage and about the full inclusion of LGBTQIA+ individuals are so diverse in different church contexts, it is advantageous to have this conversation in a Sunday school class (or classes) or small group where there is adequate space for discussion, disagreement, and dialogue.[14] It would be ideal if the person leading this conversation was a trusted member of the congregation with expertise in this area and skill in facilitating difficult conversations. Alternately, the church could bring in a guest speaker with these qualifications to conduct this important dialogue.

A different way to approach Genesis 19 would be to use it to address the problem of sexualized violence (option 5).[15] One of the most disturbing features of this story is the way Lot treats his two daughters. When the inhabitants of Sodom want to rape his male houseguests, Lot offers his two virgin daughters, with permission to "do to them as you please" (v. 8). What was Lot thinking? How could he suggest such a thing? And what effect would this have had on his relationship with his daughters?[16] Even in a patriarchal culture where women are valued less than men, and where children—especially female children—are regarded as expendable, this constitutes "an epic parenting failure."[17] Lot's behavior is unconscionable, and modern readers rightly recoil in horror.

Yet Lot's obscene offer is not just a thing of the past, a relic of a bygone era. Rather, it is a perennial problem, one that continues to plague us to this very day. Too many men today sanction—and even participate in—acts of violence against women, exerting power and control over women's bodies and sexuality just as Lot did so many years ago. We see this all the time in the world around us, both in the church and in other contexts. It happens in arranged marriages, in the production and consumption of pornography, in sex trafficking, in intimate partner violence, and in a wide range of sexual assaults that occur with alarming frequency and regularity. While the situation and context may differ—most fathers today never find themselves facing an

angry mob intent on sexually assaulting male guests staying in their home—
the harmful treatment of women today is much the same. The story of Lot's
callous disregard for the well-being of his own daughters, and his willingness
to allow them to be sexually assaulted and traumatized, creates an opportunity
for the church to talk about sexual violence against women: where it occurs,
why it occurs, and what can be done to prevent it.[18]

As part of this conversation, you might consider sharing some first-person
accounts from women who have experienced this kind of trauma and written
about it in books and online posts.[19] Putting a human face on this kind of violence is powerful and makes it personal. When names, faces, and stories are
included, it becomes more than just an abstract "issue."

Obviously, sharing first-person accounts like these will need to be done
carefully because it could be traumatic for some churchgoers to hear stories
like these. This is one of those times when it would be wise to give people
advance notice in case they feel the need to remove themselves (or their children) while stories like these are being shared.[20] But these stories should be
told, for all sorts of reasons, not least of which is their power to persuade
churchgoers to take a stand against sexualized violence.

A violent text like Genesis 19 can also be used to explore the nature and
character of God. For many readers, God's violent destruction of these cities is
typical of the way God reacts to transgressors in the Old Testament.

> Then the LORD rained on Sodom and Gomorrah sulfur and fire
> from the LORD out of heaven; and he overthrew those cities, and all
> the Plain, and all the inhabitants of the cities, and what grew on the
> ground. (vv. 24–25)

According to the story, God kills everyone and everything except Lot and his
wife and two daughters. While this might seem extreme, lethal behavior is not
unusual for God in the pages of the Old Testament. As Peter Enns puts it:

> God killing people . . . isn't a last-ditch measure of an otherwise patient
> deity. It's the go-to punishment for disobedience. To put a fine point
> on it, this God is flat-out terrifying: he comes across as a perennially
> hacked-off warrior-god, more Megatron than heavenly Father.[21]

But is this what God is really like? Is God really in the business of smiting, slaying, and slaughtering countless men, women, and children? Or is
there another way to understand these violent portrayals of God, one that
squares with images of God as loving, compassionate, and merciful (as God
was toward Lot in Gen. 19:16)? We will consider this issue at length in the next
chapter. I mention it here simply to illustrate that even if we are disturbed by

certain portrayals of God in the Old Testament—and perhaps even disagree with them—they can still be used constructively as a catalyst for clarifying what we believe to be true about God.

Obviously, we have only scratched the surface here. There are many more ways Genesis 19 could be used to encourage spiritual growth and Christian maturity. For example, ministers could use it to reflect on the importance of hospitality (option 7),[22] though Lot clearly takes this to an unhealthy extreme. And the church could also use the end of the chapter to create space to talk about the problem of sexual abuse in the home (option 4), or to consider how we view others, particularly our traditional enemies (option 7). These and other possibilities await those who are willing to wrestle with this text and to do something positive with it.

NABOTH: THE EXECUTION OF AN INNOCENT MAN (1 KGS. 21:1–16)

The story of the acquisition of Naboth's vineyard is another violent biblical text brimming with creative possibilities for use in church. In the Revised Common Lectionary, it appears as a reading in the season after Pentecost in Year C.

> Later the following events took place: Naboth the Jezreelite had a vineyard in Jezreel, beside the palace of King Ahab of Samaria. And Ahab said to Naboth, "Give me your vineyard, so that I may have it for a vegetable garden, because it is near my house; I will give you a better vineyard for it; or, if it seems good to you, I will give you its value in money." But Naboth said to Ahab, "The LORD forbid that I should give you my ancestral inheritance." Ahab went home resentful and sullen because of what Naboth the Jezreelite had said to him; for he had said, "I will not give you my ancestral inheritance." He lay down on his bed, turned away his face, and would not eat.
>
> His wife Jezebel came to him and said, "Why are you so depressed that you will not eat?" He said to her, "Because I spoke to Naboth the Jezreelite and said to him, 'Give me your vineyard for money; or else, if you prefer, I will give you another vineyard for it'; but he answered, 'I will not give you my vineyard.'" His wife Jezebel said to him, "Do you now govern Israel? Get up, eat some food, and be cheerful; I will give you the vineyard of Naboth the Jezreelite."
>
> So she wrote letters in Ahab's name and sealed them with his seal; she sent the letters to the elders and the nobles who lived with Naboth in his city. She wrote in the letters, "Proclaim a fast, and seat Naboth at the head of the assembly; seat two scoundrels opposite him, and have

them bring a charge against him, saying, 'You have cursed God and the king.' Then take him out, and stone him to death." The men of his city, the elders and the nobles who lived in his city, did as Jezebel had sent word to them. Just as it was written in the letters that she had sent to them, they proclaimed a fast and seated Naboth at the head of the assembly. The two scoundrels came in and sat opposite him; and the scoundrels brought a charge against Naboth, in the presence of the people, saying, "Naboth cursed God and the king." So they took him outside the city, and stoned him to death. Then they sent to Jezebel, saying, "Naboth has been stoned; he is dead."

As soon as Jezebel heard that Naboth had been stoned and was dead, Jezebel said to Ahab, "Go, take possession of the vineyard of Naboth the Jezreelite, which he refused to give you for money; for Naboth is not alive, but dead." As soon as Ahab heard that Naboth was dead, Ahab set out to go down to the vineyard of Naboth the Jezreelite, to take possession of it.

Although the story of Naboth's vineyard can be explored from many angles, it is essentially a story about an innocent man who is falsely accused and summarily executed. This makes it ideal for preachers and teachers who want to use it to talk about the death penalty in a sermon or Sunday school lesson (option 4). In the United States, twenty-seven states continue to practice capital punishment even though it has become increasingly obvious that many people are wrongly convicted, just like Naboth.[23] The trumped-up charges against Naboth were fabricated to facilitate an illegal land grab. His "trial" was a complete miscarriage of justice. The same is true of many capital cases today that are unduly biased by racial prejudice. As the authors of a 2015 Equal Justice Initiative report assert, "Capital punishment remains rooted in racial terror—a direct descendant of lynching."[24] The story of Naboth's vineyard reminds us that other agendas are often at work in cases like these. As such, it serves as a useful entry point into this important topic.

Ministers who want to use 1 Kings 21 to discuss the problem of capital punishment today may want to consult some other resources before stepping into the pulpit or walking into a Sunday school classroom. Two especially helpful books are *Executing Grace: How the Death Penalty Killed Jesus and Why It's Killing Us*, by Shane Claiborne, and *Just Mercy: A Story of Justice and Redemption*, the *New York Times* number-one bestseller by Bryan Stevenson, founder of the Equal Justice Initiative. Many great resources are also available online through the Equal Justice Initiative (eji.org).

The story of Naboth's vineyard is also useful for reflecting on the nature of power: how it operates, how it influences others, and how it is used and abused (option 7). One of the most intriguing features of this story is the role played by "the elders and the nobles" (vv. 8–14). They are ultimately the ones responsible for turning Jezebel's deadly desires into reality. After receiving the queen's order to kill Naboth—albeit in letters ostensibly written in Ahab's name and sealed with his official seal—they immediately do as they are told.

The story emphasizes that these "elders and the nobles" were people who "lived with Naboth in his city" (v. 8; cf. v. 11). They were obviously acquainted with Naboth and must have known what he was like. Nothing in the text suggests Naboth was sinful or evil. On the contrary, his determination to retain his "ancestral inheritance" even when he could have sold it for more than market value—or could have had better land—emphasizes his piety.[25] If Naboth was a person of good character, as the text seems to imply, and his fellow Jezreelites knew this, why did they go along with this legal charade? Why were they willing accomplices to the death of an innocent man?

Although 1 Kings 21 does not reveal their motives, their actions raise important questions that could be explored in a sermon or Sunday school lesson to encourage self-reflection. For example, what do you think *you* would have done if you were one of the elders or nobles who received these letters? Would you have complied? Why or why not? Or to ask the question more generally, how would you respond to someone who demands you do something you know is wrong? Would you do it? What if the order came from someone in authority over you, someone who could make things very difficult for you if you did not do what they want? These are important questions to consider. It is easy to allow fear to control our actions and to compromise our principles in misguided acts of self-preservation even if that means hurting other people along the way. Yet if we capitulate to those in authority, we are just like the elders and nobles of Jezreel, a group of royal lackeys without the moral courage to resist a directive they should have disobeyed.

Thankfully, not everyone in the Old Testament is as spineless as these officials. Consider the bold daring of Shiphrah and Puah, two Hebrew midwives who refuse to kill Hebrew baby boys even though Pharaoh orders them to do so. These women choose to disobey Pharaoh—at great risk to themselves—because they fear God rather than this Egyptian monarch (Exod. 1:17, 21). The actions of these midwives serve as an inspiring counterpoint to the Jezreelites' lack of courage, creativity, and conviction, making the story an ideal text to bring into conversation with 1 Kings 21.

The story of Naboth's vineyard could also be used "to demonstrate why violence is so harmful" (option 1). Apparently, Naboth was not the only casualty in Jezebel's evil scheme. Based on an oracle preserved in 2 Kings, it appears that Naboth's children suffered the same fate he did.[26]

> For the blood of Naboth and for the blood of his children that I saw yesterday, says the LORD, I swear I will repay you [Ahab] on this very plot of ground. (2 Kgs. 9:26)

Killing Naboth's children eliminated any future threat they might have posed to King Ahab by avenging their father's death—not to mention any claim they might make on the land.

We are told nothing about Naboth's wife or whether she was still living when he died. If she was, and was not subsequently killed as well, she would have been profoundly impacted by this whole sordid affair. It would have been devastating to her and would have put her at great risk. Not only would she grieve the loss of her husband and children, she would likely struggle for her own survival. With no sons to provide for her, and without the vineyard to support her, she would be extremely vulnerable.

As part of a sermon or Sunday school lesson, you might consider writing a first-person narrative from her perspective. (Alternatively, you could have people in church write something like this, which they could then share with others.) You could use this to explore the anger and grief she felt over what happened to her family and to express her anxiety over the desperate situation in which she now finds herself. This would poignantly demonstrate the harmful and destructive nature of violence, particularly against those in society who are most vulnerable.

One way you could process this tragedy liturgically would be to make lament for Naboth's children and, by extension, for all who suffer and die at the hands of those in power (option 3). Something along these lines could easily be worked into a responsive reading. Here is one example:

A Lament for Naboth's Children

Leader: We lament for the sons and daughters of Naboth, children killed for no other reason than greedy desire.

People: Lord, forgive us for our greed.

Leader: We lament for the sons and daughters of those around the world whose land has been unjustly confiscated and who struggle to survive on what little they have.

People: Lord, in your mercy, prompt us to act for justice on their behalf.

Leader: We grieve for children whose lives are cut short by acts of violence.

People: **Lord, forgive us for the violence in our own hearts, and strengthen our resolve to protect children always and everywhere.**

Leader: We condemn the use of power and privilege for personal enrichment at the expense of others.

People: **Lord, keep us from temptation to increase our wealth by harming others.**

Leader: We condemn the use of power and deceit to tarnish the good character of another.

People: **Lord, prevent us from taking advantage of others to advance our own agenda.**

All: **Lord, keep us from all evil. Teach us your ways. Help us to do what is right, now and forever.**[27]

As this simple liturgy illustrates, ministers can use the story of Naboth's vineyard to help churchgoers develop compassion for people who are disenfranchised by those in power and to admonish them not to use the power they have to harm others.

The story of Naboth's vineyard can also be used to urge Christians to take action on behalf of people, like Naboth, who are threatened by rich and powerful individuals, corporations, and governments who use their resources and connections to unjustly appropriate land that does not belong to them (option 2). This is a global problem, one that affects the poor most keenly in both rural and urban areas. To help people understand this issue more fully, and to inspire them to take action, ministers could introduce people to organizations like Solidarity Uganda that encourage nonviolent action to address the problem of land grabs.[28] This aspect of the story could be emphasized in a sermon or Sunday school class and would be especially well received by individuals committed to working for peace and justice.

Before leaving this passage, allow me to mention one more way to use it, though I realize some may feel like it is a stretch. Jezebel is always portrayed negatively in the Bible, and her own violent death is reported approvingly by the writer of Kings (2 Kgs. 9:30–37). In an effort "to develop compassion for victims of violence" (option 3), experiment with a more sympathetic reading of this Sidonian woman. Even "villains" have redeeming qualities, regardless of whether or not those are on display in the text, and it is important not to lose sight of the fact that they too are human beings. As Professor Lynn Japinga suggests:

The preacher might find it helpful to shift the perspective on Jezebel for a moment and identify her as a good wife who supported her husband and children. She was devoted to her religion, even though she was harassed for her beliefs. She was an evangelist who encouraged others to adopt her faith. To the Canaanites, she was a hero, and a model of religious devotion; but what the Canaanites saw as virtue, the Israelites saw as sin and idolatry.[29]

While Japinga recognizes Jezebel's treachery, shifting the perspective this way enables us to humanize her, to see her as a person rather than a personification of evil.

To be sure, Jezebel has blood on her hands—remember what she did to the prophets of the Lord (1 Kgs. 18:4)—and we should not whitewash, or attempt to justify, her evil deeds. Still, we should remember that the stories we have of Jezebel in the Bible were meant to cast her in the worst possible light. They were written by people who hated her. But was she worse than some of the other people we meet in Scripture, even some we often revere? Japinga thinks not:

Her crimes, though violent and ugly, were no worse than the sins committed by those labeled "men of God." She killed God's prophets; Elijah killed Baal's prophets. She had Naboth killed because she wanted his land. David had Uriah killed because he wanted his wife. She encouraged the worship of Baal, as did Solomon (1 Kgs. 11) and many of his successors.[30]

While we rightly abhor Jezebel's violent behavior, we should remember that she—just like Elijah, David, Solomon, and each one of us—was created in God's image and is loved unconditionally by the Creator. We should also be mindful that much of the hatred heaped upon Jezebel is due to the simple fact that she is a woman, and a powerful one at that. This has led to a long and ugly history of misogynistic interpretation.[31] All this should prompt us to be careful how we talk about her. At the very least, it should prevent us from demonizing her and should encourage us to view her tragic death with a degree of compassion.[32]

DANIEL: IN (AND OUT OF) THE LIONS' DEN (DAN. 6)

The final violent biblical text I would like to consider here is Daniel in the lions' den. It is one of the most well-known stories in the Old Testament, one that regularly appears in children's Bibles and Sunday school curriculum.

The story tells of a Jew named Daniel who is an official in the royal court of a Babylonian king named Darius. In time, Daniel rises to prominence "because an excellent spirit was in him" (Dan. 6:3). King Darius notices this and plans to put Daniel in charge of his entire kingdom, including Daniel's fellow royal officials (v. 3). Sensing Daniel's promotion close at hand, and not wanting to be usurped by this foreigner, these officials attempt to thwart the king's plans. To do this, they try to find dirt on Daniel but come up empty-handed. Daniel is squeaky clean with no skeletons in the closet.

So Daniel's rivals resort to Plan B. They conspire together and draft a document that would restrict his religious freedom by stipulating that for the next thirty days, prayers can be made only *to the king*. The punishment for transgressors is a one-way trip to the lions' den. Daniel is aware of this edict but is unwavering in his religious devotion. He continues his daily regimen of praying to the Lord three times a day with the windows of his house wide open (v. 10). As planned, the conspirators catch Daniel red-handed and report him to the king (vv. 11–12).

King Darius is distressed by these developments. But he has no choice other than to follow through with the punishment, since his edict is irrevo-cable. So, as decreed, Daniel is thrown into the lions' den. The king is unable to sleep all night and approaches the den of lions early the next morning to see how Daniel has fared. He is delighted to discover that Daniel has survived, and he immediately removes him from the lions' den. The king praises God for delivering Daniel and issues a decree ordering all subjects in his kingdom to "tremble and fear before the God of Daniel" (v. 26).

This is where most retellings of the story end, and there are many power-ful takeaways that can be made at this juncture. The story is routinely used to emphasize the importance of remaining faithful to God, no matter what, since God will take of you. Even in environments that are hostile to your faith, it pays to trust God. This was, after all, the key to Daniel's deliverance (v. 23).

But what interests me for our purposes is a single verse near the end of the story that is often overlooked. Right after Daniel is retrieved from the lions' den, the story takes a deadly turn.

> The king gave a command, and those who had accused Daniel were brought and thrown into the den of lions—they, their children, and their wives. Before they reached the bottom of the den the lions over-powered them and broke all their bones in pieces. (v. 24)[33]

I seriously doubt this verse is illustrated in most children's Bibles! It is extremely graphic and deeply disturbing. But in the spirit of reading the Bible honestly in a preaching or teaching context, how can pastors and lay leaders use a violent verse like this constructively?

One way to redeem this verse would be to use it to reflect on the way our sinful behavior impacts those around us (options 1 and 7). It is bad enough that the conspirators are killed for their misdeeds. But it does not end there. Their evil scheme results in the death of their wives and children as well. Yet as far as we know, they had nothing to do with this. They were innocent.[34]

That is how sin works. It has ripple effects, negative repercussions that harm many others. Just think of all the people who would have been affected by the untimely deaths of the conspirators and their families: aunts and uncles, nieces and nephews, parents and grandparents, friends—the list goes on. Their lives would be forever changed.

Pastors and lay leaders could press this point by exploring various ways our sinful behavior affects those around us. Take a hypothetical example. Imagine what might happen if I decided to commit insurance fraud. If I got caught, I would likely be prosecuted, fined, and possibly imprisoned. Even though the guilt is mine alone, my family would suffer as well. Although they would not suffer the *same* consequences as me (*they* would not be thrown in prison), they would feel the effects of my poor choices in very real ways. They would suffer financially and would bear the burden of additional responsibilities to keep the household running while I was incarcerated. They might be ridiculed and scorned, and could even lose some friends over the whole ordeal. My colleagues would have to scramble to cover my classes, and my relationship with my wife and children, along with many others, would be strained. My bad choices would inevitably have unpleasant consequences for those I care about.

These royal officials brought calamity upon their families. Their scheme dramatically demonstrates the terrible consequences our actions can have upon us and the people we love, sometimes in devastating and unforeseen ways. As such, this story becomes a cautionary tale, one we can carry around with us like a portable prophylactic against sin.[35] The next time you are tempted to cheat on your income taxes or inflate your résumé or lie about something you did, bring this story to mind. Doing so will help you remember the damaging effects your sinful actions can have on others—particularly those closest to you—and it might restrain you from doing something you will later regret. When pastors and lay leaders encourage people to use Daniel 6:24 this way, they help them move beyond the sheer horror of the verse—and it is horrifying—to ways they might benefit from it.

Coming at it from a different angle, another constructive way to use this verse is to consider how violence harms those responsible for perpetrating it (option 1). Admittedly, this will take some imagination. The executioners are never explicitly named in this verse. But they are there, barely present but clearly visible.

> The king gave a command, and those who had accused Daniel *were brought.* (v. 24, emphasis mine)

Brought *by whom?* Who were these individuals given the unenviable task of hauling men, women, and children to their death in the lions' den? Presumably they were people in the king's employ, possibly the same individuals who had brought Daniel the day before (v. 16). How did they feel about their role in this deadly assignment?

Though the text does not describe the scene, it is hard to believe the conspirators and their families came willingly—or quietly. Did they resist? Were the wives screaming? Their children crying? What effect would this have had on these unnamed executioners, especially after they witnessed the gruesome deaths of these men, women, and children? Would they ever be the same afterward? Would this incident haunt them in their dreams? Would it cause psychological trauma? Moral injury? How would they have been impacted by performing actions they may have felt were wrong?

Exploring questions like these provides a significant opportunity to reflect on the fact that violence harms both victims *and* perpetrators. Human beings are not wired to kill other human beings. When they do, trauma inevitably results. The church could emphasize this point as one way to reinforce its commitment to peace and nonviolence and to demonstrate why violence is so harmful and destructive, further problematizing all forms of state-sanctioned killing, from executing a prisoner on death row to killing a combatant on the battlefield.[36]

I realize some people may not be troubled by King Darius's command to throw the treacherous conspirators into the lions' den since they believe these men got just what they deserved. It seems only fair that the conspirators should die in the same manner they devised for Daniel. Poetic justice, they would say.

Still, while this violent punishment is unremarkable in its historical context, it is at odds with core Christian values. As this book repeatedly emphasizes, followers of Jesus are commanded to love—not kill—their enemies (Matt. 5:43–45). It is well-nigh impossible to reconcile the king's execution orders with Christian notions of grace, forgiveness, and redemption. Therefore, whenever a passage like this is used in church, a passage that seemingly sanctions retributive violence, care must be taken to avoid giving the impression that we approve of such measures. While these officials needed to be held accountable for their actions, killing them is unacceptable from the standpoint of Christian ethics.

In light of this, it would be interesting to consider crafting an alternate ending to the story that emphasizes *restorative* justice rather than *retributive* justice (option 2).[37] You could easily incorporate something like this into a sermon. Or, if you are discussing this passage in a Sunday school class or small-group setting, invite participants to write an alternate ending themselves, giving them space to imagine less violent, more conciliatory outcomes. Give them five to seven minutes to write, and then ask for volunteers to read their creative conclusion to the story. Here is an alternate ending I wrote that picks up the story immediately after verse 23:

> The king gave a command, and those who had accused Daniel were brought to be thrown into the den of lions—they, their children, and their wives. But before they were cast into the lions' den, Daniel stood up and spoke these words to the king:
>
> "Praise be to God, who miraculously delivered me this day from the jaws of death. Although these men sought to destroy me, God has delivered me. What they meant for evil, God meant for good so that all might know God's awesome power to save. Therefore, this is not a day for death, but for life. Let us celebrate together the goodness of God with food and drink."
>
> "But what of these men?" asked the king. "What should be done to them?"
>
> "Release them," said Daniel, "so they might continue to serve the king as I teach them the ways of God."
>
> After hearing Daniel's words, King Darius released the men who had entrapped Daniel. Immediately the men ran to Daniel, fell on his neck, and wept, so overcome were they with gratitude that their lives had been spared. And they went away rejoicing, along with their wives and children, amazed at Daniel's gracious words and in awe of his God.

Obviously, an alternate ending like this could be developed and expanded in all sorts of ways and many different directions. Incorporating something like this into a sermon (or Sunday school lesson) subverts the violent ideology of the text and helps people conceptualize more conciliatory endings. It demonstrates that killing wrongdoers is not the only, let alone the most desirable, way to deal with them. There are alternatives. Ministers can use creative endings like this one to encourage congregants to explore alternatives as they consider more redemptive ways to deal with "evildoers."[38]

CONCLUSION

Our exploration of Genesis 19, 1 Kings 21, and Daniel 6 has revealed many ways to use these violent biblical texts constructively. Hopefully, this has broadened your appreciation of what is possible and encouraged you to try similar things with other violent verses in the Bible.

Before bringing this book to a close, there is one very important issue yet to consider that we have touched on but haven't addressed at length: *How should ministers deal with violent portrayals of God in Scripture?* In the next chapter, this concern takes center stage as we explore various ways that pastors, Sunday school teachers, and worship leaders can deal responsibly with divine violence in the Old Testament.

8

Talking about God's Violent Behavior in the Bible

Doing Good Theology When "God" Behaves Badly

> In a world being torn apart by violence, there is no more urgent task than to counter the Bible's frequent and nauseating portraits of a ruthless and violent deity.
>
> —Jack Nelson-Pallmeyer, *Jesus against Christianity*[1]

Before reading any further, please take the following short quiz. Based on your own personal beliefs about God's character, answer yes or no to each of these questions:

- Do you think God would ever *delight* in punishing people?
- Do you think God would ever command people to kill children and infants?
- Do you think God would ever sanction sexual violence?
- Do you think God would ever send wild animals to kill people who do not worship God?
- Do you think God would ever afflict people for *no reason*?

How well do you think you did? If you answered no to all these questions, I would give you a perfect score. That's the good news.

The bad news? The biblical writers would flunk you!

In fact, if you answered no to even *one* of these questions, your view of God is at odds with the way God is sometimes portrayed in the Bible. God does *all* these terrible things—and more—in the pages of the Old Testament. If you do not believe me, take a look at the biblical references in this note.[2] They will remove all doubt.

The purpose of this little quiz is to illustrate a seldom-acknowledged reality: hardly anyone believes that every single portrayal of God in the Old Testament accurately reflects God's character.[3] Whether they are willing to acknowledge it or not is a different matter. Yet even those who make the boldest claims about the Bible's authority and reliability inevitably still pick and choose which passages they allow to inform their view of God.

This is on display every Sunday morning when prayers are offered. God is extolled for being good, loving, forgiving, compassionate, merciful, and kind. Rarely, if ever, will you hear God praised for being violent. But if everything God does is praiseworthy, and the Old Testament claims God engages in acts of violence, why not praise God for these acts as well?

> Thank you, O Lord, that in your infinite wisdom and judgment, you commanded the people of Israel to annihilate the Amalekites and leave no survivors. Thank you for ordering King Saul to slaughter every last Amalekite child and infant as punishment for sins their ancestors had committed hundreds of years earlier.[4]

> And we praise you, O God, for giving David's wives to his son Absalom, so he could have sex with them without their consent. Thank you for sanctioning the sexual assault of these women to punish David for his sin.[5]

I have gone to church all my life and have never heard a minister pray this way. Most wouldn't dare. Nor should they.

This once again illustrates that even those who insist they base their view of God on the Bible do so very selectively. We all make interpretative choices when we read Scripture. The important question is what governs the choices we make when using the Bible to think about the nature and character of God.

GOD'S VIOLENT BEHAVIOR IN THE OLD TESTAMENT

God is responsible for a lot of death and destruction in the pages of the Old Testament.[6] As noted earlier, of the approximately seventeen hundred violent passages in the Old Testament, about eleven hundred contain divine violence (acts God allegedly *commits*) or divinely sanctioned violence (acts God allegedly *commands*).[7] And the body count from these passages in which God commits or commands violence is staggering. According to calculations made by Steve Wells, God is responsible for the death of nearly 2.5 million people in the Old Testament, and that only includes the casualties that are actually reported in the text.[8] Wells believes the figure would be about ten times higher if it included estimates of those slain when no count of the dead is given (e.g., the flood narrative, the story of Sodom and Gomorrah, and so forth).[9] However you look at it, God is implicated in an enormous amount of violent behavior in the pages of the Old Testament. Here is a brief sampling:[10]

> When Pharaoh stubbornly refused to let us go, the LORD killed all the firstborn in the land of Egypt, from human firstborn to the firstborn of animals. (Exod. 13:15)

> The LORD tossed the Egyptians into the sea. The waters returned and covered the chariots and the chariot drivers, the entire army of Pharaoh that had followed them into the sea; not one of them remained. (Exod. 14:27–28)

> As they fled before Israel, while they were going down the slope of Beth-horon, the LORD threw down huge stones from heaven on them as far as Azekah, and they died; there were more who died because of the hailstones than the Israelites killed with the sword. (Josh. 10:11)

> The descendants of Jeconiah did not rejoice with the people of Beth-shemesh when they greeted the ark of the LORD; and he killed seventy men of them. The people mourned because the LORD had made a great slaughter among the people. (1 Sam. 6:19)

> When they first settled there, they did not worship the LORD; therefore the LORD sent lions among them, which killed some of them. (2 Kgs. 17:25)

> That very night the angel of the LORD set out and struck down one hundred eighty-five thousand in the camp of the Assyrians; when morning dawned, they were all dead bodies. (2 Kgs. 19:35)

What should the church to do with these violent verses and hundreds of others like them in the Old Testament?

A CHALLENGING CONVERSATION

Talking directly about God's violent behavior in the Old Testament creates all sorts of challenges for ministers, church workers, and religious educators. Stories of God smiting, slaying, and slaughtering countless individuals do not fit well with Israel's core confession that praises God for being "merciful and gracious, slow to anger, and abounding in steadfast love and faithfulness" (Exod. 34:6). Similarly, images of God behaving violently in the Old Testament do not correspond well with the way God is revealed in the New Testament through the life and teachings of Jesus.[11] How can we deal with these tensions? What is God really like?

Part of what makes this conversation so complicated is that raising questions about the nature of God inevitably raises questions about the nature of Scripture. The two are inextricably linked. If we affirm the inspiration and authority of Scripture, does that mean we are bound to accept all portrayals of God as they appear? Some believe so. Or, is it possible to have a robust view of the inspiration and authority of Scripture while at the same time asserting God did *not* actually say or do everything the Bible claims? But if we reach this conclusion, then what? How will we decide which portrayals reveal what God is like and which do not? Clearly, there are significant challenges here.

Be that as it may, it is imperative for the church to find constructive ways to deal with divine violence in the Old Testament. As we observed, people have *mis*used these texts to justify warfare and colonialism; to oppress and kill women, children, and Native peoples; and to legitimate a range of violent beliefs and practices that have done enormous harm, especially to marginalized communities. And passages containing violent portrayals of God present significant barriers to faith. According to Greg Boyd, "The violence ascribed to God in the OT has arguably been one of the greatest contributors to modern unbelief, at least in the western world."[12] As I hope I've persuaded you by now, it behooves ministers to find responsible ways to talk about these texts in church.

If the church is going to help people deal responsibly with violent portrayals of God in the Bible, it must begin by convincing people to reexamine some of their most fundamental assumptions about the nature of Scripture and the nature of God. Apart from this, little progress can be made.

IS GOD VIOLENT?

Many Christians uncritically assume that whatever the Bible says about God is true. If the Bible says God destroyed humanity in a worldwide flood, they believe that's what God actually did. If a passage in Genesis says God killed all the inhabitants of Sodom and Gomorrah, they are convinced that is what happened. And if the Old Testament declares, "The LORD is a warrior," they are certain God must be one.

Many people also believe God still initiates, sanctions, and participates in acts of violence today. Though they might balk at the idea of God killing infants or sanctioning sexual violence—as evident by the way many of them would respond to the quiz questions above—they remain convinced God sometimes uses sickness, misfortune, and natural disasters to punish "evildoers." They also believe God condones state-sanctioned violence like capital punishment and wars fought to liberate the oppressed. And they can sometimes be quite adamant that God consigns recalcitrant sinners to the eternal violence of hell.

Perhaps you agree, at least to some extent, with these individuals. Maybe you also believe God is violent or behaves violently at times, even if you think God forbids *people* from behaving this way in most cases. If so, you are not alone. Violent views of God like these are common, and even prevalent, in many segments of the church.

But are these views accurate? Is God violent? Does God, the *living* God, the God revealed in Jesus, behave this way? I do not think so. Why? For one simple reason.

God is not violent because God is love.[13]

There is nothing loving about violence. On the contrary, it is *antithetical* to love, even if used for noble purposes. Violence, by its very nature, *always* does harm to some even when it might be used to help others. It involves domination and control, whereas love is exactly the opposite. Love serves others and promotes their well-being. In the words of the apostle Paul, "Love is patient; love is kind. . . . It does not insist on its own way" (1 Cor. 13:4–5). Love is noncoercive and unselfish. It puts others first and looks out for their interests (Phil. 2:4). Whereas love is the chief virtue (1 Cor. 13:13), violence is no virtue at all. Since God is fundamentally, essentially a God of love, God is not violent. As theologian Tom Oord observes, "God's unchanging nature is love. . . . Love is what God does. . . . Love comes logically first among divine attributes. . . . God cannot not love."[14]

God's love is evident in numerous Old Testament passages (e.g., Pss. 86:15; 146:5–8; Lam. 3:22–23; Hos. 11:1; 14:4–7), and Christians believe it is displayed with particular clarity through Jesus, "the exact imprint of God's very being" (Heb. 1:3). Jesus' life and teachings make the love of God manifest in various ways, and this helps us see the true nature and character of God. This is a crucial point that we will revisit later.

The conviction that God is love leads me to reject the notion that God, the living God, is a violent God or a purveyor of violence. God does not justify, celebrate, or participate in any acts of violence. Never has—never will. Such behavior is utterly inconsistent with the nature of a God who is love. Thus, violent portrayals of God in the both the Old and New Testaments distort God's good character and do not reflect what God is really like.

I realize I have just made some rather large theological claims here, claims that many will strenuously disagree with, and claims that deserve far more attention than I will give them in the pages to follow. But I wanted to lay my cards on the table at the outset so you know where I stand and why I believe it is so terribly important to handle violent Old Testament portrayals of God with great care.

But if God is not violent, as I have asserted, what should ministers do with violent portrayals of God, especially those appearing in the Old Testament? How should they use biblical passages containing divine violence and divinely sanctioned violence? Here's my proposal. I believe one of the most important things we can do with these problematic portrayals of God is to use them to deconstruct the violent views of God so many people continue to embrace. They provide opportunities to talk about the true nature of God, which is defined by love, not violence. By demonstrating what God is *not* like, these troubling images can help us sharpen our understanding of what God really *is* like. This, I submit, is incredibly important work because having an accurate view of God is essential to our spiritual health and well-being.

DECONSTRUCTING VIOLENT VIEWS
ABOUT GOD: FOUR KEY IDEAS

In what follows, I will discuss four ideas that can be introduced in church through sermons, Sunday school classes, and small-group discussions, ideas that mitigate some of the hazards associated with these violent texts and clear the way for a more accurate view of God to emerge. Given limitations of space, and the fact that I have written extensively on this topic elsewhere, I won't develop these ideas at great length here.[15] Still, what is said here should be enough to point you in the right direction as you consider what to do with violent portrayals of God in the Old Testament.

Contextualize Violent Portrayals of God

One way to begin deconstructing violent views of God is to help people understand *why* God is sometimes portrayed behaving this way in the Old Testament. We know that ancient Israelites were deeply influenced by their historical and cultural context and shared many of the same assumptions about the world as their neighbors. As Peter Enns reminds us, "Israel's culture developed the way every other culture in the history of humanity has developed: as part of a larger cultural environment."[16]

People across the ancient Near East believed God punished individuals, communities, and even entire countries by sending plagues and sickness and by causing natural disasters. They also believed that the gods not only *engaged* in warfare but were ultimately responsible for victory and defeat in battle. The violent nature of the gods was a theological given, unquestioned and embraced by people everywhere. As Charlie Trimm expresses it in his massive study of warfare in the ancient Near East:

All armies in the ancient Near East viewed warfare as fundamentally religious. Kings and warriors frequently praised the divine warriors [i.e., gods and goddesses], called on them for help, received messages from them, lamented their occasional divine abandonment, gratefully accepted divine weapons (linking their actions with the tales of divine combat), and saw their hand in battle.[17]

This can easily be demonstrated with numerous texts and inscriptions from the ancient world, and I would encourage you to use some of these in sermons or Sunday school classes so people can see the similarities for themselves.[18] Introducing congregants to something like the Moabite Stone (Mesha Inscription), for example, would be particularly illuminating since it describes the Moabite god Chemosh acting in ways that resemble some of God's behavior in the Old Testament.[19]

Since Israel was part and parcel of a world that believed the gods behaved violently and participated in warfare, it is unsurprising to discover that Israel conceived of God in similar ways. This is a very important point, one that has huge ramifications for how we evaluate violent Old Testament portrayals of God. Rather than revealing something unique about God's character, these violent portrayals more likely reflect the historical milieu from which they emerged. In other words, the reason Israel portrayed God behaving violently is because that's what everyone did in the ancient world. Thus, violent depictions of God in the Old Testament say more about the cultural context from which they emerged than they do about the true nature of the living God.

Recognize God Did Not Do Everything the Old Testament Claims

To successfully deconstruct violent views of God, it is necessary to demonstrate that God did not say or do everything the Old Testament claims. Many pieces of evidence point in this direction. We just noted one of them: Israel's culturally conditioned portrayals of God. The results of archaeological study and the nature of ancient historiography provide two more.

Archaeological excavations from the second half of the twentieth century have demonstrated, rather conclusively, that some stories in the Bible never actually happened. Take, for example, the so-called conquest narrative in Joshua 6–11. Ostensibly, this is the story of how the Israelites conquered Canaanite cities and took possession of their land. Yet the archaeological evidence does not support this version of events. As American archaeologist William Dever says, "There is little that we can salvage from Joshua's stories of the rapid, wholesale destruction of Canaanite cities and the annihilation of the local population. *It simply did not happen; the archaeological evidence is indisputable.*"[20]

Here's what we know. The first two cities the Israelites are said to have destroyed, Jericho and Ai, were uninhabited at the time these events purportedly happened. If nobody was living in these cities, as archaeological research at these sites suggests, then it stands to reason that God never "handed Jericho over" to Joshua (Josh. 6:2) or told him to "do to Ai and its king as you did to Jericho and its king" (8:2). In short, these violent portrayals of God have no basis in historical reality.[21]

The nature of ancient historiography also raises questions about the reliability of some of the Old Testament's claims about God. Historiography relates to the practice of writing history, of using the past to tell the story of particular people, places, and events. Ancient historiographers were guided by theological assumptions that often differ quite dramatically from our own. For example, in the Old Testament, God is routinely portrayed as directing human affairs by opening and closing wombs, blessing obedience with success and material prosperity, and punishing human sinfulness through famines, plagues, and natural disasters. But today, if a couple has difficulty conceiving, they are likely to seek help at a fertility clinic. Why? Because they understand the root cause of their problem to be biological (e.g., a low sperm count, endometriosis) rather than theological (a divine decision to "close" a womb). While the couple certainly might pray and seek divine guidance, most Christians who struggle with infertility seek medical assistance.

Similarly, most Christians I know would be very reluctant to say COVID-19, which has killed millions of people worldwide, was an act of divine punishment. Yet this is *exactly* how a "plague" like this would have been interpreted in the ancient world, as divine punishment for human sinfulness.[22] This idea is reflected in numerous Old Testament passages, such as this one from the book of Deuteronomy:

> If you do not diligently observe all the words of this law that are written in this book, fearing this glorious and awesome name, the LORD your God, then the LORD will overwhelm both you and your offspring with severe and lasting afflictions and grievous and lasting maladies. He will bring back upon you all the diseases of Egypt, of which you were in dread, and they shall cling to you. Every other malady and affliction, even though not recorded in the book of this law, the LORD will inflict on you until you are destroyed. Although once you were as numerous as the stars in heaven, you shall be left few in number, because you did not obey the LORD your God. (Deut. 28:58–62)

Ancient Israelites connected disease, sickness, and plagues with human disobedience. We have more scientific explanations for such things today. We are aware of microorganisms and understand that germs and viruses cause many of our ailments. Thus, just because a biblical passage claims a plague or natural disaster was caused by God does not mean it actually was. It may simply reflect theological assumptions about the way God works in the world that many people no longer accept as valid.

By discussing relevant archaeological discoveries, and considering the nature of ancient historiography, pastors and lay leaders can help people evaluate various claims about God in the Old Testament more knowledgeably. Once people realize God did not say and do everything the Old Testament claims, they are much better able to deconstruct the violent views of God they encounter there.

Admittedly, teaching people about these things takes time, effort, and intentionality. But it is important, and it is time well spent. As long as people are convinced that God said and did everything the Old Testament claims, they will continue to believe God sanctions and participates in acts of violence. Providing evidence to the contrary is precisely what many churchgoers will need before they will be ready to consider abandoning their violent views of God.

Differentiate between the Textual and Actual God

Since not every Old Testament portrayal of God accurately reveals God's character, people who want to use the Bible to learn about God must distinguish "between the textual God and the actual God," to borrow language from Old Testament scholar Terence Fretheim.[23] The "textual God" refers to the literary representation of God as words on a page in the Bible. The actual God is a living reality, the creator of heaven and earth, the One to whom all worship and praise should be directed. Embracing this distinction is essential for deconstructing violent views of God.

Demonstrating the need to make this distinction between the textual and actual God is relatively easy, since it is built into the very fabric of Scripture itself. Even a cursory reading of the Old Testament reveals that some portrayals of God stand in stark contrast with others. For example, one passage claims God punishes "children for the iniquity of parents" while another emphatically states "a child shall not suffer for the iniquity of a parent" (Exod. 20:5; Ezek. 18:20). One passage says God's mind won't change, while another clearly says God's mind actually did change (1 Sam. 15:29; Jonah 3:10). One passage declares God to be gracious and merciful, while another says God hardens people's hearts for the express purpose of allowing them to be mercilessly slaughtered (Exod. 34:6; Josh. 11:20). Competing and contrasting views of God are canonized in the pages of the Old Testament.

This contrast becomes even more striking when images of God in the Old Testament are compared to images of God in the New Testament (more on this in a moment). Unless we are willing to concede that God's character is utterly inconsistent, these diverse assertions about God cannot all be accurate. Some are mutually exclusive, forcing us to make choices about what God is really like.

While some people might find this theological diversity unsettling, it is not really all that surprising. The Bible was written over a thousand years, by scores of people living in different times and places. It would be extremely naive to expect them all to conceive of God in the same way. Part of our job as theologically responsible readers is to evaluate these competing portrayals of God in order to determine which ones most clearly reflect the true character of God.

When I read the Bible, I want to use it to help me "think rightly about God."[24] At times, it does just that. But not always. I do not assume I can simply open the Bible, read what it says about God, and then move directly from the textual God to the actual God. Things are far more complicated than that. Sometimes the Bible reveals God's character; other times it distorts it.[25] If we want to think rightly about God, we need to do the hard work of figuring out which portrayals reveal God's character and which do not. Ministers can be very helpful in guiding people in this regard.

To do this work most effectively, we need to develop a principled interpretive approach that enables us to negotiate the distance between the textual and actual God. This allows us to determine what is reliable and what is not without picking and choosing based on our own personal preferences. For me, this principled approach is grounded in the person of Jesus.

Evaluate Portrayals of God by the God Jesus Reveals

A principled interpretive approach faithful to my own theological heritage involves using a christocentric hermeneutic, or Christ-centered method of interpretation. This approach privileges the life and teachings of Jesus for biblical interpretation and is particularly helpful in deconstructing violent views of God. This interpretive approach, as I develop it, is based on three major premises.

Premise 1. God's moral character is most clearly and completely revealed through the person of Jesus.

This premise emphasizes that Jesus is the key to understanding what God is like. It is important to note that this premise focuses on God's *moral* character. As such, it refers to the way God behaves toward people and creation with regard to such things as justice, mercy, goodness, and love. It does not refer to attributes like God's eternal nature, omnipresence, or omniscience.

To put this premise most simply, it asserts that seeing Jesus is seeing God. In other words, if you want to know what God is like and how God behaves, look at Jesus. Why? Because Jesus is "the image of the invisible God" (Col. 1:15). When Philip asks Jesus to "show us the Father," Jesus replies,

> Have I been with you all this time, Philip, and you still do not know me? Whoever has seen me has seen the Father. How can you say, "Show us the Father"? (John 14:9)

To see Jesus is to see God. But what kind of God do we see in Jesus?

Premise 2. Jesus reveals a God of love, one who heals rather than harms, is kind rather than cruel, forgives rather than retaliates, and behaves nonviolently rather than violently.

The God that Jesus reveals shares both similarities and dissimilarities with portrayals of God in the Old Testament. Some of the most striking differences concern God's relation to violence. In Jesus we see a God who absorbs violence rather than sanctions it, a God who loves enemies rather than kills them.

While it is clear that Jesus builds his view of God from the Old Testament,[26] Jesus feels no compulsion to accept every portrayal he finds there. Rather, he uses these images of God selectively, affirming some while distancing himself from others. Jesus promoted Old Testament views of God that reflect God's love, compassion, and mercy, while largely ignoring those portraying God's wrath, violence, and retribution.[27] Apparently, Jesus believed some Old Testament views of God were serviceable, while others were not. In this way, Jesus demonstrates deep respect for the Scripture without perpetuating some of its most problematic views of God.

The Old Testament portrays God as antagonistic toward the wicked and those who do evil. In Zephaniah 1:3, for example, God is depicted as one who "will make the wicked stumble," and in Psalm 3:7 God is described as one who will "break the teeth of the wicked."

Yet Jesus seems to have had a different view of God's attitude toward Israel's enemies and toward "sinners" generally. Jesus describes God as one who "is kind to the ungrateful and wicked" (Luke 6:35). And Jesus commands his followers to love their enemies because that's what God does.

> Love your enemies and pray for those who persecute you, so that you may be children of your Father in heaven; for he makes his sun rise on the evil and on the good, and sends rain on the righteous and on the unrighteous. (Matt. 5:44–45)

In this saying, Jesus challenges violent views of God rooted in beliefs held by many Israelites about divine reward and punishment. Despite the Old

Testament's frequent insistence that God punishes sinners and rewards the righteous,[28] Jesus claims that God extends goodness to all people regardless of how they behave. When Jesus says God "makes his sun rise on the evil and on the good, and sends rain on the righteous and on the unrighteous," he is saying God gives good gifts to everyone indiscriminately. God is not nice to the righteous and mean to the wicked. God is kind to all, and graciously cares for all, however worthy or unworthy they may be.[29]

The parables of Jesus also tend to promote a different vision of God than the one suggested by violent images of God in the Old Testament portrayals. It is a vision of God more in line with Old Testament portrayals of divine love and mercy than with portrayals of divine wrath and destruction.[30] The parables of the Lost Sheep, the Lost Coin, and the Lost Son (the Prodigal Son) in Luke 15, for example, make it clear that God pursues "sinners" to save and deliver, not to smite and kill.

Not only did Jesus teach and preach in ways that deconstructed violent portrayals of God, he embodied the nonviolent love of God in the manner of his life and death. People in the first century were expecting the Messiah to be a conquering king, a military commander who would free them from foreign occupation by slaughtering their Roman oppressors. But Jesus had not come as a conquering king. He came as a suffering servant. That is why Jesus told his disciples "that the Son of Man must undergo great suffering, . . . be rejected . . . , and be killed."[31] Jesus, the son of God, dies with words of forgiveness on his lips, not words of revenge and retribution. Ultimately, God overcomes evil and death through suffering love, not through acts of brutal force and violence.

To be sure, not everyone agrees with the depiction of Jesus I have just outlined. Some regard it as skewed and incomplete, arguing that certain passages in the Gospels indicate Jesus sometimes behaved violently and conceived of God doing likewise. I have responded to these challenges more fully elsewhere, but want to offer a few very brief thoughts here before proceeding.[32]

With respect to Jesus and violence, some point to the incident in the temple, where Jesus overturns tables. According to the version of the story in the Gospel of John, Jesus even uses a whip to drive out animals (2:15). Doesn't that suggest Jesus was violent? I don't think so. As one of my former colleagues likes to say, "What was the body count?" Nobody is killed, and people do not stagger out of the temple precincts bloody and bruised. Jesus does not physically harm anyone. While his behavior certainly challenges sentimental perceptions of Jesus "meek and mild," his actions are not violent. Disruptive? Yes. Forceful? Absolutely. Violent? No. Jesus' behavior is consistent with the prophets of old who sometimes engaged in symbolic prophetic actions like this.

Others accuse Jesus of being violent because of his words in Matthew 10:34 about not coming "to bring peace, but a sword." But the context here surely indicates these words are meant to be taken metaphorically. Jesus is simply talking about the divisive effects the gospel has on families when some family members decide to follow Jesus and others do not. In my estimation, attempts like these to describe Jesus as violent seem strained.

I am also not convinced that words of eschatological judgment ascribed to Jesus in the Gospels—such as those that describe people weeping and gnashing teeth (Matt. 8:11–12; 13:41–42) or the teaching about the separation of the sheep and the goats (Matt. 25:31–46)—undermine what I have said about the kind of God Jesus reveals. To begin, there is some debate about the provenance of these sayings. Numerous scholars have argued that most, or all, of the pronouncements of eschatological judgment found in the Gospels did not originate with the historical Jesus but were attributed to Jesus later by the church.[33] If these pronouncements are not from Jesus, this removes the objection entirely.

Those who do believe these sayings come from Jesus should bear a number of points in mind. First, Jesus often spoke using hyperbole and metaphor, and this certainly seems characteristic of his language about final judgment. We must be careful not to take literally words meant to be understood symbolically. Also, whenever Jesus spoke about final judgment it was always in the service of calling people to live faithfully in the present. That was the purpose of these sayings. They were not intended to give listeners futuristic and otherwise secretive information about the hereafter. Those who do believe these words of eschatological judgment originate with Jesus should be extremely cautious about trying to use them to argue that God is violent, because they refer to a yet-to-happen, completely unique, end-time event described in symbolic language.[34] These passages use language and imagery that is not meant to be read literally.

If we really want to know what God is like, we should look at the way Jesus lived his life on earth, in time and space. When we do, we see a God of infinite love, grace, and compassion.

Premise 3. God's moral character is consistent throughout time.

My third and final premise has to do with the consistency of God's moral character. The basic idea here is that whatever God is like, God has always been like and will always be like. God is not merciful one day and malicious the next. Therefore, the God Jesus reveals does not only provide a snapshot of what God was like in the first century. Rather, it demonstrates what God has *always* been like and will *always* be like. Because God's moral character is unchanging, the God we see in Jesus reveals God's true nature and character for all time: past, present, and future.

Interpretive Conclusions

Taken together, these three premises lead to an important interpretive conclusion: the God Jesus reveals should be the standard, or measuring rod, by which the accuracy of all biblical portrayals of God are evaluated. Portrayals that correspond to the God Jesus reveals are reliable; those that are at odds with the revelation of God in Jesus are not. In the words of C. S. Cowles:

> If ours is a Christlike God, then we can categorically affirm that God is not a destroyer. . . . God does not engage in punitive, redemptive, or sacred violence. . . . God does not proactively use death as an instrument of judgment.[35]

God does not murder Egyptian babies, strike people with a skin disease, or send poisonous snakes to kill grumbling Israelites—literary portrayals of God behaving this way in the Old Testament notwithstanding. For this reason, it is crucial to distinguish carefully between the textual and actual God lest we confuse the two and conceive of the God we worship as the author of unspeakable evil.

Helping people see the kind of God Jesus reveals, and then using that as an interpretive guide, is one of the best tools available for deconstructing violent views of God.

PRACTICAL SUGGESTIONS

Having considered several things that can be done to deconstruct violent views of God, we are now ready to talk more directly about what this looks like in the context of the church. The practical suggestions that follow build upon what we have already discussed and expand it in some new directions. It constitutes my earnest appeal to all ministers who talk about God's violent behavior in the Old Testament.

Don't Defend "God's" Violent Behavior

When pastors and lay leaders deal with divine violence in the Old Testament, it is absolutely imperative to avoid the temptation to defend it or to suggest it is OK. There is nothing "OK" about soldiers being drowned (Exod. 14:26–31), a family being stoned (Josh. 7:16–26), infants being slain (1 Sam. 15:3), women being sexually assaulted (2 Sam. 12:11), people being mercilessly slaughtered (Lam. 2:21), or refugees being killed by lions (2 Kgs. 17:24–28). Yet the Old

Testament claims *God* is responsible for all of these horrors—and many, many more.

When we talk about these texts, we should *not* rush to God's defense and attempt to explain why it was good and right for God to smite *this* individual or to destroy *that* city. Yet this happens all the time. And it is not only pastors and Sunday school teachers who try to exonerate God. Many biblical scholars, theologians, and religious leaders do this as well. Some go to great lengths to defend God's character, using a variety of approaches to justify God's violent words and deeds. With regard to the conquest of Canaan in Joshua 6–11, for example, they say things like, "The Canaanites were exceedingly wicked and deserved to die." Or they claim that killing Canaanites was for a "greater good." Whatever reason, or combination of reasons, is given, these individuals try to defend God's goodness by justifying "God's" violence in the Old Testament. It is a losing proposition.

I certainly understand the motivation behind these efforts—I do not want to believe in an unjust, immoral, vengeful deity any more than they do. But efforts to defend God's violent behavior in the Old Testament are doomed to fail for one simple reason: God, the living God, does not behave violently.

Perhaps an analogy will help. I am the parent of three children, ages seventeen, fifteen, and ten. Thankfully I can honestly say I have never physically beaten or abused them (though there have been moments when they have sorely tested my commitment to nonviolence!). But let's imagine I come home from work one day and learn I have been accused of this very thing, of abusing my children. I am summoned to appear in court to answer the charges against me. Given the grave ramifications of such an accusation, I would immediately secure a lawyer to help me face these unwelcome legal challenges.

Suppose my lawyer's strategy to exonerate me—and hopefully keep me out of jail—is to present the best possible reasons for why I beat my children. My lawyer plans to tell the court that the reason I beat my children is because they are exceedingly bad and they deserve it. My lawyer will also argue that I "discipline" my children severely for the greater good of society. By correcting their behavior at a young age, I am keeping them from being a negative influence on others. Using these and similar arguments, my lawyer plans to do everything possible to put my *alleged* abusive behavior in the best possible light.

While I might appreciate these strenuous efforts on my behalf, it's obvious that my lawyer's overall strategy is fundamentally flawed. Wouldn't it be better if my lawyer simply demonstrated that the charges against me are totally and completely false? *Why try to put a positive spin on evil actions I never committed in the first place?* Yet that is precisely what so many interpreters do when it comes to God's violent behavior in the Old Testament. They tie themselves in knots trying to justify violent acts God never committed.

Rushing to defend God for violent acts God never committed is fundamentally misguided and counterproductive. If you want to help people know who God really is, you should avoid doing this at all costs.

Critique Violent Portrayals of God Publicly

Rather than defending God's violent behavior in the Bible, we should be critiquing it—publicly. We have already talked about ways to deconstruct violent views of God, including contextualizing violent Old Testament portrayals of God, acknowledging God didn't say or do everything the Old Testament claims, distinguishing between the textual and actual God, and using a christocentric hermeneutic to govern our reading of these passages.

Now we are ready to add one more piece to this. If we are convinced that portrayals of God slaying and smiting do not reflect divine reality, we must be willing to go on record and say so. When we read stories of a God who slaughters every firstborn child of Egypt in a single night (Exod. 12:29), we say, "This is not God." When the Old Testament claims that God commanded Israel to kill Canaanites without mercy (Deut. 7:2), we say, "This is not God." When we encounter a prophet who declares that God will "devour" Israel "like a lion" and "mangle them" like "a wild animal" (Hos. 13:8), we say, "This is not God." God, the living God, the creator of the universe, does not behave this way.

Despite what violent biblical texts suggest, God is not a deadly lawgiver, an instant executioner, a mass murderer, a divine warrior, or a genocidal general. Whenever the Old Testament portrays God in these ways, it fundamentally misrepresents God's true nature and character, and we should have the courage to say so. I would even say that if you are a religious educator, a member of the clergy, a mentor, a spiritual director, or a person of influence in your place of worship, you have a *moral obligation* to help people see God as clearly as possible. It is irresponsible to leave violent portrayals of God unchallenged.

Like it or not, we are the experts. If we do not help people in the church wrestle with these images and the problems they raise, who will? Some random blogger? A fundamentalist pastor who has never seriously examined the issue? Popular authors who claim to be defending the authority of Scripture by perpetuating violent and vile images of God?

If you believe God is good and loving, and you want people to know that, you have a responsibility to deconstruct violent images of God in the Bible. If you are a scholar or theologian, research and write about it. If you are a pastor or priest, preach about it. If you are a teacher or professor, teach about it.

Given the enormous confusion, harm, and suffering these texts have inspired, it is imperative that we speak up and speak out.

But be warned.

Deconstructing violent views of God may come at a significant cost. Many people are not open to the kind of critique I am proposing. They do not want their view of God deconstructed, and they have no interest in having their view of the Bible challenged. People have paid a high price, personally and professionally, for being honest about their convictions about the nature of Scripture and the nature of God. This is especially true in religious contexts where individuals are required to adhere to a certain set of doctrinal beliefs or affirm particular confessional statements as a requirement of their employment or membership. If you find yourself in one of these contexts and dare to critique violent portrayals of God in the Bible, expect some pushback. Some will call you a heretic. Others will accuse you of undermining biblical authority. Don't let that stop you. The stakes are too high and the issues are too important to capitulate to religious gatekeepers.

Of course, if you suspect that publicly critiquing violent portrayals of God in the Bible might cause you to lose your job or put your ministerial credentials at risk, you will have some hard choices to make. This is especially fraught for people whose position may already be tenuous because of their identity (e.g., being queer, Black, or a woman in a ministry assignment where that is not fully accepted or appreciated). I would certainly not encourage you to behave rashly. Take some time to consult with trusted friends and mentors. Examine your own heart and motives. Be wise, prayerful, and discerning as you consider how to proceed, and reflect on the words of Jesus, who instructs us to "be wise as serpents and innocent as doves" (Matt. 10:16). Then, with eyes wide open, do as much as you can to deconstruct violent views of God that cause so much harm to so many people.

Construct a More Accurate View of God

As you deconstruct violent images of God, you should simultaneously be reconstructing an alternate view of God, one that is free from the violent cultural trappings that have distorted the truth about God's character for so long. The good news is there are many biblical passages that provide excellent resources for doing so. The Old Testament is home to many of these. Some of the most tender and beautiful portrayals of God in all of human literature are found in its pages.[36]

For example, speaking of Israel's early years, God says through the prophet Hosea, "I led them with cords of human kindness, with bands of love. I was to them like those who lift infants to their cheeks. I bent down to them and fed them" (Hos. 11:4). And the psalmist speaks of God's great mercy and grace in Psalm 103:

> He does not deal with us according to our sins,
>   nor repay us according to our iniquities.
> For as the heavens are high above the earth,
>   so great is his steadfast love toward those who fear him;
> as far as the east is from the west,
>   so far he removes our transgressions from us.
> As a father has compassion for his children,
>   so the LORD has compassion for those who fear him.
>   Ps. 103:10–13

There are literally hundreds of Old Testament passages like these that describe God's grace, love, loyalty, commitment, and faithfulness. We can—and should—emphasize *these* positive images and use them to construct a more accurate view of God's character.

To return briefly to a point made earlier, we should help people understand that God is first and foremost defined as love, "self-giving, others-empowering love."[37] This is the God we serve and confess. A God who is in the business of saving people, not slaying them, and one who is passionate about reconciliation and redemption, not retaliation and revenge. The God in whom "we live, and move, and have our being" is a God of peace and justice who does no violence, certain Old Testament portrayals of God notwithstanding.[38]

SOME FINAL THOUGHTS

Before concluding, I want to make two additional proposals and suggest several resources for dealing with divine violence in the Old Testament. In chapter 4, I mentioned that Sunday school teachers could use a multiple-option approach by introducing the class to various ways Christians have dealt with violent portrayals of God over the years. The same thing could be done in a sermon or sermon series. It is a relatively low-risk approach that introduces people to various "explanations" or "solutions." This provides an opportunity to discuss strengths and weaknesses of various ways individuals have dealt with God's violent behavior in the Old Testament, and it encourages people to wrestle seriously with this important issue as they arrive at their own conclusions (ideally, that God did not behave violently, despite what the text claims). There are convenient surveys showing a range of approaches to this topic that can help pastors and lay leaders who wish to do this in church.[39]

While I ultimately hope ministers will *deconstruct* violent views of God, and encourage others to do the same, this multiple-option approach has its usefulness. It is helpful for people to know there is a long and diverse history of interpretation surrounding this issue. Seeing different possibilities encourages critical thinking as people weigh the pros and cons of various approaches, and it fosters understanding toward Christians who see the issue differently than they do. It is also beneficial for pastors and lay leaders who might be uncomfortable staking out their own position on this topic for some of the reasons discussed above. And it is certainly preferable to ignoring these violent verses altogether.

Another way to handle passages containing violent Old Testament portrayals of God is to use a both-and approach. This approach involves *both* critique *and* embrace. Problematic parts of a passage (e.g., images of God behaving violently) are critiqued, while other parts of the passage are embraced for whatever positive spiritual lessons and applications can be derived from it. This strikes me as an honest, expedient, and prudent way to handle Old Testament texts containing divine violence. It allows minsters, Sunday school teachers, and liturgists to acknowledge some of the difficulties raised by violent images of God without always feeling the need to devote an entire sermon, or Sunday school class, to them. In many cases, just a relatively brief acknowledgment of the problems associated with a violent portrayal of God will be enough said before moving on to other aspects of the text that can be used constructively. I took this approach when preaching on the near sacrifice of Isaac in Genesis 22 and found it quite useful.[40]

Finally, I want to highlight a few resources that should be helpful as you deconstruct violent views of God in order to help people see God more clearly. If you are interested in exploring recent scholarship on the loving, nonviolent nature of God—and I would certainly encourage you in this direction—there are a number of excellent books to consider, including *The Uncontrolling Love of God* by Thomas Oord, *A Nonviolent Theology of Love* by Sharon Putt, and *Sinners in the Hands of a Loving God* by Brian Zahnd. J. Denny Weaver has also written books emphasizing the nonviolent nature of God, including *The Nonviolent God* and *God without Violence: A Theology of the God Revealed in Jesus*. For efforts to use Jesus as a guide to reading Scripture responsibly, see Derek Flood's excellent book *Disarming Scripture: Cherry-Picking Liberals, Violence-Loving Conservatives, and Why We All Need to Learn to Read the Bible Like Jesus Did*, along with the essay by C. S. Cowles, "The Case for Radical Discontinuity," in *Show Them No Mercy: Four Views on God and Canaanite Genocide*. Jack Nelson-Pallmeyer's book *Jesus against Christianity: Reclaiming the Missing Jesus* is also extremely helpful in wrestling honestly with violent biblical texts and working toward a more accurate way of seeing God through the pages of Scripture. My book *Disturbing Divine Behavior: Troubling Old Testament Images of God* also explores this issue at length.

CONCLUSION

Although biblical passages containing divine violence are among some of the most difficult to address, there are ways to use them responsibly in church. I am hopeful that the resources and suggestions offered in this chapter will be helpful to you as you deconstruct violent portrayals of God in the Old Testament and beyond.

9

Bringing Violent Verses Back to Church

*Concluding Reflections on Using Violent
Biblical Texts Responsibly*

> Although some Christians may resort to rejecting whole sections of
> the Bible, such denial is unnecessary. However hard it may seem to
> accommodate the texts of terror, the task is not in fact impossible, and
> the results are entirely worthwhile.
> —Philip Jenkins, *Laying Down the Sword*[1]

Throughout this book, I have encouraged pastors and lay leaders to find ways
to use violent biblical texts responsibly in church and ministry. I realize doing
this does not come naturally for many Christian leaders. It is much easier
to focus on passages of Scripture that offer clear messages of comfort, hope,
and encouragement than it is to grapple with biblical texts dealing with the
unpleasant realities of warfare, rape, and murder. Many ministers understandably struggle with violent verses, uncertain where to begin or how to use
them effectively in public settings.

Hopefully, this book has cleared away some of this uncertainty by offering numerous suggestions for using these texts in various settings. This was,
after all, the purpose stated in chapter 1: to help religious practitioners—pastors, priests, church leaders, Christian educators, lay leaders, and ministers
of all stripes—find constructive ways to use violent biblical texts responsibly
through preaching, teaching, and worship.

SOME FINAL WORDS OF ADVICE

Before bringing this study to a close, a few remaining items need our attention. These are largely pragmatic in nature and provide some additional things to consider as you begin working with violent biblical texts.

Develop a Plan for Using Violent Verses

Given the heavy demands on a pastor's time, I understand why dealing with violence in the Bible is not often at the top of the to-do list. Still, for reasons discussed earlier, it is unwise and potentially dangerous to ignore it.[2] Those who minister have a responsibility to help people know what to do with these troublesome texts.

Since figuring out how to incorporate violent verses into sermons, worship services, and Christian education programs takes careful thought and planning, it will be helpful to set some goals for yourself. What do you want to do with violent biblical texts in church over the next few years, and how do you plan to accomplish that? Here are a number of things you might consider doing to strengthen your ministry in this area:

- Read a book that provides a general overview of violence in the Bible to help orient you to this content (you might consider Jerome Creach's *Violence in Scripture*).
- Commit to preaching sermons each year from violent biblical texts (see chap. 6 for some specific suggestions).
- Form a "violent texts" support group (described below).
- Conduct a training retreat for lay leaders that provides practical suggestions for using violent passages in church.
- Find (or create) Sunday school curriculum for children and young adults that handles violent biblical texts well.
- Offer an adult Sunday school elective that explores the problem of divine violence in Scripture (consider using Brian Zahnd's book *Sinners in the Hands of a Loving God* or my *Disturbing Divine Behavior*).
- Incorporate violent biblical texts into prayers and responsive readings you write for worship.
- Distribute and discuss this book (or another, such as Philip Jenkins's *Laying Down the Sword: Why We Can't Ignore the Bible's Violent Verses*) with church board members so they can be informed (and hopefully supportive) of your efforts to use violent biblical texts in church. See the discussion guide at www.wjkbooks.com/RedeemingViolentVerses.

Obviously, this is just a sampling of possible activities, but hopefully enough to stimulate your thinking as you begin setting goals for how you will integrate violent verses into your ministry.

As you consider the possibilities, focus on items you think are most important and that you are most likely to do. It is much better to set a few modest goals you can actually achieve than to set too many goals that will be hard to reach. Since you know your own capacity and rhythm better than anyone else, customize a plan that works well for you. And as you move forward, choose a pace that is appropriate for your congregation or ministry, not going too fast or too slow. I suggest setting goals for a two- to three-year time period. Try to be as specific as possible in your plan about exactly *what* you hope to accomplish *when*. At the end of this time, reflect on what you have accomplished and evaluate the extent to which you met your goals. Then, consider what the next few years might look like as you continue to explore ways to use violent verses regularly in church and ministry.

Equip Lay Leaders

Not every church is fortunate enough to have more than one paid minister on staff, and many use lay leaders to facilitate worship or deliver Christian education. Yet most lay leaders have little, if any, formal biblical or theological training. While some may have taken a Bible or religion class in college, most are unlikely to have had any instruction in how to handle violent biblical texts. Therefore, you will need to provide some guidance for lay leaders.

This could take different forms. You might consider discussing a book or article on this topic with Sunday school teachers, children's church leaders, and other individuals who are involved in Christian education. One convenient resource would be the chapter on teaching contained in this book. Even if there is not some sort of "required reading," you can still gather these individuals together from time to time to discuss how things are going as they attempt to use violent biblical texts responsibly. Invite them to talk about what is working well and what is not. What challenges have they faced? What questions do they have? What success stories can they share? This sort of conversation would be both validating and instructional. Teachers would leave encouraged and equipped with new ideas and practices. They would also be reminded that they are not alone in this important work.

Another way to support lay leaders is to help them select Sunday school curriculum that does a good job of handling violence in the Old Testament responsibly. A senior pastor or Christian education director could look over the curriculum with these teachers, noting places where they will have opportunities to discuss violent verses. If the curriculum omits or glosses over these texts, they could encourage teachers to still find ways to incorporate them into their lesson. Or, if the curriculum sanctions or celebrates violence in the Bible, they can offer suggestions for how teachers can deal with these violent texts in ways that do not reinforce the notion of "virtuous" violence.

Another way the church could equip lay leaders (and ministers) would be to have a retreat or workshop devoted to using violent verses in ministry. The discussion guide for *Redeeming Violent Verses*, available at www.wjkbooks .com/RedeemingViolentVerses, is ideal for this group training. If feasible, you might consider inviting a guest speaker who is knowledgeable about troubling Old Testament texts so people can benefit from his or her expertise and experience. An event like this could be exclusively for leaders in one particular church, or it could be open to other churches and ministers in the area. Either way, providing this kind of training and support will go a long way toward ensuring violent biblical texts are handled well in the church and other ministry settings.

Find Support among Peers

Given the unique challenges associated with using violent biblical texts well in church, you might find it beneficial to assemble a "violent verse support group" that consists of individuals like you who have reason to use these challenging passages in public settings. Members could include fellow pastors, spiritual mentors, biblical scholars, theologians, and others. I would suggest meeting with this group regularly (perhaps three or four times a year) to swap ideas and to talk about how things are going with your efforts to include violent verses in church. Specifically, you could (1) discuss how you have incorporated violent verses into your liturgies and share some original material you have created, (2) describe ways you have dealt with some of these texts in sermons, (3) identify Sunday school curriculum you have found useful for addressing violence in Scripture, (4) ask for help and ideas regarding how to use a particularly difficult passage in worship, (5) seek advice for how to minister to a parishioner having a faith crisis due to their encounter with violent portrayals of God in Scripture, and (6) introduce a book or article on the topic that you have found particularly enlightening.

Having a supportive community with whom you can process and refine your work with violent biblical texts will help sustain you over the long haul. Not only will you pick up tips to enhance your ability to use these passages when you minister, you will be encouraged by interacting with women and men like you who also desire to work responsibly with some of the Bible's most difficult texts.

Being part of a support group like this also provides a means of accountability. Knowing that people are going to ask you what you have been doing to accomplish your goals will—or at least should—prompt you to keep finding ways to use these texts in sermons, liturgies, and Sunday school classes.

If possible, it is ideal to meet in person, since there is a certain energy in the room that is difficult to replicate online—plus you can share food together. But if that is impractical based on where you live or other factors, forming an online support group is a great alternative. Either way, don't go it alone! Find people who can come alongside you on the journey. They will be a source of significant help and blessing to you—as you will be to them.

Keep Violent Verses in Perspective

As important as I believe it is to use violent verses in church and ministry—and I believe it is *very* important—it is crucial to keep this in perspective. I am *not* suggesting that pastors and lay leaders should flood every worship service with nothing but violent verses. Nor am I proposing that Sunday school teachers devote half of their classes each year to nothing but the most difficult passages. Similarly, I would not advocate adorning our churches with gruesome images such as a graphic painting of Samuel slaying Agag for the sanctuary, or a life-size illustration of David beheading Goliath in the children's wing. And there is no need to include violent verses on the marquee board outside the church, since it is doubtful many will be drawn inside by reading, "The Lord will take delight in bringing you to ruin and destruction" (Deut. 28:63)!

While it is important to incorporate violent verses into Sunday morning worship, there is no merit in being known as a church that talks about nothing *but* violent biblical texts. Although it is essential for church leaders to find ways to utilize these texts in public worship and Christian education—I wouldn't have written this book otherwise—it is one part of the much larger mission of the church. The heart of Christian faith involves love for God and others. This should be the primary focus and consistent emphasis of the church. While pastors, Sunday school teachers, and worship leaders should find ways to give attention to violent biblical texts, they should do so without overemphasizing them or allowing them to obscure other central themes of Scripture.

A FINAL APPEAL

Most violent verses have not been to church for a very long time, at least not in any meaningful way. They get little airtime on Sunday morning and rarely appear in worship services or Christian education programs. As Philip Jenkins observes, "In modern times, Western Christian churches have largely

dropped the most frightening and troubling passages from their public readings, and generally from preaching."[3] This is unfortunate, to say the least.
These troublesome texts have much to offer us, and ignoring them deprives
people of benefiting from them. Although bringing violent verses out of the
shadows and into the light might feel risky, it is well worth the effort.

One of the best ways to help people have a positive experience with violent
biblical texts is to show them creative ways to use these passages constructively. Through courageous sermons, engaging Sunday school classes, and
creative liturgies, you can demonstrate the value these texts have for people
of faith. As pastors, lay leaders, and ministers, you are uniquely positioned to
show people how to use violent verses in ways that help rather than harm. In
so doing, you provide an example to follow.

Churchgoers need to encounter these texts, and they need guidance for
how to read them responsibly. By using troubling texts for preaching, teaching, and leading worship, you prove that these often-neglected passages can be
applied in ways that are both life-affirming and spiritually edifying. As such,
you demonstrate the truth of 2 Timothy 3:16. *All* Scripture is useful for the life
of faith—even those parts we might be tempted to ignore.

So let us give thanks for the Bible we have in all its marvelous richness,
beauty, and complexity. And let us be diligent to use it all for the glory of God
as we love and serve others in church, ministry, and beyond.

Notes

Chapter 1: A Violent Bible and Vanishing Verses

1. Jerome F. D. Creach, *Violence in Scripture* (Louisville, KY: Westminster John Knox, 2013), 1.

2. Mark McEntire, *The Blood of Abel: The Violent Plot in the Hebrew Bible* (Macon, GA: Mercer University Press, 1999), 6, emphasis mine.

3. Matt. 14:1–12; 27:27–54; Acts 7:54–60; 12:20–23. For a discussion of violence in the New Testament generally, see Thomas R. Yoder Neufeld, *Killing Enmity: Violence and the New Testament* (Grand Rapids: Baker, 2011); and for the Gospels particularly, see David J. Neville, *The Vehement Jesus: Grappling with Troubling Gospel Texts* (Eugene, OR: Cascade, 2017).

4. Randal Rauser, *What's So Confusing about Grace?* (Canada: 2 Cup Press, 2017), 125–26, emphasis original.

5. See John Shelby Spong, *The Sins of Scripture: Exposing the Bible's Texts of Hate to Reveal the God of Love* (San Francisco: HarperSanFrancisco, 2005); and Adrian Thatcher, *The Savage Text: The Use and Abuse of the Bible* (Malden, MA: Wiley-Blackwell, 2008).

6. For an insightful discussion of how the church often mishandles violent verses by "omission," "misrepresentation," "distraction," and "blunted affect," see Randal Rauser, *Jesus Loves Canaanites: Biblical Genocide in the Light of Moral Intuition* (Canada: 2 Cup Press, 2021), 21–38.

7. The idea of the Bible being "Disneyfied" is from Rauser, *What's So Confusing about Grace?*, 124–25.

8. For more on this point, see chap. 4.

9. See chap. 8 for an extensive discussion of this issue.

10. Chap. 2 provides an extensive rationale for addressing violent biblical texts in church rather than ignoring them.

11. One area I have not explored in this study relates to the way violent biblical texts can be used to process trauma, particularly trauma that results from participation in war. For an excellent study in this regard, see Brad E. Kelle, *The Bible and Moral Injury: Reading Scripture alongside War's Unseen Wounds* (Nashville: Abingdon, 2020), esp. 139–68. For a more general treatment of how troubling texts may aid in trauma recovery, see Christopher G. Frechette, "The Old Testament as Controlled Substance: How Insights from Trauma Studies Reveal Healing Capacities in Potentially Harmful Texts," *Interpretation: A Journal of Bible and Theology* 69:1 (2015): 20–34. For an extensive exploration of how to use a single violent biblical text (1 Sam. 21) to process trauma in a group setting, see Sharon

A. Buttry and Daniel L. Buttry, *Daughters of Rizpah: Nonviolence and the Transformation of Trauma* (Eugene, OR: Wipf & Stock, 2020).

12. See, e.g., Eric A. Seibert, *Disturbing Divine Behavior: Troubling Old Testament Images of God* (Minneapolis: Fortress, 2009); M. Daniel Carroll R. and J. Blair Wilgus, eds., *Wrestling with the Violence of God: Soundings in the Old Testament* (Winona Lake, IN: Eisenbrauns, 2015); Gregory A. Boyd, *The Crucifixion of the Warrior God: Interpreting the Old Testament's Violent Portraits of God in Light of the Cross*, 2 vols. (Minneapolis: Fortress, 2017); L. Daniel Hawk, *The Violence of the Biblical God: Canonical Narrative and Christian Faith* (Grand Rapids: Eerdmans, 2019); Paul Copan, *Is God a Vindictive Bully? Reconciling Portrayals of God in the Old and New Testaments* (Grand Rapids: Baker, 2022).

13. I realize the title "Old Testament" is not entirely satisfactory, partly because "old" sometimes connotes something outdated and irrelevant. Though many scholars customarily refer to these books as the Hebrew Bible, most churchgoers still refer to it as the Old Testament, and this is the designation I will use in this book.

14. For a broader discussion of these issues, see Eric A. Seibert, *The Violence of Scripture: Overcoming the Old Testament's Troubling Legacy* (Minneapolis: Fortress, 2012), 10 and throughout.

15. For a collection of essays dealing with animal care, see Tripp York and Andy Alexis-Baker, eds., *A Faith Embracing All Creatures: Addressing Commonly Asked Questions about Christian Care for Animals* (Eugene, OR: Cascade, 2012). For a collection of essays dealing with creation care, see York and Alexis-Baker, eds., *A Faith Encompassing All Creation: Addressing Commonly Asked Questions about Christian Care for the Environment* (Eugene, OR: Cascade, 2014).

16. See Paul Douglas and Mitch Hescox, *Caring for Creation: The Evangelical's Guide to Climate Change and a Healthy Environment* (Bloomington, MN: Bethany House, 2016); Sharon Delgado, *Love in a Time of Climate Change: Honoring Creation, Establishing Justice* (Minneapolis: Fortress, 2017); Douglas J. Moo and Jonathan A. Moo, *Creation Care: A Biblical Theology of the Natural World* (Grand Rapids: Zondervan, 2018).

17. For a recent attempt to argue that the Old Testament is not as violent as often perceived, see Brent A. Strawn, *Lies My Preacher Told Me: An Honest Look at the Old Testament* (Louisville, KY: Westminster John Knox, 2021), 41–53.

18. McEntire, *Blood of Abel*, 160, emphasis mine.

19. Raymund Schwager, *Must There Be Scapegoats? Violence and Redemption in the Bible*, trans. Maria L. Assad (New York: Crossroad, 2000), 47, emphasis original.

20. Schwager, *Must There Be Scapegoats?*, 55, emphasis original. "Yahweh" is the way biblical scholars typically vocalize YHWH, the personal name of Israel's God in the Old Testament, though observant Jews traditionally do not speak the name aloud out of reverence.

21. Schwager, *Must There Be Scapegoats?*, 60.

22. The only exception in these examples is Moses being told to "stretch out your hand over the sea" (Exod. 14:26). Even in this case, the ensuing violence is still attributed to God (see vv. 27, 30–31).

23. See chap. 8.

24. What follows is adapted from Seibert, *Violence of Scripture*, 28.

25. For further discussion and elaboration, see Seibert, *Violence of Scripture*, 28–43.

26. Eric A. Seibert, *Disarming the Church: Why Christians Must Forsake Violence to Follow Jesus and Change the World* (Eugene, OR: Cascade, 2018).

Chapter 2: Why Bother with Violent Verses?

1. Rauser, *What's So Confusing about Grace?*, 138–39, emphasis original.
2. What follows is adapted from Seibert, *Violence of Scripture*, 41. The tendency to omit violent parts of the Old Testament is also prevalent in the Roman Catholic Mass and the Liturgy of the Hours. See Michael Prior, *The Bible and Colonialism: A Moral Critique* (Sheffield: Sheffield Academic, 1997), 273–78. Gordon H. Matties, in *Joshua* (Harrisonburg, VA: Herald, 2012), 27, refers to the process of omitting something objectionable from the Bible as a "textectomy," a term he adapted from Eugene Peterson, who memorably refers to the removal of difficult parts of Psalms as "psalmectomies." See Eugene H. Peterson, *Answering God: The Psalms as Tools for Prayer* (San Francisco: Harper & Row, 1989), 98.
3. John L. Thompson, *Reading the Bible with the Dead: What You Can Learn from the History of Exegesis That You Can't Learn from Exegesis Alone* (Grand Rapids: Eerdmans, 2007), 2.
4. Barbara Brown Taylor, "Hard Words," *Christian Century* 118 (May 2001): 24.
5. Julia M. O'Brien, *Challenging Prophetic Metaphor: Theology and Ideology in the Prophets* (Louisville, KY: Westminster John Knox, 2008), 101, emphasis mine.
6. Brent A. Strawn, *The Old Testament Is Dying: A Diagnosis and Recommended Treatment* (Grand Rapids: Baker, 2017), 19–58.
7. In addition to Strawn, *Old Testament Is Dying*, see Ellen F. Davis, "Losing a Friend: The Loss of the Old Testament to the Church," in *Jews, Christians, and the Theology of the Hebrew Scriptures*, ed. Alice Ogden Bellis and Joel S. Kaminsky, Society of Biblical Literature Symposium Series 8 (Atlanta: Society of Biblical Literature, 2000), 83–94.
8. To learn what a particular church or denomination believes about the Bible, consult their statement of faith.
9. I am not suggesting there is anything wrong with questioning what we are taught by religious leaders. On the contrary, I believe cultivating a healthy faith requires us to do precisely that. What complicates things tremendously is when people suspect their religious leaders have intentionally misled them, either by providing them with misinformation or by not telling them the whole story. When that happens, it becomes very difficult to continue to trust these individuals and the institutions they serve.
10. David Kinnaman, in *You Lost Me: Why Young Christians Are Leaving Church . . . and Rethinking Faith* (Grand Rapids: Baker, 2011), 89–198, says people ages eighteen to twenty-nine are leaving the church because they view it as overprotective, shallow, antiscience, repressive, exclusive, and doubtless. In his chapter on "doubtless," Kinnaman indicates that a third (36 percent) of the Christians surveyed in this age-group agreed with the statement "I don't feel that I can ask my most pressing life questions in church" (190). While Kinnaman discusses a variety of reasons that young people feel this way, he acknowledges that sometimes the church is directly to blame (see esp. 193).
11. For an extended discussion of why violence is off-limits for Christians, see Seibert, *Disarming the Church*, 97–113.
12. Seibert, *Violence of Scripture*, 54–57.
13. Seibert, *Violence of Scripture*, 54.
14. Seibert, *Violence of Scripture*, 56.
15. Rauser, *What's So Confusing about Grace?*, 129. For a sampling of Rauser's interactions with atheists, see John W. Loftus and Randal Rauser, *God or Godless? One Atheist. One Christian. Twenty Controversial Questions* (Grand Rapids: Baker, 2013);

and Randal Rauser and Justin Schieber, *An Atheist and a Christian Walk into a Bar: Talking about God, the Universe, and Everything* (Amherst, NY: Prometheus, 2016).

16. The following two examples, from David Plotz and Ted Grimsrud, also appear in Eric A. Seibert, "The Violent Legacy of the Old Testament (and What to Do about It)," *Listening: Journal of Communication Ethics, Religion, and Culture* 56:3 (2021): 219.

17. David Plotz, *Good Book: The Bizarre, Hilarious, Disturbing, Marvelous, and Inspiring Things I Learned When I Read Every Single Word of the Bible* (New York: Harper, 2009), 302.

18. Ted Grimsrud, "Is God Nonviolent?," *Conrad Grebel Review* 21:1 (2003): 13–14.

19. See chap. 8.

20. Steve Wells, *Drunk with Blood: God's Killings in the Bible* (USA: Giordano, 2010), 1–2.

21. Richard Dawkins, *The God Delusion* (Boston: Mariner, 2008), 51.

22. Dan Barker, *God: The Most Unpleasant Character in All Fiction* (New York: Sterling, 2016).

23. For a response to the New Atheists' critique of the Old Testament, see Katharine Dell, *Who Needs the Old Testament? Its Enduring Appeal and Why the New Atheists Don't Get It* (Eugene, OR: Cascade, 2017).

24. Boyd, *Crucifixion of the Warrior God*, 25.

25. See Seibert, *Violence of Scripture*, 15–26; and Seibert, "Violent Legacy of the Old Testament," 215–28.

26. William W. Emilsen and John T. Squires, introduction to *Validating Violence— Violating Faith? Religion, Scripture and Violence*, ed. William W. Emilsen and John T. Squires (Adelaide: ATF, 2008), xiii.

Chapter 3: Seven Constructive Ways to Use a Violent Biblical Text

1. O'Brien, *Challenging Prophetic Metaphor*, 101.

2. 2 Sam. 11:26; 12:18.

3. See Seibert, *Disarming the Church*, 46–59, for a discussion of the negative effects of violence. As noted there, violence breeds more violence, escalates dangerous situations, harms countless people, wounds those who use it, and is unnatural and extremely costly.

4. Compare Rahab's actions on behalf of the spies in Josh. 2.

5. Compare the story of Joseph and Mary taking Jesus to Egypt to escape Herod's grasp (Matt. 2:13–15).

6. For another example, see 2 Chron. 33:1–13, which describes Manasseh repenting after being captured and exiled by the king of Assyria.

7. See, e.g., Pss. 78:38; 103:13; 106:45; 145:9; and Matt. 9:36; 14:14; 15:32; 20:34.

8. See Seibert, *Violence of Scripture*, 81–85, 121–22.

9. There is debate about whether Jephthah actually offered his daughter as a burnt offering because the text never directly describes Jephthah performing this dastardly deed. Still, we are told that he "did with her according to the vow he had made" (Judg. 11:39), which seems to imply he sacrificed her.

10. Studies indicate that people who read literary fiction demonstrate higher degrees of empathy and compassion than those who do not. While I am not suggesting that reading the Bible is identical to reading literary fiction, it seems reasonable to assume that reading stories in the Bible also has the potential to encourage readers to develop empathy and compassion. For a summary of the research with respect to literary fiction, see Megan Schmidt, "How Reading Fiction Increases

Empathy and Encourages Understanding." *Discover Magazine*, August 28, 2020, https://www.discovermagazine.com/mind/how-reading-fiction-increases -empathy-and-encourages-understanding; and Claudia Hammond, "Does Reading Fiction Make Us Better People?," *BBC Future*, June 2, 2019, https://www.bbc.com/future/article/20190523-does-reading-fiction-make-us -better-people.

11. See chap. 6 for more about issuing trigger warnings.
12. According to the National Coalition against Domestic Violence (NCADV), in the United States, "1 in 4 women and 1 in 9 men experience severe intimate partner physical violence, intimate partner contact sexual violence, and/or intimate partner stalking." NCADV, "Statistics," accessed May 16, 2023, https://ncadv .org/statistics.
13. According to Catherine Clark Kroeger and Nancy Nason-Clark, "Researchers in the field of family violence have consistently argued that abuse crosses all religious boundaries and that the rates inside and outside the walls of the church are similar." *No Place for Abuse: Biblical and Practical Resources to Counteract Domestic Violence*, 2nd ed. (Downers Grove, IL: InterVarsity, 2010), 50.
14. I am indebted to Dr. David Bosworth for this idea, which he demonstrated in a paper titled "Teaching Intimate Partner Violence in Hosea 1–3," presented in the Academic Teaching and Biblical Studies section of the Society of Biblical Literature Annual Meeting in San Antonio, Texas, on November 19, 2016.
15. One complicating factor when using the passage this way is that God is portrayed as the abusive husband. This should be acknowledged, but it need not be the focal point of the sermon or Sunday school lesson.
16. See Rachael A. Keefe, *The Lifesaving Church: Faith Communities and Suicide Prevention* (St. Louis: Chalice, 2018), for guidance about dealing with this issue in the church. More generally, see Stacey Freedenthal, *Loving Someone with Suicidal Thoughts: What Family, Friends, and Partners Can Say and Do* (Oakland, CA: New Harbinger, 2023).
17. "Scope of the Problem: Statistics," Rape, Abuse and Incest National Network, accessed May 16, 2023, https://www.rainn.org/statistics/scope-problem.
18. Phyllis Trible, *Texts of Terror: Literary-Feminist Readings of Biblical Narratives* (Philadelphia: Fortress, 1984).
19. Rachel Held Evans, *Inspired: Slaying Giants, Walking on Water, and Loving the Bible Again* (Nashville: Nelson Books, 2018), 75. For a fuller description of this event, see Evans, *A Year of Biblical Womanhood: How a Liberated Woman Found Herself Sitting on Her Roof, Covering Her Head, and Calling Her Husband "Master"* (Nashville: Thomas Nelson, 2012), 61–66.
20. Evans, *Inspired*, 75.
21. Evans, *Inspired*, 76. For more on how to use stories of violence against women responsibly, see Seibert, *Violence of Scripture*, 143–46.
22. For a general overview of ways biblical texts have been misused, see Seibert, *Violence of Scripture*, 15–26. For a detailed discussion of how one particular set of biblical texts has been used violently through history, see Christian Hofreiter, *Making Sense of Old Testament Genocide: Christian Interpretations of Herem Passages* (Oxford: Oxford University Press, 2018), 160–213.
23. For an extensive discussion of how Christians and Jews have appropriated and weaponized this story of the annihilation of Amalek, see Philip Jenkins, *Laying Down the Sword: Why We Can't Ignore the Bible's Violent Verses* (New York: HarperOne, 2011), 123–63.

24. Susan Niditch, *War in the Hebrew Bible: A Study of the Ethics of Violence* (Oxford: Oxford University Press, 1983), 3–4.
25. David F. Dawes, "Rwanda's Genocide: 'Never Again,' Says Pastor," *BC Christian News* 21:6 (June 2001), https://web.archive.org/web/20210301151453/https://www.canadianchristianity.com/cgi-bin/bc.cgi?bc/bccn/0601/intrwanda. Cited in Jenkins, *Laying Down the Sword,* 141.
26. This quote is attributed to Sun Tzu, author of *The Art of War.*
27. Some of what follows in this section is adapted from Seibert, *Disturbing Divine Behavior,* 214.
28. Ellen F. Davis, "Critical Traditioning: Seeking an Inner Biblical Hermeneutic," *Anglican Theological Review* 82 (2000): 734.
29. Davis, "Critical Traditioning," 749.
30. Thomas G. Long, "The Fall of the House of Uzzah . . . and Other Difficult Preaching Texts," *Journal for Preachers* 7 (Advent 1983): 17, emphasis mine.
31. This will be discussed in chap. 5.

Chapter 4: Teaching Violent Bible Stories to Children

1. Elizabeth F. Caldwell, *I Wonder: Engaging a Child's Curiosity about the Bible* (Nashville: Abingdon, 2016), xiv.
2. Catherine Maresca, *Violence and Nonviolence in Scripture: Helping Children Understand Challenging Stories* (Chicago: Liturgy Training, 2019), v.
3. Maresca, *Violence and Nonviolence,* v, emphasis mine.
4. Rosemary Cox, "Using the Bible with Children," *Journal of Education and Christian Belief* 5:1 (2001): 49. Although this observation was made a couple decades ago, it still seems like very little has been done in this regard.
5. Peter Enns gives similar counsel to parents when they teach the Bible to their children: "As we teach the youngest children—those in grades one through four—the primary emphasis should be on Jesus." *Telling God's Story: A Parents' Guide to Teaching the Bible* (Charles City, VA: Olive Branch, 2010), 29–35; quote, 29.
6. This question is adapted from the title of Francis Landy's article, "Do We Want Our Children to Read This Book?," in *Bible and Ethics of Reading,* ed. Danna Nolan Fewell and Gary A. Phillips, *Semeia* 77 (1997): 157–76. As Landy acknowledges, this question is raised by Fewell and Gunn in their book *Gender, Power, and Promise,* though they are speaking more specifically about whether we want our children to read Genesis–Kings, since it is so thoroughly patriarchal.
7. "Sunday school" refers to classes held for people of all ages for about an hour, typically right before the Sunday morning worship service. "Children's church" is a special worship service for children held during all, or part, of the main worship service. I will use this terminology for convenience' sake, though I realize there are various designations for these ministries.
8. Parents looking for a guide to help them teach the Bible to their children could consult Enns, *Telling God's Story.* Though *Telling God's Story* is not about teaching violent verses to children, it contains many helpful ideas that parents could apply when they do.
9. For a summary and critique of some prominent stage theorists, see Melody R. Briggs, *How Children Read Biblical Narrative: An Investigation of Children's Readings of the Gospel of Luke* (Eugene, OR: Pickwick, 2017), 33–52.
10. For dealing with suicidal ideation, see Keefe, *Lifesaving Church.* For information on sexual assault, see Al Miles, *Ending Violence in Teen Dating Relationships: A Resource Guide for Parents and Pastors* (Minneapolis: Augsburg Fortress, 2005). For general

awareness about how to respond to various mental health concerns, consider the training offered by Mental Health First Aid (https://www.mentalhealthfirstaid .org).

11. For an extensive discussion of how people often fail to deal honestly with the Bible as it is, see Mark Roncace, *Raw Revelation: The Bible They Never Tell You About* (North Charleston, SC: CreateSpace, 2012).

12. Sarah Hinlicky Wilson, "R-rated: How to Read the Bible with Children," *Christian Century* 130 (March 6, 2013): 25.

13. For a very accessible and incredibly helpful book that gives people permission to ask questions and express doubt, see Rachel Held Evans, *Faith Unraveled: How a Girl Who Knew All the Answers Learned to Ask Questions* (Grand Rapids: Zondervan, 2010).

14. As discussed in chap. 2, one of the reasons it is so important for ministers to use violent verses in worship services and Christian education programs is to avoid creating doubts about the church's credibility.

15. See Peter King, "Sunday School Hero or Suicide Bomber? Reading Samson Responsibly," in *The Bible on Violence: A Thick Description*, ed. Helen Paynter and Michael Spalione (Sheffield: Sheffield Phoenix, 2020), 238–57.

16. Exod. 21:22–25; Lev. 24:17–20; Deut. 19:15–21.

17. Seibert, *Violence of Scripture*, 153 (with a typo corrected and a word changed). See Judg. 4 (Jael), 1 Sam. 25 (Abigail) and 17 (David), and Gen. 45 and 50 (Joseph). In addition to Abigail and Joseph, people like Shiphrah and Puah, Obadiah, and Jehosheba, who were mentioned in chap. 2, would be good candidates for inclusion in a book about (nonviolent) Bible heroes.

18. For a critique of violence along with nonviolent alternatives for responding to difficult or dangerous situations, see Seibert, *Disarming the Church*, esp. 46–59, 151–204.

19. Cited in Terry L. Brensinger, "War in the Old Testament: A Journey toward Nonparticipation," in *A Peace Reader*, ed. E. Morris Sider and Luke Keefer Jr. (Nappanee, IN: Evangel, 2002), 23.

20. See John J. Collins, *What Are Biblical Values? What the Bible Says on Key Ethical Issues* (New Haven, CT: Yale University Press, 2019).

21. These differences could be multiplied many times over. The idea of Sheol is another good example. Israelites believed *all* people, good and bad alike, went to this shadowy underground world when they died (Eccl. 9:1–10). Jacob, who thinks Joseph has been killed by a wild animal, expresses his belief that he will join his favorite son in Sheol when he dies (Gen. 37:35). Belief in Sheol is widely attested in the Old Testament and never condemned or refuted. Yet Christians do not believe in Sheol. They have other ideas about what happens to people after they die.

22. For Joseph, see Gen. 45 and 50; for Jonah, see esp. Jonah 4; and for Abigail, see 1 Sam. 25.

23. Howard Worsley, *How Not to Totally Put Your Children off God: A Conversation on Christian Parenting between a Father and His Sons* (Oxford: Lion Hudson, 2020), 35–37.

24. Worsley, *How Not to Totally Put Your Children off God*, 36–37. For a brief discussion of this tendency to view biblical characters more virtuously than the text warrants, see Seibert, *Violence of Scripture*, 39–41.

25. Jerome W. Berryman, *Teaching Godly Play: How to Mentor the Spiritual Development of Children* (Denver, CO: Morehouse Education Resources, 2009).

26. Caldwell, *I Wonder,* 47–48.
27. This language of taming the text comes from Caldwell, *I Wonder.* See, e.g., 10, 13, 18.
28. Caldwell, *I Wonder,* 40–41. See also 131–34. Caldwell acknowledges some of these questions may work better than others, depending on the age of the child.
29. This illustration is adapted from Seibert, *Violence of Scripture,* 153.
30. Rauser, *Jesus Loves Canaanites,* 23. Another song to avoid is "Arky, Arky," a catchy tune about the flood that completely ignores all the tremendous harm it causes.
31. While this song has a long and rich history in African American communities, especially in the context of oppression, it functions rather differently when sung by children in a music video or Sunday school class.
32. Rauser, *Jesus Loves Canaanites,* 23. You can watch this video at https://www.youtube.com/watch?v=MdQy2l8BegA.
33. These online images are also available in print in books Spurling has published under her birth name, Brendon Powell Smith.
34. The artwork of Gustave Doré also provides sobering and more realistic portrayals of the violent aspects of various biblical stories. See Gustave Doré, *The Doré Bible Illustrations* (Mineola, NY: Dover, 1974).
35. Even though I am unpersuaded by attempts to defend God's violent behavior in the Old Testament, a point that will become obvious in chap. 8, I introduce this perspective (along with others) in the entry-level Bible class I teach to undergraduate students.
36. See chap. 8 for brief discussion of this point. For an exploration of these tensions in academia, see Brandon G. Withrow and Menachem Wecker, *Consider No Evil: Two Faith Traditions and the Problem of Academic Freedom in Religious Higher Education* (Eugene, OR: Cascade, 2014).
37. For more on this, see Catherine Stonehouse and Scottie May, *Listening to Children on the Spiritual Journey: Guidance for Those Who Teach and Nurture* (Grand Rapids: Baker, 2010), 131–34.
38. If you are working with teens, you could direct them to Brian Zahnd's excellent book, *Sinners in the Hands of a Loving God: The Scandalous Truth of the Very Good News* (Colorado Springs, CO: WaterBrook, 2017).
39. See chap. 9 for a brief discussion of equipping lay leaders and others.

Chapter 5: Using Violent Verses in Worship

1. Jack Nelson-Pallmeyer and Bret Hesla, *Worship in the Spirit of Jesus: Theology, Liturgy, and Songs without Violence* (Eugene, OR: Wipf & Stock, 2005), 96.
2. Created by Eric A. Seibert. See Gen. 45 and 50 for Joseph forgiving his brothers, Josh. 22 for the conversation that stopped a war, and 1 Sam. 25 for Abigail's inspiring intervention. The words about living peaceably with all are from Rom. 12:18.
3. Created by Eric A. Seibert. See Gen. 4:8; Ps. 51:10; 2 Sam. 11:14–15; 1 Kgs. 21:1–16; and John 8:11.
4. See Gen. 4:13–16; and 2 Sam. 12:10–12; 15:13–18; 16:22.
5. Isa. 61:2.
6. For a discussion of possible explanations of why Jesus stopped reading here and what is meant by the key phrase he omits, see Richard B. Hays, *Echoes of Scripture in the Gospels* (Waco, TX: Baylor University Press, 2016), 226–30.
7. The term "psalmectomies" is from Peterson, *Answering God,* 98. He is opposed to them.
8. For an excellent resource on this topic, see David Batstone, *Not for Sale: The Return of the Global Slave Trade—and How We Can Fight It* (New York: HarperSanFrancisco, 2007).

9. There is debate about whether the psalmist prays these words or if the psalmist is quoting someone else who has prayed these words against him. For a discussion of various options, see David Tuesday Adamo, "Reading Psalm 109 in African Christianity," *Old Testament Essays* 21:3 (2008): 580–81. However this is understood, the problem of imprecation remains.

10. Boyd, *Crucifixion of the Warrior God,* 29.

11. John N. Day, *Crying for Justice: What the Psalms Teach Us about Mercy and Vengeance in an Age of Terrorism* (Grand Rapids: Kregel, 2005), 109, emphasis original.

12. For more on the nonviolent way of Jesus and the nonviolent nature of Christian discipleship, see Seibert, *Disarming the Church,* 60–113.

13. Ellen F. Davis, *Getting Involved with God: Rediscovering the Old Testament* (Cambridge, MA: Cowley, 2001), 28, emphasis mine.

14. Davis, *Getting Involved with God,* 28–29. The translation of Ps. 109:16 is her own.

15. See Ps. 139:23–24.

16. Matthew Richard Schlimm, *This Strange and Sacred Scripture: Wrestling with the Old Testament and Its Oddities* (Grand Rapids: Baker, 2015), 72–73, emphasis mine.

17. Davis, *Getting Involved with God,* 28.

18. Both Davis (*Getting Involved with God,* 21–29) and Schlimm (*Strange and Sacred,* 71–72) believe it is sometimes appropriate for Christians to pray these prayers against their enemies. While I affirm we should be honest with God in our prayers, and should find appropriate ways to express our anger and outrage, asking God to send evil upon others strikes me as incompatible with the teachings of Jesus.

19. Created by Eric A. Seibert. See John 8:11 for the language of going and sinning no more.

20. I am indebted to Ted Davis for identifying the songwriter of "Warrior."

21. This is from b. Megillah 10b, cited in James L. Kugel, *Traditions of the Bible: A Guide to the Bible as It Was at the Beginning of the Common Era* (Cambridge, MA: Harvard University Press, 1998), 609.

22. Noted in examples in the previous chapter.

23. For examples of songs promoting peace and justice, see hymns 56–66 in Jane Parker Huber, *A Singing Faith* (Philadelphia: Westminster, 1987). For a resource that recognizes the problematic nature of violent verses and provides nonviolent resources for worship, see Nelson-Pallmeyer and Hesla, *Worship in the Spirit of Jesus.*

Chapter 6: Preaching from Violent Passages

1. Jenkins, *Laying Down the Sword,* 227–28.

2. Taylor, "Hard Words," 24. Parts of this chapter are adapted from Eric A. Seibert, "Preaching from Violent Biblical Texts: Helpful Strategies for Addressing Violence in the Old Testament," *Perspectives in Religious Studies* 42 (2015): 247–57.

3. Taylor, "Hard Words," 24.

4. Taylor, "Hard Words," 24.

5. Joseph R. Jeter Jr., *Preaching Judges* (St. Louis: Chalice, 2003), 20. See throughout for helpful suggestions for preaching from the book of Judges and its many violent verses.

6. Material in this paragraph and the next is adapted from Seibert, *Violence of Scripture,* 42–43.

7. See Jim Hill and Rand Cheadle, *The Bible Tells Me So: Uses and Abuses of Holy Scripture* (New York: Doubleday, 1996); Spong, *Sins of Scripture;* Thatcher, *Savage Text;* Jenkins, *Laying Down the Sword;* Seibert, *Violence of Scripture,* 15–26.

8. For specific historical examples, see Prior, *Bible and Colonialism.*
9. Verses about using "the rod" on children include Prov. 13:24; 22:15; 23:13–14; 29:15. For more on this topic generally, see William J. Webb, *Corporal Punishment in the Bible: A Redemptive-Movement Hermeneutic for Troubling Texts* (Downers Grove, IL: InterVarsity), 2011.
10. For a brief discussion of some of the ways the conquest narrative (Josh. 6–11) has been misused historically, see John J. Collins, *Does the Bible Justify Violence?* (Minneapolis: Fortress, 2004), 19–20. For various ways 1 Sam. 15 has been misused by Christians and Jews, see Jenkins, *Laying Down the Sword,* 123–63.
11. Cheryl B. Anderson, *Ancient Laws and Contemporary Controversies: The Need for Inclusive Biblical Interpretation* (Oxford: Oxford University Press, 2009), 67. Material in this paragraph is adapted from Seibert, *Violence of Scripture,* 89.
12. Anderson, *Ancient Laws,* 67.
13. Material in this paragraph is adapted from Seibert, *Violence of Scripture,* 142.
14. Linda Day, "Rhetoric and Domestic Violence in Ezekiel 16," *Biblical Interpretation* 8 (2000): 214–16.
15. Renita J. Weems, *Battered Love: Marriage, Sex, and Violence in the Hebrew Prophets* (Minneapolis: Fortress, 1995), 68–83, esp. 72; and Katharine Doob Sakenfeld, *Just Wives? Stories of Power and Survival in the Old Testament and Today* (Louisville, KY: Westminster John Knox, 2003), 103–6.
16. For a collection of sermons on this topic, see "100 Sermons against Domestic and Sexual Violence," *Sojourners,* https://sojo.net/resources/100-sermons-against -domestic-and-sexual-violence.
17. On suicide, see Keefe, *Lifesaving Church.* On capital punishment, see Shane Claiborne, *Executing Grace: How the Death Penalty Killed Jesus and Why It's Killing Us* (San Francisco: HarperOne, 2016). On child abuse, see Jeanette Harder, *Let the Children Come: Preparing Faith Communities to End Child Abuse and Neglect* (Scottdale, PA: Herald, 2010).
18. Material in this paragraph is adapted from Seibert, *Violence of Scripture,* 120.
19. I believe it is dangerous to view any sentient life as irredeemable. On the question of whether Tolkien was racist, including whether his depiction of orcs is racist, see Anderson M. Rearick III, "Why Is the Only Good Orc a Dead Orc?," in *Inklings Forever: Published Colloquium Proceedings 1997–2016,* vol. 4 (2004): article 10, https://pillars.taylor.edu/inklings_forever/vol4/iss1/10.
20. Daniel L. Buttry, *First-Person Preaching: Bringing New Life to Biblical Stories* (Valley Forge, PA: Judson, 1998); and J. Kent Edwards, *Effective First-Person Biblical Preaching: The Steps from Text to Narrative* (Grand Rapids: Zondervan, 2005). For examples of this type of writing, see Philip R. Davies, ed., *First Person: Essays in Biblical Autobiography* (Sheffield: Sheffield Academic, 2002); and Julie Faith Parker, ed., *My So-Called Biblical Life: Imagined Stories from the World's Bestselling Book* (Eugene, OR: Wipf & Stock, 2017).
21. Ulrike Bechmann, "The Woman of Jericho: Dramatization and Feminist Hermeneutics," in *Faith and Feminism: Ecumenical Essays,* ed. B. Diane Lipsett and Phyllis Trible (Louisville, KY: Westminster John Knox, 2014), 185.
22. For another example of this kind of storytelling, see Clara Garnier-Amouroux, "What about Me? The Tale of the Forgotten Sister (Genesis 29:1–30)," in *My So-Called Biblical Life: Imagined Stories from the World's Best-Selling Book,* ed. Julie Faith Parker (Eugene, OR: Wipf & Stock, 2017), 12–21. Garnier-Amouroux poignantly retells the story of Jacob's first wedding from the perspective of Leah, the unloved sister whose deceitfully arranged marriage causes tremendous heartache and grief.

23. Carol Lakey Hess, *Caretakers of Our Common House: Women's Development in Communities of Faith* (Nashville: Abingdon, 1997), 202.

24. Hess, *Caretakers of Our Common House*, 193, emphasis mine.

25. Compare the discussion in chap. 4 about how our views of violence differ from ancient Israel's.

26. For an excellent discussion of this point, see Eryl W. Davies, *The Immoral Bible: Approaches to Biblical Ethics* (London: T & T Clark, 2010), 120–38.

27. See Seibert, *Violence of Scripture*, 61–72. The quoted material is from 67.

28. As Eryl W. Davies observes, employing a reader-response approach to the Bible "serves to remind readers that they have a duty to enter into dialogue with the text. . . . Their task is to engage in a vigorous debate with the Hebrew Bible, resisting statements that appear to be morally objectionable." "The Morally Dubious Passages of the Hebrew Bible: An Examination of Some Proposed Solutions," *Currents in Biblical Research* 3 (2005): 219.

29. See Simon Joseph, *The Nonviolent Messiah: Jesus, Q, and the Enochic Tradition* (Minneapolis: Fortress, 2014). "If Jesus was consistent about anything," argues Joseph, "it seems to have been his commitment to nonviolence" (230).

30. For an extensive discussion of the nonviolent nature of Christian discipleship, see Seibert, *Disarming the Church*, 97–113 and throughout.

31. For discussion of a christocentric hermeneutic, see Seibert, *Disturbing Divine Behavior*, 183–207.

32. Material in this paragraph is adapted from Seibert, *Violence of Scripture*, 154.

33. See Seibert, *Violence of Scripture*, 9.

34. Frances Taylor Gench, *Encountering God in Tyrannical Texts: Reflections on Paul, Women, and the Authority of Scripture* (Louisville, KY: Westminster John Knox, 2015), 13.

35. James L. Crenshaw, *A Whirlpool of Torment: Israelite Traditions of God as an Oppressive Presence* (Philadelphia: Fortress, 1984), 12.

36. Terence E. Fretheim and Karlfried Froehlich, *The Bible as Word of God: In a Postmodern Age* (Minneapolis: Fortress, 1998), 100.

37. Adapted from Seibert, *Disturbing Divine Behavior*, 218–20.

38. Material in this paragraph is adapted from Seibert, *Disturbing Divine Behavior*, 220.

39. For a much less favorable reading of Abraham's behavior in this passage (and elsewhere), see David M. Gunn and Danna Nolan Fewell, *Narrative in the Hebrew Bible* (Oxford: Oxford University Press, 1993), 90–100.

40. Judg. 19:22–30. See chap. 4 for a discussion about teaching violent texts to children in age-appropriate ways.

41. For examples of atrocities committed by Assyrians and others in the ancient world, see William J. Webb and Gordan K. Oeste, *Bloody, Brutal, and Barbaric? Wrestling with Troubling War Texts* (Downers Grove, IL: InterVarsity, 2019), 263–87.

42. For a brief but helpful article about this, see Mike Woodruff, "Difficult Sermon? Call in a Team," *CT Pastors*, July 11, 2008, https://www.christianitytoday.com/pastors/2008/spring/24.47.html.

Chapter 7: Exploring Selected Passages for Use in Church

1. This is suggested, for example, by Jesus' use of the story in Matt. 10:1–15 and 11:20–24.

2. The NRSV translates the reason for their demand as "so that we may know them." The Hebrew word *yada'*, "to know," is sometimes used euphemistically for sexual relations (see, e.g., Gen. 4:1).

3. For a discussion of Gen. 19:30–38 that engages with interpreters who believe this passage misconstrues what really happens in incestuous situations (i.e., it is initiated by the father, *not* his daughters), see Susanne Scholz, *Sacred Witness: Rape in the Hebrew Bible* (Minneapolis: Fortress, 2010), 169–73.

4. This term is problematic, but it continues to be used by many people to describe same-sex attraction and behavior. For a discussion of the word's origin, see Kathy Baldock, *Walking the Bridgeless Canyon: Repairing the Breach between the Church and the LGBT Community* (Reno, NV: Canyonwalker, 2014), 17–23.

5. For an attempt to argue this way, see Kevin DeYoung, *What Does the Bible Really Teach about Homosexuality?* (Wheaton, IL: Crossway, 2015), 33–38. DeYoung draws the following conclusion: "While the violence associated with homosexual behavior in Sodom certainly made the offense worse, *the nature of the act itself contributed to the overwhelmingly negative assessment of the city*" (38, emphasis mine). While the latter part of this statement would most likely be true for ancient readers (as it is for many modern ones, like DeYoung), that does not constitute a basis upon which one can argue that same-sex sex is inherently sinful. At most, it provides insight into the way this kind of sexual activity was regarded in the ancient world. But it says nothing about *why* people held these views. Without knowing this, it is extremely difficult to use this passage in any meaningful way in conversations about same-sex attraction or same-sex sexual behavior today.

6. Matthew Vines, *God and the Gay Christian: The Biblical Case for Same-Sex Relationships* (New York: Convergent, 2014), 59.

7. Collins, *What Are Biblical Values?*, 66.

8. In the New Testament, Jude 7 assigns blame to Sodom for sexual immorality (cf. 2 Pet. 2:4–10), though the nature of this is unspecified. It most likely does not refer to same-sex sexual activity, but probably refers to illicit sexual unions between angels and human women (see Gen. 6:1–4). For discussion, see Richard J. Bauckham, *Jude, 2 Peter* (Waco, TX: Word, 1983), 50–55, esp. 54.

9. Some scholars believe "homosexuality" is implied by the reference to "abominable things" (*toevah*) in v. 50, though this seems unlikely. While it is true that *toevah* can refer to same-sex behavior (as it does in Lev. 18:22 and 20:13) or various sexual transgressions, the word also is often used in connection with a wide range of nonsexual acts as well. Moreover, as Matthew Vines points out, "In the immediate context of Ezekiel 16, the word *toevah* refers to idolatry and adultery (verses 2, 22, 36, 43, 47, 51, and 58), not to same-sex behavior. So it's contextually unlikely that Ezekiel's reference . . . in verse 50 represents a condemnation of same-sex behavior" (*God and the Gay Christian*, 196).

10. For a fuller exposition of this passage from an affirming perspective, see, e.g., Vines, *God and the Gay Christian*, 59–75; and Colby Martin, *Unclobber: Rethinking Our Misuse of the Bible on Homosexuality* (Louisville, KY: Westminster John Knox, 2016), 47–60.

11. For a more extensive discussion of how Christians have used Scripture against LGBTQIA+ individuals, see Linda J. Patterson, *Hate Thy Neighbor: How the Bible Is Misused to Condemn Homosexuality* (West Conshohocken, PA: Infinity, 2009).

12. For an accessible treatment of human sexuality that creates space for less traditional viewpoints, see Nadia Bolz-Weber, *Shameless: A Case for Not Feeling Bad about Feeling Good (about Sex)* (New York: Convergent, 2020).

13. For an excellent resource that would be ideal for discussion in the context of the church, see David P. Gushee, *Changing Our Mind: Definitive 3rd Edition of the*

Landmark Call for Inclusion of LGBTQ Christians with Response to Critics (Canton, MI: Read the Spirit, 2022).

14. See Harold Heie, *Respectful LGBT Conversations: Seeking Truth, Giving Love, and Modeling Christian Unity* (Eugene, OR: Cascade, 2018), 161–204 and passim.

15. On the importance of approaching Genesis 19 this way, see Sonia E. Waters, "Reading Sodom through Sexual Violence against Women," *Interpretation: A Journal of Bible and Theology* 71:3 (2017): 274–83.

16. It is unclear whether Lot's daughters hear him make this offer since he is outside with the mob while they remain inside behind closed doors. They make no mention of it when they devise their plan to sleep with Lot in the cave (vv. 30–38). If they did hear Lot say this, or if they somehow became aware of it later, the resulting psychological, emotional, and relational damage would have been severe.

17. Lynn Japinga, *Preaching the Women of the Old Testament: Who They Were and Why They Matter* (Louisville, KY: Westminster John Knox, 2017), 23.

18. See John S. McClure and Nancy J. Ramsay, eds., *Preaching about Sexual and Domestic Violence* (Cleveland: United Church, 1998); and Marie M. Fortune, *Sexual Violence: The Sin Revisited* (Cleveland: Pilgrim, 2005).

19. For first-person accounts online, see, e.g., the website for Into Accounts, intoaccount.org/reports.

20. See the discussion about issuing trigger warnings in chap. 6.

21. Peter Enns, *The Bible Tells Me So: Why Defending Scripture Has Made Us Unable to Read It* (San Francisco: HarperOne, 2014), 31.

22. See Gen. 19:30–38.

23. At the time of this writing, the governors of three of those states—California, Oregon, and Pennsylvania—have issued a moratorium.

24. Quoted in Claiborne, *Executing Grace*, 172. The report, "Lynching in America: Confronting the Legacy of Racial Terror," can be found at https://eji.org /reports/lynching-in-america/.

25. See Lev. 25:8–34, esp. v. 23.

26. See Jesse C. Long Jr., *1 & 2 Kings* (Joplin, MO: College Press, 2002), 368.

27. Created by Eric A. Seibert.

28. Solidarity Uganda, "The Anti-Land Grabbing Bicycle Riding Caravan," August 20, 2021, https://solidarityuganda.org/the-anti-land-grabbing-bicycle-riding -caravan/.

29. Japinga, *Preaching the Women of the Old Testament*, 146.

30. Japinga, *Preaching the Women of the Old Testament*, 145.

31. See, e.g., Robyn J. Whitaker, "Invoking Jezebel, Invoking Terror: The Threat of Sexual Violence in the Apocalypse to John," in *Terror in the Bible: Rhetoric, Gender, and Violence*, ed. Monica Jyotsna Melanchthon and Robyn J. Whitaker (Atlanta: Society of Biblical Literature, 2021), 107–20.

33. As a point of comparison, consider the sympathetic portrayals of Goliath in Jonathan L. Friedmann, *Goliath as Gentle Giant: Sympathetic Portrayals in Popular Culture* (Lanham, MD: Rowman & Littlefield, 2022).

33. For another version of this story, see Bel and the Dragon 23–42. The final verse also describes the death of those who sought to kill Daniel: "Then he [the king] pulled Daniel out, and threw into the den those who had attempted his destruction, and they were instantly eaten before his eyes."

34. For another Old Testament story that illustrates how one person's misdeeds had lethal consequences for his family, see Josh. 7:22–26. As the story goes, after the

Israelites destroy Jericho, a man named Achan takes some forbidden spoils of war. When his transgression is discovered, he is stoned to death, and his sons and daughters are burned along with him.

35. As the psalmist declares, "I treasure your word in my heart, so that I may not sin against you" (Ps. 119:11). Compare 1 Cor. 10:1–13, esp. v. 11.

36. For an excellent resource about the horrific toll that killing takes upon soldiers, see David A. Grossman, *On Killing: The Psychological Cost of Learning to Kill in War and Society*, rev. ed. (New York: Back Bay, 2009).

37. For a helpful introduction to restorative justice, see Howard Zehr, *The Little Book of Restorative Justice*, rev. and updated (New York: Good Books, 2015).

38. For discussion of a broad range of alternatives to violence, see Seibert, *Disarming the Church*, esp. 134–290. For some prominent historical examples of nonviolent action, see Ronald J. Sider, *Nonviolent Action: What Christian Ethics Demands but Most Christians Have Never Really Tried* (Grand Rapids: Brazos, 2015).

Chapter 8: Talking about God's Violent Behavior in the Bible

1. Jack Nelson-Pallmeyer, *Jesus against Christianity: Reclaiming the Missing Jesus* (Harrisburg, PA: Trinity Press International, 2001), 21.

2. Deut. 28:6,; 1 Sam. 15:3; 2 Sam. 12:11; 2 Kgs. 17:25; Job 2:3.

3. Mark Roncace is a notable exception. In *Raw Revelation*, Roncace says, "We must take the Bible—all of it—as fundamental revelation about our God" (77). For Roncace, this means understanding the character of God as the Bible explains it, warts and all! "For me," Roncace writes, "the paradoxical God of Scripture—kind and cruel, good and genocidal, present and absent—is the true nature of the God of the universe. God is not all good, powerful, holy, and loving; he's partly those things and partly their opposite" (80). In fairness to Roncace, he calls these ideas "totally expendable." Still, they represent an attempt to take biblical statements about God at face value despite what results—namely, a very conflicted portrait of God.

4. See Exod. 17:8–16; Deut. 25:17–19; and 1 Sam. 15:1–3.

5. See 2 Sam. 12:11–12; 16:20–23.

6. Parts of this chapter are adapted from Seibert, *Disturbing Divine Behavior*.

7. See chap. 1.

8. Wells, *Drunk with Blood*, 3.

9. Wells, *Drunk with Blood*, 4–5.

10. For more extensive lists, see Seibert, *Disturbing Divine Behavior*, 15–34; Nelson-Pallmeyer, *Jesus against Christianity*, 24–62; Roncace, *Raw Revelation*, 41–77; Boyd, *Crucifixion of the Warrior God*, 279–333.

11. For an alternative viewpoint that emphasizes continuity between the portrayal of God in the Old and New Testaments, see Tremper Longman III, *Confronting Old Testament Controversies: Pressing Questions about Evolution, Sexuality, History, and Violence* (Grand Rapids: Baker, 2019), 123–206, esp. 176–95.

12. Boyd, *Crucifixion of the Warrior God*, 32–33.

13. 1 John 4:7–12.

14. Thomas Jay Oord, *Open and Relational Theology: An Introduction to Life-Changing Ideas* (Grasmere, ID: SacraSage, 2021), 124.

15. See Seibert, *Disturbing Divine Behavior*.

16. Enns, *Bible Tells Me So*, 56.

17. Charlie Trimm, *Fighting for the King and the Gods: A Survey of Warfare in the Ancient Near East* (Atlanta: Society of Biblical Literature, 2017), 553.

18. For an extensive treatment of how the gods were understood to be involved in warfare in the ancient Near East, see Trimm, *Fighting for the King and the Gods*, 553–625. See also Sa-Moon Kang, *Divine War in the Old Testament and in the Ancient Near East*, Beihefte zur Zeitschrift für die alttestamentliche Wissenschaft 177 (Berlin: de Gruyter, 1989).

19. For a brief discussion, see Seibert, *Disturbing Divine Behavior*, 157–59.

20. William G. Dever, *Who Were the Early Israelites and Where Did They Come From?* (Grand Rapids: Eerdmans, 2003), 227–28, emphasis mine.

21. For a much fuller discussion of how archaeological discoveries contradict the basic story of Josh. 6–11, see Dever, *Who Were the Israelites?*, 37–74. See also Israel Finkelstein and Neil Asher Silberman, *The Bible Unearthed: Archaeology's New Vision of Ancient Israel and the Origin of Its Sacred Texts* (New York: Free Press, 2001), 72–96.

22. See, e.g., Num. 16:49; 2 Sam. 24:15; Amos 4:10.

23. Fretheim and Froehlich, *Bible as Word of God*, 116.

24. A. W. Tozer, *The Knowledge of the Holy: The Attributes of God; Their Meaning in the Christian Life* (New York: Harper & Row, 1961), 7.

25. This language of revealing and distorting God's character is from Nelson-Pallmeyer, *Jesus against Christianity*. See, e.g., 16, 65, 88, 137.

26. This is evident, for example, in Jesus' use of two Old Testament stories in Luke 4 that were mentioned earlier. Both stories speak of God's inclusivity by demonstrating God's mercy to foreigners. Of course, there was no finalized "Old Testament" in Jesus' day. I use this designation for convenience to refer to books that would have been regarded as Scripture at the time, many of which would later become part of the Old Testament.

27. When Jesus referred to stories of divine destruction from the Old Testament (e.g., the flood narrative and the story of Sodom and Gomorrah), these were used to describe eschatological realities rather than present ones. For discussion, see Seibert, *Disturbing Divine Behavior*, 245–54.

28. The book of Job is a notable exception to this. Clearly, not everyone in Israel subscribed to the theology of retribution.

29. Adapted from Seibert, *Disarming the Church*, 69.

30. For a study of Jesus' teachings that some people believe portray God violently or sanction violence, see Neville, *Vehement Jesus*.

31. Mark 8:31.

32. For a more complete response to these kinds of objections, see Seibert, *Disarming the Church*, 82–96; Boyd, *Crucifixion of the Warrior God*, 563–82; and Neville, *Vehement Jesus*.

33. See, e.g., Walter Wink, *Engaging the Powers: Discernment and Resistance in a World of Domination* (Minneapolis: Fortress, 1992), 135–36; and esp. Joseph, *Nonviolent Messiah*, 71–89 and passim.

34. For an extensive treatment of this topic, see David J. Neville, *A Peaceable Hope: Contesting Violent Eschatology in New Testament Narratives* (Grand Rapids: Baker, 2013).

35. C. S. Cowles, "The Case for Radical Discontinuity," in *Show Them No Mercy: Four Views on God and Canaanite Genocide*, ed. Stanley N. Gundry (Grand Rapids: Zondervan, 2003), 30.

36. See Seibert, *Disturbing Divine Behavior*, 230–31.

37. Thomas Jay Oord, *The Uncontrolling Love of God: An Open and Relational Account of Providence* (Downers Grove, IL: InterVarsity, 2015), 170.

38. Acts 17:28 KJV.

39. See, e.g., Eric A. Seibert, "Recent Research on Divine Violence in the Old Testament (with Special Attention to Christian Theological Perspectives)," *Currents in Biblical Research* 15 (2016): 8–40. For a more extensive discussion (and evaluation) of various views, see Boyd, *Crucifixion of the Warrior God*, 335–511.
40. See chap. 6.

Chapter 9: Bringing Violent Verses Back to Church

1. Jenkins, *Laying Down the Sword*, 209.
2. See chap. 2.
3. Jenkins, *Laying Down the Sword*, 14.

Bibliography

Adamo, David Tuesday. "Reading Psalm 109 in African Christianity." *Old Testament Essays* 21:3 (2008): 575–92.

Anderson, Cheryl B. *Ancient Laws and Contemporary Controversies: The Need for Inclusive Biblical Interpretation.* Oxford: Oxford University Press, 2009.

Baldock, Kathy. *Walking the Bridgeless Canyon: Repairing the Breach between the Church and the LGBT Community.* Reno, NV: Canyonwalker, 2014.

Barker, Dan. *God: The Most Unpleasant Character in All Fiction.* New York: Sterling, 2016.

Batstone, David. *Not for Sale: The Return of the Global Slave Trade—and How We Can Fight It.* New York: HarperSanFrancisco, 2007.

Bauckham, Richard J. *Jude, 2 Peter.* Waco, TX: Word, 1983.

Bechmann, Ulrike. "The Woman of Jericho: Dramatization and Feminist Hermeneutics." Pages 183–86 in *Faith and Feminism: Ecumenical Essays.* Edited by B. Diane Lipsett and Phyllis Trible. Louisville, KY: Westminster John Knox, 2014.

Berryman, Jerome W. *Teaching Godly Play: How to Mentor the Spiritual Development of Children.* Denver, CO: Morehouse Education Resources, 2009.

Bolz-Weber, Nadia. *Shameless: A Case for Not Feeling Bad about Feeling Good (about Sex).* New York: Convergent, 2020.

Boyd, Gregory A. *The Crucifixion of the Warrior God: Interpreting the Old Testament's Violent Portraits of God in Light of the Cross.* 2 vols. Minneapolis: Fortress, 2017.

Brensinger, Terry L. "War in the Old Testament: A Journey toward Nonparticipation." Pages 22–31 in *A Peace Reader.* Edited by E. Morris Sider and Luke Keefer Jr. Nappanee, IN: Evangel, 2002.

Briggs, Melody R. *How Children Read Biblical Narrative: An Investigation of Children's Readings of the Gospel of Luke.* Eugene, OR: Pickwick, 2017.

Buttry, Daniel L. *First-Person Preaching: Bringing New Life to Biblical Stories.* Valley Forge, PA: Judson, 1998.

Buttry, Sharon A., and Daniel L. Buttry. *Daughters of Rizpah: Nonviolence and the Transformation of Trauma.* Eugene, OR: Wipf & Stock, 2020.

Caldwell, Elizabeth F. *I Wonder: Engaging a Child's Curiosity about the Bible.* Nashville: Abingdon, 2016.

Carroll R., M. Daniel, and J. Blair Wilgus, eds. *Wrestling with the Violence of God: Soundings in the Old Testament.* Winona Lake, IN: Eisenbrauns, 2015.

Claiborne, Shane. *Executing Grace: How the Death Penalty Killed Jesus and Why It's Killing Us.* San Francisco: HarperOne, 2016.

Collins, John J. *Does the Bible Justify Violence?* Minneapolis: Fortress, 2004.

————. *What Are Biblical Values? What the Bible Says on Key Ethical Issues.* New Haven, CT: Yale University Press, 2019.

Copan, Paul. *Is God a Vindictive Bully? Reconciling Portrayals of God in the Old and New Testaments.* Grand Rapids: Baker, 2022.

Cowles, C. S. "The Case for Radical Discontinuity." Pages 13–44 in *Show Them No Mercy: Four Views on God and Canaanite Genocide.* Edited by Stanley N. Gundry. Grand Rapids: Zondervan, 2003.

Cox, Rosemary. "Using the Bible with Children." *Journal of Education and Christian Belief* 5:1 (2001): 41–49.

Creach, Jerome F. D. *Violence in Scripture.* Louisville, KY: Westminster John Knox, 2013.

Crenshaw, James L. *A Whirlpool of Torment: Israelite Traditions of God as an Oppressive Presence.* Philadelphia: Fortress, 1984.

Davies, Eryl W. *The Immoral Bible: Approaches to Biblical Ethics.* London: T & T Clark, 2010.

————. "The Morally Dubious Passages of the Hebrew Bible: An Examination of Some Proposed Solutions." *Currents in Biblical Research* 3 (2005): 197–228.

Davies, Philip R., ed. *First Person: Essays in Biblical Autobiography.* Sheffield: Sheffield Academic Press, 2002.

Davis, Ellen F. "Critical Traditioning: Seeking an Inner Biblical Hermeneutic." *Anglican Theological Review* 82 (2000): 733–51.

————. *Getting Involved with God: Rediscovering the Old Testament.* Cambridge, MA: Cowley, 2001.

————. "Losing a Friend: The Loss of the Old Testament to the Church." Pages 83–94 in *Jews, Christians, and the Theology of the Hebrew Scriptures.* Edited by Alice Ogden Bellis and Joel S. Kaminsky. Society of Biblical Literature Symposium Series 8. Atlanta: Society of Biblical Literature, 2000.

Dawes, David F. "Rwanda's Genocide: 'Never Again,' Says Pastor." *BC Christian News* 21:6 (June 2001), https://web.archive.org/web/20210301151453 /https://www.canadianchristianity.com/cgi-bin/bc.cgi?bc/bccn/0601 /intrwanda.

Dawkins, Richard. *The God Delusion.* Boston: Mariner, 2008.

Day, John N. *Crying for Justice: What the Psalms Teach Us about Mercy and Vengeance in an Age of Terrorism.* Grand Rapids: Kregel, 2005.

Day, Linda. "Rhetoric and Domestic Violence in Ezekiel 16." *Biblical Interpretation* 8 (2000): 205–30.

Delgado, Sharon. *Love in a Time of Climate Change: Honoring Creation, Establishing Justice.* Minneapolis: Fortress, 2017.

Dell, Katharine. *Who Needs the Old Testament? Its Enduring Appeal and Why the New Atheists Don't Get It.* Eugene, OR: Cascade, 2017.

Dever, William G. *Who Were the Early Israelites and Where Did They Come From?* Grand Rapids: Eerdmans, 2003.

DeYoung, Kevin. *What Does the Bible Really Teach about Homosexuality?* Wheaton, IL: Crossway, 2015.

Doré, Gustave. *The Doré Bible Illustrations.* Mineola, NY: Dover, 1974.

Douglas, Paul, and Mitch Hescox. *Caring for Creation: The Evangelical's Guide to Climate Change and a Healthy Environment.* Bloomington, MN: Bethany House, 2016.

Edwards, J. Kent. *Effective First-Person Biblical Preaching: The Steps from Text to Narrative.* Grand Rapids: Zondervan, 2005.

Emilsen, William W., and John T. Squires. Introduction. Pages xiii–xvi in *Validating Violence—Violating Faith? Religion, Scripture and Violence.* Edited by William W. Emilsen and John T. Squires. Adelaide: ATF, 2008.

Enns, Peter. *The Bible Tells Me So: Why Defending Scripture Has Made Us Unable to Read It.* San Francisco: HarperOne, 2014.

———. *Telling God's Story: A Parents' Guide to Teaching the Bible.* Charles City, VA: Olive Branch, 2010.

Evans, Rachel Held. *Faith Unraveled: How a Girl Who Knew All the Answers Learned to Ask Questions.* Grand Rapids: Zondervan, 2010.

———. *Inspired: Slaying Giants, Walking on Water, and Loving the Bible Again.* Nashville: Nelson Books, 2018.

———. *A Year of Biblical Womanhood: How a Liberated Woman Found Herself Sitting on Her Roof, Covering Her Head, and Calling Her Husband "Master."* Nashville: Thomas Nelson, 2012.

Finkelstein, Israel, and Neil Asher Silberman. *The Bible Unearthed: Archaeology's New Vision of Ancient Israel and the Origin of Its Sacred Texts.* New York: Free Press, 2001.

Fortune, Marie M. *Sexual Violence: The Sin Revisited.* Cleveland: Pilgrim, 2005.

Flood, Derek. *Disarming Scripture: Cherry-Picking Liberals, Violence-Loving Conservatives, and Why We All Need to Learn to Read the Bible Like Jesus Did.* San Francisco: Metanoia, 2014.

Frechette, Christopher G. "The Old Testament as Controlled Substance: How Insights from Trauma Studies Reveal Healing Capacities in Potentially Harmful Texts." *Interpretation: A Journal of Bible and Theology* 69:1 (2015): 20–34.

Freedenthal, Stacey. *Loving Someone with Suicidal Thoughts: What Family, Friends, and Partners Can Say and Do.* Oakland, CA: New Harbinger, 2023.

Fretheim, Terence E., and Karlfried Froehlich. *The Bible as Word of God: In a Postmodern Age.* Minneapolis: Fortress, 1998.

Friedmann, Jonathan L. *Goliath as Gentle Giant: Sympathetic Portrayals in Popular Culture.* Lanham, MD: Rowman & Littlefield, 2022.

Garnier-Amouroux, Clara. "What about Me? The Tale of the Forgotten Sister (Genesis 29:1–30)." Pages 12–21 in *My So-Called Biblical Life: Imagined Stories from the World's Bestselling Book.* Edited by Julie Faith Parker. Eugene, OR: Wipf & Stock, 2017.

Gench, Frances Taylor. *Encountering God in Tyrannical Texts: Reflections on Paul, Women, and the Authority of Scripture.* Louisville, KY: Westminster John Knox, 2015.

Grimsrud, Ted. "Is God Nonviolent?" *Conrad Grebel Review* 21:1 (2003): 13–17, 54–55.

Grossman, David A. *On Killing: The Psychological Cost of Learning to Kill in War and Society.* Rev. ed. New York: Back Bay, 2009.

Gunn, David M., and Danna Nolan Fewell. *Narrative in the Hebrew Bible.* Oxford: Oxford University Press, 1993.

Gushee, David P. *Changing Our Mind: Definitive 3rd Edition of the Landmark Call for Inclusion of LGBTQ Christians with Response to Critics.* Canton, MI: Read the Spirit, 2022.

Hammond, Claudia. "Does Reading Fiction Make Us Better People?" *BBC Future,*

June 2, 2019. https://www.bbc.com/future/article/20190523-does-reading
    -fiction-make-us-better-people.

Harder, Jeanette. *Let the Children Come: Preparing Faith Communities to End Child Abuse and
    Neglect.* Scottdale, PA: Herald, 2010.

Hawk, L. Daniel. *The Violence of the Biblical God: Canonical Narrative and Christian Faith.*
    Grand Rapids: Eerdmans, 2019.

Hays, Richard B. *Echoes of Scripture in the Gospels.* Waco, TX: Baylor University Press,
    2016.

Heie, Harold. *Respectful LGBT Conversations: Seeking Truth, Giving Love, and Modeling
    Christian Unity.* Eugene, OR: Cascade, 2018.

Hess, Carol Lakey. *Caretakers of Our Common House: Women's Development in Communities
    of Faith.* Nashville: Abingdon, 1997.

Hill, Jim, and Rand Cheadle. *The Bible Tells Me So: Uses and Abuses of Holy Scripture.*
    New York: Doubleday, 1996.

Hofreiter, Christian. *Making Sense of Old Testament Genocide: Christian Interpretations of
    Herem Passages.* Oxford: Oxford University Press, 2018.

Huber, Jane Parker. *A Singing Faith.* Philadelphia: Westminster, 1987.

Japinga, Lynn. *Preaching the Women of the Old Testament: Who They Were and Why They
    Matter.* Louisville, KY: Westminster John Knox, 2017.

Jenkins, Philip. *Laying Down the Sword: Why We Can't Ignore the Bible's Violent Verses.* New
    York: HarperOne, 2011.

Jeter, Joseph R., Jr. *Preaching Judges.* St. Louis: Chalice, 2003.

Joseph, Simon. *The Nonviolent Messiah: Jesus, Q, and the Enochic Tradition.* Minneapolis:
    Fortress, 2014.

Kang, Sa-Moon. *Divine War in the Old Testament and in the Ancient Near East.* Beihefte
    zur Zeitschrift für die alttestamentliche Wissenschaft 177. Berlin: de Gruyter,
    1989.

Keefe, Rachael A. *The Lifesaving Church: Faith Communities and Suicide Prevention.* St.
    Louis: Chalice, 2018.

Kelle, Brad E. *The Bible and Moral Injury: Reading Scripture alongside War's Unseen Wounds.*
    Nashville: Abingdon, 2020.

King, Peter. "Sunday School Hero or Suicide Bomber? Reading Samson
    Responsibly." Pages 238–57 in *The Bible on Violence: A Thick Description.* Edited
    by Helen Paynter and Michael Spalione. Sheffield: Sheffield Phoenix, 2020.

Kinnaman, David. *You Lost Me: Why Young Christians Are Leaving Church . . . and
    Rethinking Faith.* Grand Rapids: Baker, 2011.

Kroeger, Catherine Clark, and Nancy Nason-Clark. *No Place for Abuse: Biblical and
    Practical Resources to Counteract Domestic Violence.* 2nd ed. Downers Grove, IL:
    InterVarsity, 2010.

Kugel, James L. *Traditions of the Bible: A Guide to the Bible as It Was at the Beginning of the
    Common Era.* Cambridge, MA: Harvard University Press, 1998.

Landy, Francis. "Do We Want Our Children to Read This Book?" In *Bible and Ethics
    of Reading.* Edited by Danna Nolan Fewell and Gary A. Phillips. *Semeia* 77
    (1997): 157–76.

Loftus, John W., and Randal Rauser. *God or Godless? One Atheist. One Christian. Twenty
    Controversial Questions.* Grand Rapids: Baker, 2013.

Long, Jesse C., Jr. *1 & 2 Kings.* Joplin, MO: College Press, 2002.

Long, Thomas G. "The Fall of the House of Uzzah . . . and Other Difficult
    Preaching Texts." *Journal for Preachers* 7 (Advent 1983): 13–19.

Longman, Tremper, III. *Confronting Old Testament Controversies: Pressing Questions about Evolution, Sexuality, History, and Violence.* Grand Rapids: Baker, 2019.

Maresca, Catherine. *Violence and Nonviolence in Scripture: Helping Children Understand Challenging Stories.* Chicago: Liturgy Training, 2019.

Martin, Colby. *Unclobber: Rethinking Our Misuse of the Bible on Homosexuality.* Louisville, KY: Westminster John Knox, 2016.

Matties, Gordon H. *Joshua.* Harrisonburg, VA: Herald, 2012.

McClure, John S., and Nancy J. Ramsay, eds. *Preaching about Sexual and Domestic Violence.* Cleveland: United Church, 1998.

McEntire, Mark. *The Blood of Abel: The Violent Plot in the Hebrew Bible.* Macon, GA: Mercer University Press, 1999.

Miles, Al. *Ending Violence in Teen Dating Relationships: A Resource Guide for Parents and Pastors.* Minneapolis: Augsburg Fortress, 2005.

Moo, Douglas J., and Jonathan A. Moo. *Creation Care: A Biblical Theology of the Natural World.* Grand Rapids: Zondervan, 2018.

Nelson-Pallmeyer, Jack. *Jesus against Christianity: Reclaiming the Missing Jesus.* Harrisburg: PA: Trinity Press International, 2001.

Nelson-Pallmeyer, Jack, and Bret Hesla. *Worship in the Spirit of Jesus: Theology, Liturgy, and Songs without Violence.* Eugene, OR: Wipf & Stock, 2005.

Neufeld, Thomas R. Yoder. *Killing Enmity: Violence and the New Testament.* Grand Rapids: Baker, 2011.

Neville, David J. *A Peaceable Hope: Contesting Violent Eschatology in New Testament Narratives.* Grand Rapids: Baker, 2013.

———. *The Vehement Jesus: Grappling with Troubling Gospel Texts.* Eugene, OR: Cascade, 2017.

Niditch, Susan. *War in the Hebrew Bible: A Study of the Ethics of Violence.* Oxford: Oxford University Press, 1983.

O'Brien, Julia M. *Challenging Prophetic Metaphor: Theology and Ideology in the Prophets.* Louisville, KY: Westminster John Knox, 2008.

Oord, Thomas Jay. *Open and Relational Theology: An Introduction to Life-Changing Ideas.* Grasmere, ID: SacraSage, 2021.

———. *The Uncontrolling Love of God: An Open and Relational Account of Providence.* Downers Grove, IL: InterVarsity, 2015.

Parker, Julie Faith, ed. *My So-Called Biblical Life: Imagined Stories from the World's Bestselling Book.* Eugene, OR: Wipf & Stock, 2017.

Patterson, Linda J. *Hate Thy Neighbor: How the Bible Is Misused to Condemn Homosexuality.* West Conshohocken, PA: Infinity, 2009.

Peterson, Eugene H. *Answering God: The Psalms as Tools for Prayer.* San Francisco: Harper & Row, 1989.

Plotz, David. *Good Book: The Bizarre, Hilarious, Disturbing, Marvelous, and Inspiring Things I Learned When I Read Every Single Word of the Bible.* New York: Harper, 2009.

Prior, Michael. *The Bible and Colonialism: A Moral Critique.* Sheffield: Sheffield Academic Press, 1997.

Putt, Sharon L. Baker. *A Nonviolent Theology of Love: Peacefully Confessing the Apostles' Creed.* Minneapolis: Fortress, 2021.

Rauser, Randal. *Jesus Loves Canaanites: Biblical Genocide in the Light of Moral Intuition.* Canada: 2 Cup Press, 2021.

———. *What's So Confusing about Grace?* Canada: 2 Cup Press, 2017.

Rauser, Randal, and Justin Schieber. *An Atheist and a Christian Walk into a Bar:*

　　　Talking about God, the Universe, and Everything. Amherst, NY: Prometheus, 2016.

Rearick, Anderson M., III. "Why Is the Only Good Orc a Dead Orc?" *Inklings Forever: Published Colloquium Proceedings 1997–2016,* vol. 4 (2004): article 10, https://pillars.taylor.edu/inklings_forever/vol4/iss1/10.

Roncace, Mark. *Raw Revelation: The Bible They Never Tell You About.* North Charleston, SC: CreateSpace, 2012.

Sakenfeld, Katharine Doob. *Just Wives? Stories of Power and Survival in the Old Testament and Today.* Louisville, KY: Westminster John Knox, 2003.

Schlimm, Matthew Richard. *This Strange and Sacred Scripture: Wrestling with the Old Testament and Its Oddities.* Grand Rapids: Baker, 2015.

Schmidt, Megan. "How Reading Fiction Increases Empathy and Encourages Understanding." *Discover Magazine,* August 28, 2020. https://www.discover magazine.com/mind/how-reading-fiction-increases-empathy-and-encourages -understanding.

Scholz, Susanne. *Sacred Witness: Rape in the Hebrew Bible.* Minneapolis: Fortress, 2010.

Schwager, Raymund. *Must There Be Scapegoats? Violence and Redemption in the Bible.* Translated by Maria L. Assad. New York: Crossroad, 2000.

Seibert, Eric A. *Disarming the Church: Why Christians Must Forsake Violence to Follow Jesus and Change the World.* Eugene, OR: Cascade, 2018.

———. *Disturbing Divine Behavior: Troubling Old Testament Images of God.* Minneapolis: Fortress, 2009.

———. "Preaching from Violent Biblical Texts: Helpful Strategies for Addressing Violence in the Old Testament." *Perspectives in Religious Studies* 42 (2015): 247–57.

———. "Recent Research on Divine Violence in the Old Testament (with Special Attention to Christian Theological Perspectives)." *Currents in Biblical Research* 15 (2016): 8–40.

———. *The Violence of Scripture: Overcoming the Old Testament's Troubling Legacy.* Minneapolis: Fortress, 2012.

———. "The Violent Legacy of the Old Testament (and What to Do about It)." *Listening: Journal of Communication Ethics, Religion, and Culture* 56:3 (2021): 215–28.

Sider, Ronald J. *Nonviolent Action: What Christian Ethics Demands but Most Christians Have Never Really Tried.* Grand Rapids: Brazos, 2015.

Spong, John Shelby. *The Sins of Scripture: Exposing the Bible's Texts of Hate to Reveal the God of Love.* San Francisco: HarperSanFrancisco, 2005.

Stevenson, Bryan. *Just Mercy: A Story of Justice and Redemption.* New York: Spiegel & Grau, 2015.

Stonehouse, Catherine, and Scottie May. *Listening to Children on the Spiritual Journey: Guidance for Those Who Teach and Nurture.* Grand Rapids: Baker, 2010.

Strawn, Brent A. *Lies My Preacher Told Me: An Honest Look at the Old Testament.* Louisville, KY: Westminster John Knox, 2021.

———. *The Old Testament Is Dying: A Diagnosis and Recommended Treatment.* Grand Rapids: Baker, 2017.

Taylor, Barbara Brown. "Hard Words." *Christian Century* 118 (May 2001): 24.

Thatcher, Adrian. *The Savage Text: The Use and Abuse of the Bible.* Malden, MA: Wiley-Blackwell, 2008.

Thompson, John L. *Reading the Bible with the Dead: What You Can Learn from the History of Exegesis That You Can't Learn from Exegesis Alone.* Grand Rapids: Eerdmans, 2007.

Tozer, A. W. *The Knowledge of the Holy: The Attributes of God; Their Meaning in the Christian Life.* New York: Harper & Row, 1961.

Trible, Phyllis. *Texts of Terror: Literary-Feminist Readings of Biblical Narratives.* Philadelphia: Fortress, 1984.

Trimm, Charlie. *Fighting for the King and the Gods: A Survey of Warfare in the Ancient Near East.* Atlanta: Society of Biblical Literature, 2017.

Vines, Matthew. *God and the Gay Christian: The Biblical Case for Same-Sex Relationships.* New York: Convergent, 2014.

Waters, Sonia E. "Reading Sodom through Sexual Violence against Women." *Interpretation: A Journal of Bible and Theology* 71:3 (2017): 274–83.

Weaver, J. Denny. *God without Violence: A Theology of the God Revealed in Jesus.* 2nd ed. Eugene, OR: Cascade, 2020.

———. *The Nonviolent God.* Grand Rapids: Eerdmans, 2013.

Webb, William J. *Corporal Punishment in the Bible: A Redemptive-Movement Hermeneutic for Troubling Texts.* Downers Grove, IL: InterVarsity, 2011.

Webb, William J., and Gordan K. Oeste. *Bloody, Brutal, and Barbaric? Wrestling with Troubling War Texts.* Downers Grove, IL: InterVarsity, 2019.

Weems, Renita J. *Battered Love: Marriage, Sex, and Violence in the Hebrew Prophets.* Minneapolis: Fortress, 1995.

Wells, Steve. *Drunk with Blood: God's Killings in the Bible.* USA: Giordano, 2010.

Whitaker, Robyn J. "Invoking Jezebel, Invoking Terror: The Threat of Sexual Violence in the Apocalypse to John." Pages 107–20 in *Terror in the Bible: Rhetoric, Gender, and Violence.* Edited by Monica Jyotsna Melanchthon and Robyn J. Whitaker. Atlanta: Society of Biblical Literature, 2021.

Wilson, Sarah Hinlicky. "R-rated: How to Read the Bible with Children." *Christian Century* 130 (March 6, 2013): 22–25.

Wink, Walter. *Engaging the Powers: Discernment and Resistance in a World of Domination.* Minneapolis: Fortress, 1992.

Withrow, Brandon G., and Menachem Wecker. *Consider No Evil: Two Faith Traditions and the Problem of Academic Freedom in Religious Higher Education.* Eugene, OR: Cascade, 2014.

Woodruff, Mike. "Difficult Sermon? Call in a Team." *CT Pastors,* July 11, 2008, https://www.christianitytoday.com/pastors/2008/spring/24.47.html.

Worsley, Howard. *How Not to Totally Put Your Children off God: A Conversation on Christian Parenting between a Father and His Sons.* Oxford: Lion Hudson, 2020.

York, Tripp, and Andy Alexis-Baker, eds. *A Faith Embracing All Creatures: Addressing Commonly Asked Questions about Christian Care for Animals.* Eugene, OR: Cascade, 2012.

———, eds. *A Faith Encompassing All Creation: Addressing Commonly Asked Questions about Christian Care for the Environment.* Eugene, OR: Cascade, 2014.

Zahnd, Brian. *Sinners in the Hands of a Loving God: The Scandalous Truth of the Very Good News.* Colorado Springs, CO: Waterbrook, 2017.

Zehr, Howard. *The Little Book of Restorative Justice.* Rev. ed. New York: Good Books, 2015.

Scripture Index

.

Author and Subject Index

Abigail (wife of Nabal), 71
Abimelech (king), 35
Abraham (patriarch), 98–99
Absalom (brother of Tamar), 31
abuser, God as, 92. *See also* God, as violent
abusers, characteristics of, 35
actual God, 133–34
adult education, 65
adultery, 162n9
Ahab (king), 40–42, 113
Ai (Canaanite city), 132
Amalekites, annihilation of, 38–39, 91
Amnon (son of David), 31
ancient vs. modern violence, 55–57, 97–98
Anderson, Cheryl, 92
angels (men in Sodom), 108–9
applications, personal biblical, 40–42
archaeological studies, 131–33
attention, of churchgoers, during sermon, 88–89
authority, biblical, 21, 96, 126, 128
authority, those in, 114–17

Babylonians, 32
Barker, Dan, 24
Bathsheba (wife of Uriah/David), 30–31
Bechmann, Ulrike, 95
Ben-ammi (son of Lot), 109
Berryman, Jerome, 57
betrayal by church, feelings of, 20, 22–23, 52, 153n10

Bible
authority of, 21, 96, 126, 128
children's, 58
children's reading of, 46–47, 62, 156n6
contradictions in, 133–34
data of violence in, 126–27
deaths in, number of, 126–27
as God-inspired, 19–20
honesty on, 89
human formation of, 21–22
as justification for violence, 5, 24–25, 38–39, 90–92, 138–40
as literal, 128, 131–33
personal connections with, 40–42, 113–14, 120
reader-types of, 22
responsible reading of, 18–19, 89–90, 96, 134
suicides in, 4, 35–36, 51, 54, 92
teaching, 57–58 (*see also* education, Christian)
See also New Testament; Old Testament
Bible Heroes of the Old Testament (Little Golden Book), 53–54
Bible study, 4–5, 20–21, 89–90, 126
both-and approach, 143
Boyd, Greg, 25, 128
Brick Bible, 60–61
Buttry, Daniel, 95

Printed in the USA
CPSIA information can be obtained
at www.ICGtesting.com
JSHW061159041123
51260JS00016B/93